THE REBBE, THE MESSIAH
AND THE SCANDAL OF
ORTHODOX INDIFFERENCE

THE LITTMAN LIBRARY OF
JEWISH CIVILIZATION

MANAGING EDITOR
Connie Webber

Dedicated to the memory of
LOUIS THOMAS SIDNEY LITTMAN
*who founded the Littman Library for the love of God
and as an act of charity in memory of his father*
JOSEPH AARON LITTMAN
יהא זכרם ברוך

*'Get wisdom, get understanding:
Forsake her not and she shall preserve thee'*
PROV. 4:5

*The Littman Library of Jewish Civilization is a registered UK charity
Registered charity no.* 1000784

THE REBBE
THE MESSIAH
AND THE
SCANDAL
OF ORTHODOX
INDIFFERENCE

◆

DAVID BERGER

London · Portland, Oregon
The Littman Library of Jewish Civilization
2001

The Littman Library of Jewish Civilization
74 Addison Road
London W14 8DJ, UK

———

Published in the United States and Canada by
The Littman Library of Jewish Civilization
c/o ISBS 5824 N.E. Hassalo Street
Portland, Oregon 97213-3644

A catalogue record for this book is available from the British Library

Library of Congress cataloging-in-publication data
Berger, David, 1943–
The Rebbe, the Messiah, and the scandal of orthodox indifference / David Berger.
p. cm. Includes bibliographical references (p.) and index.
1. Messiah—Judaism—History of doctrines—20th century.
2. Habad. 3. Schneersohn, Menahem Mendel, 1902—Influence.
4. Eschatology, Jewish. 5. Orthodox Judaism—History—20th century.
I. Title.
BM615.B37   2001   296.3'36—dc21   2001041412

ISBN 1–874774–88–9

Publishing co-ordinator: Janet Moth
Copy-editing: Bonnie Blackburn
Proof-reading: Colin Baldwin
Indexing: Sarah Ereira
Production: John Saunders
Designed and typeset by Pete Russell, Faringdon, Oxon.
Printed in Great Britain on acid-free paper by
Biddles Ltd., King's Lynn, www.biddles.co.uk

לז"נ חמי הרה"ג רב ברוך מאיר רבינוביץ ז"ל

בן הרה"ק רבי גדליהו אהרן הי"ד

נצר לשושלת מאנאסטרישטש

למלאת שנה לפטירתו

"אפילו כל הרוחות שבעולם באות ונושבות בו

אין מזיזין אותו ממקומו"

Acknowledgements

ACKNOWLEDGEMENTS customarily contain an expression of thanks, often perfunctory, to the author's spouse. In this instance, however, my gratitude to Pearl runs especially deep. The campaign described in this book has generated vehement, public denunciations; expressions of agreement, on the other hand, though numerous and laudatory, have generally remained in the private sphere. While I effectively asked for these tribulations, Pearl, who did not, has had to live with them. Despite moments of deep ambivalence, she has extended much-needed support, and her agreement that I had to write this book notwithstanding the inevitable turmoil that it will reintroduce into our lives has provided me with indispensable encouragement and some measure of peace of mind. In addition, she read the manuscript with characteristic perceptiveness and made a suggestion that greatly improved its structure and readability. The remainder of my debt to her cannot be captured in words.

Professor Mark Steiner's contribution also extends well beyond his reading of the manuscript. Years before this affair began we studied sections of the Talmud together, including parts of the especially relevant tractate *Avodah zarah*. To see a difficulty in a rabbinic text yield to the onslaught of Mark's brilliant and tenacious intellect is to experience the millennial Jewish engagement with Torah at its highest level. As my concern with the issues addressed in this book grew, Mark regularly sent me material from Jerusalem and provided moral and intellectual support. Finally, he read the manuscript and made two important suggestions that led me to introduce a structural change and to add a substantive argument. Needless to say—and here I see no way to avoid the stock formula—ultimate responsibility for the content is mine alone.

At the Littman Library, Connie Webber has done everything that an author could ask and more. She has granted the book the priority that its urgent content requires, responded to queries with alacrity, and made substantive proposals reflecting her insight, her experience as editor, and her knowledge of the Jewish world. Ludo Craddock has guided many of the technical and business aspects of publication with expertise, efficiency, and empathy. Bonnie Blackburn copy-edited the manuscript and Sarah Ereira indexed the final version with the meticulous care and genuine understanding essential for tasks whose creative challenges often go unappreciated. Janet Moth drew upon the very same qualities as she supervised the final stages of production. I am grateful to them all.

Contents

Note on Style and Transliteration

THE transliteration of Hebrew in this book reflects its purpose, the history of its content, and the culture of a significant segment of its intended readership. The book contains substantial quotations from correspondence and from material published elsewhere, where the style of transliteration represents standard practice for the organization or individual concerned. Elsewhere a more academic approach to transcription has been adopted, representing the pronunciation prescribed for modern Hebrew rather than that of Ashkenazi Hebrew or Yiddish. However, some of the Hebrew terms used are so familiar to the English-speaking Jewish reader as to be widely regarded in such circles as English words, and it was consequently considered unnecessary to impose an unfamiliar spelling or transcription. These conflicting considerations inevitably result in inconsistent transliterations. In order to keep such inconsistencies to a minimum, the transliteration in the four chapters that have previously appeared elsewhere has been lightly edited.

As a noun, the term 'messianist' is used to mean a believer in the messiahship of the Rebbe. As an adjective, it characterizes an entity marked by this belief.

Introduction

THIS BOOK is a memoir, a history, a religious tract. It is an indictment, a lament, and an appeal. It records the shattering of a core belief of a major faith, and the remarkable equanimity with which the standard-bearers of that faith have allowed one of its key pillars to be undermined. This tree has fallen during the last few years not in a deserted forest but in the midst of the madding crowd, yet the multitudes of observers somehow imagine that it continues to stand.

Since the religion in question is my own, I do not write as a dispassionate observer. I write, rather, with the hope that this account will awaken believing Jews from their torpor, alert them to the catastrophe that has befallen their faith, and inspire them to take the simple yet difficult steps needed to transform this moment from a turning point into an episode. To adapt a formulation originally applied to the abortive European revolutions of 1848 and 1849, we still have the opportunity to make this the turning point where Judaism failed to turn. If we do not seize this opportunity, a nearly irrevocable transformation will have been effected, and by the time the truth sinks in, it may well be too late to act.

As I write, two propositions from which every mainstream Jew in the last millennium would have instantly recoiled have become legitimate options within Orthodox Judaism:

1. A specific descendant of King David may be identified with certainty as the Messiah even though he died in an unredeemed world. The criteria always deemed necessary for a confident identification of the Messiah—the temporal redemption of the Jewish people, a rebuilt Temple, peace and prosperity, the universal recognition of the God of Israel—are null and void.

2. The messianic faith of Judaism allows for the following scenario: God will finally send the true Messiah to embark upon his redemptive mission. The long-awaited redeemer will declare that all preparations for the redemption have been completed and announce without qualification that the fulfilment is absolutely imminent. He will begin the process of

gathering the dispersed of Israel to the Holy Land. He will proclaim himself a prophet, point clearly to his messianic status, and declare that the only remaining task is to greet him as Messiah. And then he will die and be buried without having redeemed the world. To put the matter more succinctly, the true Messiah's redemptive mission, publicly proclaimed and vigorously pursued, will be interrupted by death and burial and then consummated through a Second Coming.

While the vast majority of Jews instinctively recognize the alienness of these propositions, and the Rabbinical Council of America has declared that there is no place for such a doctrine in Judaism, the assertion that contemporary Orthodox Jewry effectively legitimates these beliefs rests on a simple observation: a large segment—almost certainly a substantial majority —of a highly significant Orthodox movement called Lubavitch, or Chabad, hasidism affirms that the Lubavitcher Rebbe, Rabbi Menachem Mendel Schneerson, who was laid to rest in 1994 without leaving a successor, did everything subsumed under proposition 2 and will soon return to complete the redemption in his capacity as the Messiah. Hasidim who proclaim this belief, including those who have ruled that it is required by Jewish law, routinely hold significant religious posts sanctioned by major Orthodox authorities with no relationship to their movement. These range from the offices of the Israeli rabbinate to the ranks of mainstream rabbinical organizations to the chairmanship of rabbinical courts in both Israel and the diaspora, not to speak of service as scribes, ritual slaughterers, teachers, and administrators of schools and religious organizations receiving support from mainstream Orthodoxy. With very important exceptions, this support comes even from circles generally marked by zealous denunciation of minor deviations from their religious worldview. Shortly after signing a public ruling that Jewish law obligates all Jews to accept the messiahship of the deceased Rebbe, a Montreal rabbi was appointed head of the rabbinical court of the entire city. For much of Orthodox Jewry, the classic boundaries of the messianic faith of Israel are no more.

What follows is an account of this historic mutation of Judaism seen through the prism of a personal odyssey that moved me from almost unalloyed admiration for Lubavitch and its leader to a public campaign which has led many hasidim to see me as an inveterate enemy of Chabad using messianism as a convenient vehicle to vent longstanding hatred. I am acutely aware that the personal perspective of this book courts the danger of deflecting the focus from the monumental issues at stake to immeasurably more trivial matters, as if the evolution of the views of a professor of Jewish history has any intrinsic importance in determining the ultimate course of the messianic faith of Judaism.

Nonetheless, several considerations impel me to write this work as a memoir. First, while my fields of expertise include the highly relevant areas of messianism and the Jewish–Christian debate, they do not embrace either hasidism in general or Chabad in particular; thus, despite the considerable education that I have received in the last few years, I do not feel competent to write a full analytical history of messianic ideas and activities in the Lubavitch movement. Second and more important, I do not aspire to write such a work. The history in this narrative serves as the handmaiden of a religious objective, and while I strive for rigorous honesty in setting out both facts and interpretation, this is unavoidably a deeply personal work. Third and most important, when I lamented my failure some years ago to elicit the response I sought, a sympathetic rabbi emphasized that one cannot realistically expect to change ingrained sympathies towards a major movement in a single article or a handful of letters. This is a long and arduous process. By inviting the reader to share my own journey, I hope that a personal transformation which took place over a period of years—and still leaves me sympathetic to the genuinely uncorrupted element in Chabad—can be negotiated in the course of a single account describing the difficult but inexorable steps leading to that transformation.

The obstacles along this road are daunting. I am not only an admirer of Lubavitch achievements who now seeks to delegitimate its largest element. I am an advocate of tolerance urging intolerance, a believer in inclusiveness preaching exclusion, an adherent of unity fomenting division. When I expressed my discomfort over these tensions to a friend, he referred me to Ronald Reagan's response when asked how he could justify dismissing all air-traffic controllers who had engaged in an illegal strike. 'I didn't fire them', he said. 'They quit.'

Admiration, tolerance, inclusiveness, and unity have thus far produced a consequence that can be stated with stark simplicity. Virtually all Orthodox Jews, whether they believe in the messiahship of the Rebbe or not, belong to a profoundly different religion from the one they adhered to in 1993. Though largely ignored thus far, this is a development of striking importance for the history of world religions, and it is an earthquake in the history of Judaism. This book presents some of the early chapters of the story. The final chapter, shrouded in the mysteries of a future that is ours to mould, is yet to be written.

ONE

From Heroism to Heterodoxy: The Crisis of a Movement and the Danger to a Faith

H ASIDISM, arguably the most vibrant religious movement in the history of modern Jewry, was born in eighteenth-century Poland with the teachings of Rabbi Israel Ba'al Shem Tov (Master of the Good Name, or, better, Good Master of the Name). Emphasizing the centrality of joy in the service of God, the crucial role of prayer, and the opportunity to cleave to the divine through a tzaddik, or rebbe—a charismatic leader seen as a conduit between the heavenly and earthly realms—the Ba'al Shem Tov and his successors fashioned a message that energized and redirected Jewish piety, ritual, and social institutions. The Chabad stream originated in the career of Rabbi Shneur Zalman (1745–1813), originally of Liozna, later of Lyady, a towering figure expert in Jewish law and mysticism who infused a movement marked by pietistic enthusiasm with a strongly intellectual component.[1] Indeed, the

---

[1] Readers interested in learning more about R. Shneur Zalman, Chabad thought, and the history and messianic orientation of the movement may wish to consult some of the following secondary works: Naftali Loewenthal, *Communicating the Infinite: The Emergence of the Habad School* (Chicago, 1990); id., 'The Neutralization of Messianism and the Apocalypse', in Rachel Elior and Joseph Dan (eds.), *Kolot Rabim: Memorial Volume to Rivkah Shatz-Uffenheimer*, Jerusalem Studies in Jewish Thought 13 (Jerusalem, 1996), 2*–14* (English section); Nissan Mindel, *R. Schneur Zalman of Liadi* (New York, 1971, 1973); Roman A. Foxbrunner, *The Hasidism of R. Shneur Zalman of Lyady* (Tuscaloosa, Ala. and London, 1992); Immanuel Etkes, 'Rabbi Schneur Zalman of Lyady's Career as a Hasidic Leader' (Heb.), *Tziyon*, 50 (1985), 321–54; Rachel Elior, *The Theory of the Divine in the Second Generation of Chabad Hasidism* (Heb.) (Jerusalem, 1982); ead., *The Paradoxical Ascent to God: The Kabbalistic Theosophy of Habad Hasidism* (Albany, NY, 1993); ead., 'The Lubavitch Messianic Resurgence: The Historical and Mystical Background 1939–1996', in Peter Schaefer and Mark Cohen (eds.), *Toward the Millennium: Messianic Expectations from the Bible to Waco* (Leiden, Boston, and Cologne, 1998), 383–408; Shalom Dov Baer Levin, *The History of Chabad in the United States, 1900–1950* (Heb.) (Brooklyn, 1988); id., *The History of Chabad in Soviet Russia, 1917–1950* (Heb.) (Brooklyn, 1989); Menachem Friedman, 'Habad as Messianic Fundamentalism: From Local Particularism to Universal Jewish Mission', in Martin E. Marty and R. Scott Appleby (eds.), *Accounting for Fundamentalisms: The Dynamic Character of Movements* (Chicago, 1994), 328–57; Aviezer Ravitzky, *Messianism, Zionism, and Jewish Religious Radicalism* (Chicago, 1996), 181–206; id.,

term Chabad itself is an acronym for the Hebrew words, *ḥokhmah, binah, da'at* (wisdom, understanding, knowledge) as used in Jewish mysticism. A host of factors rendered hasidism highly controversial, and the Chabad group, centred in Lithuania, found itself at the vortex of a campaign spear-headed by the Vilna Gaon (Rabbi Elijah ben Solomon Zalman, 1720–97), the greatest talmudist of his and all subsequent generations and the driving force behind a series of bans against nascent hasidism in the 1770s and thereafter.

With the dawn of the next century, hasidim did more than weather these attacks. As a multitude of rebbes founded proliferating dynasties in towns and hamlets throughout the Jewish Pale of Settlement, the movement spread through eastern Europe and became the dominant form of Judaism in much of the heartland of nineteenth-century Jewry. Opponents (*mitnagedim*, or, in the pronunciation that prevailed among these Jews, 'misnagdim') did not entirely abandon the cause, but opposition waned in the face of new social and religious realities.

First, it became very difficult to delegitimate a movement that commanded the allegiance of so many observant Jews. Second, the radicalism of early hasidism diminished as it was transformed from a movement of rebellion against the Jewish communal establishment into an established order of its own. No longer did hasidim engage in embarrassingly wild behaviour when they prayed, nor did they extend what misnagdim saw as violations of Jewish law beyond the few matters, such as ignoring the times of prayer set by the Talmud and codes, that had triggered some of the early controversies. Finally, the spread of the Jewish Enlightenment, or Haskalah, to eastern Europe posed so serious a threat that hasidim and misnagdim, for all their profound differences, came to see themselves as allies in a struggle to preserve their common culture, educational systems, and fundamental beliefs against the onslaught of scepticism, secularism, and acculturation working to undermine the very foundations of traditional Jewish society.

The Chabad movement, now also known as Lubavitch from the town where the group's leaders resided from 1813 to 1915, played a significant role in that resistance. This was true in the nineteenth century, when the distinguished rebbes of Chabad worked in tandem with other traditionalist leaders,

'The Contemporary Lubavitch Hasidic Movement: Between Conservatism and Messianism', in Marty and Appleby (eds.), *Accounting for Fundamentalisms*, 303–27; Gershon Greenberg, 'Machane Israel-Lubavitch, 1940–1945: Actively Responding to Khurban', in Alan A. Berger (ed.), *Bearing Witness to the Holocaust, 1939–1989* (Lewiston, NY, 1991), 141–63; id., 'Redemption after the Holocaust according to Machane Israel-Lubavitch, 1940–1945', *Modern Judaism*, 12 (1992), 61–84; Joseph Dan, *Modern Jewish Messianism* (Heb.) (Tel Aviv, 1999); Avrum M. Ehrlich, *Leadership in the Habad Movement* (Northvale, NJ, 2000).

and it was all the more true in the twentieth, when resistance meant a heroic stand, fought for decades in lonely isolation, not against Jewish modernists but against a totalitarian Soviet regime bent on the complete eradication of Jewish observance. Only the hardest of hearts could fail to be moved by accounts of self-sacrifice on the part of Lubavitch hasidim struggling for the preservation of tiny pockets of Judaism in the depths of Stalinist and post-Stalinist Russia—the commitment against all odds to the exclusive mainten-ance of a kosher diet, the avoidance of writing during enforced attendance at classes on the Sabbath and festivals, months or even years of celibacy by married couples because of the unavailability of ritual baths necessary for the resumption of marital relations. I vividly remember the emotional impact of such stories as I responded to appeals for Lishkas Ezras Achim, a Chabad organization that shipped kosher food to Jews in the darkest days of the Soviet tyranny.

In early 1989 I had the unforgettable experience of serving as one of four teachers during the inaugural mini-semester of the first officially approv-ed yeshiva in Soviet history. The school, formally called the Judaica Section of the Institute for World Civilizations, was a product of the early stage of Mikhail Gorbachev's *glasnost* and of intense negotiations between Rabbi Adin Steinsaltz of Jerusalem and an influential Soviet official. Near the beginning of February, I received a call from Jerusalem strongly urging me to participate so that the yeshiva would have at least one faculty member with standard academic credentials in addition to rabbinical ordination. My initial reaction was that despite the historic importance of the initiative, I could not leave on two weeks' notice at the beginning of the spring semester; my wife, however, persuaded me that I had no right to refuse, and I continue to be grateful for her intervention.

Rabbi Steinsaltz himself has strong loyalties to Lubavitch, though neither the school nor its student body was affiliated with the movement. One of the full-time students, however, was a Lubavitch hasid, as was one of the fac-ulty members, and we made a point of visiting the unofficial but tolerated Chabad synagogue and yeshiva. My already substantial admiration for the movement's steadfastness under the shadow of Communism was reinforced, and in public talks upon my return, I emphasized that the striking accom-plishments of the new school must be seen against the background of both the remarkable achievements of recent refuseniks and the longstanding, awe-inspiring devotion of Lubavitch hasidim.

In addition to this opportunity for a closer look at Chabad activity in the Soviet Union, I was casually aware of its American and global programmes to

the degree typical of an interested Modern Orthodox Jew. While I occasionally heard complaints about Lubavitch emissaries entering a community with
established Jewish institutions, sometimes even Orthodox institutions, and
refusing to cooperate with the existing leadership, the impressive portrait of
an army of devoted hasidim forsaking all the comforts of home to spread
observance of the Torah easily overwhelmed sporadic negative reports.

To be sure, this portrait was further challenged by extremely hostile
statements about Lubavitch emanating from two Orthodox circles. Satmar
hasidim issued attacks which appeared to result from ideological differences
about Israel as well as narrower, personal matters. My own sympathies on
the subject of Israel were far removed from the fiercely anti-Zionist Satmar
position, some of the attacks appeared scurrilous or amusing (Jews have not
been waiting, said one of the broadsides, for a Messiah whose wife drives a
car), and on rare occasions they crossed the line into violence. For all these
reasons, I was not inclined to take them seriously.

The second source appeared weightier. A half-century ago, Rabbi Aharon
Kotler (1892–1962), founder of the Lakewood yeshiva in New Jersey and
probably the most influential figure in Traditionalist Orthodox circles,[2] was
severely critical of Lubavitch, in part because of the extreme emphasis on
messianism evident even at that time. In the 1980s Rabbi Elazar Menahem
Schach, the venerable head of one of the major yeshivas in Israel and the
rabbinical authority of a significant non-Zionist religious party, vigorously
denounced the Lubavitch movement as well as the Rebbe himself for false
messianism and worse. Pointing to an assertion by the Rebbe in a passage
dealing primarily with his predecessor that a rebbe is 'the Essence and Being
[of God] placed into a body', Rabbi Schach spoke of nothing less than
avodah zarah (literally, foreign worship), which roughly though imprecisely
means idolatry. His followers refused to eat meat slaughtered by Lubavitch
shochetim (ritual slaughterers) or to recognize Chabad hasidim as adherents
of authentic Judaism. A comment widely attributed to Rabbi Schach (though
also to others) was that the religion most similar to Judaism is Chabad.

We shall see that these positions need to be examined with the utmost

---

[2] Discourse about Orthodoxy is bedevilled by a difficult problem of terminology. There is clearly a
rough division between 'Modern Orthodoxy' and the streams to its religious right centring to a
greater or lesser degree on the intrinsic value of higher secular education, the religious status of the
State of Israel, the role of women, attitudes towards non-Jews and non-Orthodox Jews, the absolute
authority of leading rabbis in matters of public policy, and involvement in the surrounding culture.
Efforts to capture the Orthodoxy or orthodoxies of the right in a single term—ultra-Orthodox, rigorously Orthodox, fervently Orthodox—invariably offend one group or another. My solution is
'Traditionalist Orthodox', which bears no invidious implications but reflects a degree of resistance to
change that is a key, though by no means infallible, marker of these differences.

seriousness, but at the time, along with the vast majority of Orthodox Jews, I dismissed them. I did not want to believe that the Rebbe had really used that expression about the essence of God, and I told myself that if he had, it must have a non-literal meaning. On several occasions in Russia, I almost asked Rabbi Steinsaltz about this, but hesitated to raise what might have been a sensitive matter at such a delicate moment. I also did not want to believe that more than a tiny minority of hasidim affirmed the Rebbe's messiahship with certainty, and I surely did not think that the Rebbe himself approved of this. Since Rabbi Schach zealously upheld other views that were uncongenial to me, I was inclined to see this position as a grievous overreaction to genuine problems. Like most observers, I respected both parties without identifying with either and was saddened by what looked like another unfortunate example of Jewish divisiveness.

As recently as late 1994, when my concern about persistent messianism just a few months after the Rebbe's death was becoming more and more acute, I lost my temper while reading a Jewish author's hostile depiction of a Lubavitch emissary. *The New York Times* had asked me to review Howard M. Sachar's *Farewell España: The World of the Sephardim Remembered*. As I neared the end of the book close to midnight a few days before Yom Kippur, a passage leapt off the page that provoked me to formulate an extraordinarily vigorous response.

After noting the author's apparent lack of familiarity with classical Judaism and its texts, I concluded the review as follows:

Sachar's seeming ignorance of traditional Judaism is compounded by his hostility to contemporary Orthodox Jews. He tells of entering a synagogue in Spain and finding an overweight young man stacking chairs; his shirttail was hanging out and he had food residue on his mouth. Conversation revealed that he was an American Lubavitcher hasid who had left his home nine years earlier to dedicate himself to the rekindling of Jewish observance in Spain. The hasid told the author that he avoided mingling with Gentiles and spoke Yiddish to his family.

Here is Sachar's comment: 'One foot rooted in garlic and chicken soup, the other in sanctimonious ignorance', this hasid 'is an intriguing variant of Jewish revival in Spain. I wonder what Maimonides, ibn Ezra, Judah Halevi, or others of the Golden Age's austere humanists would have made of this gelatinous mess.'

I don't know. But I think I do know what they would have made of a man setting out to write their history armed with minimal knowledge of Jewish tradition and capable of such cruel outbursts directed at its most devoted adherents.[3]

---

[3] *The New York Times Book Review*, 27 Nov. 1994, p. 18. While Maimonides and this Lubavitch emissary would indeed have been less than compatible, this does not excuse the bitter sarcasm and utter lack of empathy in Sachar's characterization.

And this was after I had calmed down.

Notwithstanding these deep reservoirs of sympathy, I grew more and more disturbed as assertions of the Rebbe's messiahship began to proliferate in the last decade and a half of his life. On the one hand, I sometimes reacted to queries about my view of these claims by saying that I hoped the believers turned out to be correct. In a scholarly article, I noted a parallel between Lubavitch hasidim and followers of the seventeenth-century Messiah Shabetai Tzevi but insisted on adding *lehavdil*, a word traditionally used to indicate that the phenomena being discussed are morally, religiously, or existentially incommensurate, despite the editor's objection that such a term was inappropriate in an academic setting.[4] On the other hand, the confident coronation of a man who had not achieved any of the key accomplishments required of the Messiah was so patently alien to Jewish tradition that equanimity began to desert me.

As we shall see, Maimonides (Rambam, 1138–1204) ruled that a king from the House of David attains the status of presumptive Messiah if he studies and observes the Torah assiduously, compels all Israel to follow it, and fights the wars of the Lord. In the article reproduced in the following chapter, I employed a magnanimous formulation about the messianists' utilization of this passage, writing that although they needed to reinterpret four words ('king', 'compels', 'all', and 'wars') in the space of a single sentence, 'the Rebbe's genuine achievements enabled many Chabad rabbinical courts in the nineties to issue what was labelled a legal ruling that he had met the Maimonidean criteria'.

This does not mean that I ever regarded this assertion as genuinely plausible, or even reasonable. By 'king' Maimonides surely meant a temporal ruler with genuine powers of compulsion who fought real wars, not someone who is a king only by virtue of the rabbinic dictum that rabbis are called kings, nor was Maimonides thinking of a man who persuades a few thousand Jews to observe the Torah and whose battles are fought with vans called 'mitzvah tanks' and soldiers belonging to a youth movement named 'the armies of the Lord'.

A distinguished rabbi has told me that he considers this military terminology, endorsed by the Rebbe himself, to have been motivated by the desire to fulfil the Maimonidean criterion, and I am afraid that he is probably correct. In any event, this artificial stratagem does nothing to render the assertion that the Rebbe was presumptive Messiah any more plausible, and by the late

[4] 'Some Ironic Consequences of Maimonides' Rationalistic Messianism' (Heb.), *Maimonidean Studies*, 2 (1991), 1–8 at 4 (Hebrew section).

1980s the categories of 'presumptive' and 'definite' became so blurred that they flowed into one another. In effect, a ruling that the Rebbe could be presumed to be the Messiah was tantamount to the definitive assertion that he was.

At this point, I stopped contributing to Chabad organizations that I knew to be messianist, and I recently unearthed a cancelled cheque dated two months before the Rebbe's death on which I had written 'not to be used for any messianic message'. When I saw a sign at the local mikveh (ritual bath) inviting people to a Passover event in the Chabad House honouring 'the Rebbe the King Messiah', I removed it after calling the proper authorities for permission. In a public talk, I expressed the belief that some hasidim might continue to affirm the messiahship of the Rebbe after his death since one cannot point to a specific text saying in so many words that this belief is outright heresy; nonetheless, I added, such people would surely be read out of the Jewish community. A friend who heard the lecture later confessed that he had thought the first assertion was crazy, though it of course turned out to be correct on a far larger scale than I had dreamt. It is the second expectation that was mistaken.

Many observers, especially after the strokes that disabled the Rebbe not long before his death, put forth a variety of confident prognostications. Upon his passing, some said, we would see large numbers of suicides. (The City of New York designated specially trained counsellors to help hasidim, especially children, to cope with the trauma of the Rebbe's death.) Others asserted that the movement would disintegrate. Still others, immediately after his death, affirmed that the messianist belief might last for a transitional period of a few months, but it would surely disappear when the Rebbe did not return by the first anniversary of the tragic event. I listened politely, wondering at the certainty with which these pronouncements were issued. Even without recourse to scholarly literature on the reaction of believers to the passing of apocalyptic dates,[5] common sense dictated a more cautious approach to the dynamic of such a crisis. As a historian with an interest in both the rise of Christianity and the course of Jewish messianic movements, I awaited developments with curiosity and eager anticipation; as a believing Jew, I looked ahead with more than a touch of angst and trepidation.

There was, as it turned out, ample reason for both the curiosity and the angst. I attended the Rebbe's funeral not to engage in a fact-finding mission

---

[5] The classic study is Leon Festinger, Henry W. Riecken, and Stanley Schachter, *When Prophecy Fails: A Social and Psychological Study of a Modern Group that Predicted the Destruction of the World* (New York, 1956).

but to pay final respects to a great Jewish leader, and I did not see the small group that reportedly danced to the song 'May our Master, Teacher, and Rabbi, the King Messiah, live for ever'. For me, the first indication that belief in the Rebbe's messiahship had withstood his demise came four or five days later when I saw a full-page advertisement in the *Jewish Press*, an Orthodox weekly published in New York and very widely circulated. The ad, which announced 'Good Tidings of Redemption', presented the programme of an afternoon-long event to be held in Oholei Torah, the major Lubavitch yeshiva in Crown Heights, on Sunday, 19 June 1994, precisely a week after the Rebbe's death. The text ended, 'With broken hearts we reaffirm our faith that we will at once witness Techiyas Hameisim [the resurrection of the dead] and we will have the Rebbe lead us out of Golus [exile] immediately, and together we continue to proclaim, *Yechi adonenu morenu verabbenu melech hamoshiach leolam voed* [May our Master, Teacher, and Rabbi, the King Messiah, live for ever].'[6]

At this point, I wrote the following letter to the *Jewish Press*, which was published on 1 July:

It is not yet clear, at least to an outsider, what percentage of the Lubavitch community is represented by the full-page advertisement in your June 17 issue proclaiming that the resurrected Rebbe will reveal himself as the Messiah and lead us to redemption. What is clear is the urgent need for the leadership of Habad to denounce this position in the strongest terms and to guarantee that not a single penny of the community's resources will be made available to anyone espousing it.

More than a decade ago, the Jewish Community Relations Council of New York asked Michael Wyschogrod and me to write a short book addressed to Jews attracted by Jews for Jesus and other Christian missionary groups (*Jews and Jewish Christianity*). In the chapter entitled 'Jesus and the Messiah', we retold a story about an encounter between R. Chaim Soloveitchik and a Christian missionary: R. Chaim was riding on a train and overheard a conversation between the missionary and a group of Jews. When one of the Jews expressed his confidence in the judgment of *Ḥazal* [the talmudic Sages] regarding the Messiah, the missionary responded, 'In that case, how can you explain the fact that R. Akiva initially thought that Bar Kokhba was the Messiah?' The Jews were taken aback and could find no answer. R. Chaim then turned to the missionary and asked, 'How do you know that Bar Kokhba was not the Messiah?' 'That's obvious', he replied. 'Bar Kokhba died without bringing the redemption.' R. Chaim smiled and walked away.

There exist some kabbalistic ideas about King David himself as the final redeemer, but there is no more fundamental Messianic belief in Judaism than the conviction that the Davidic Messiah who appears at the end of days will not die before completing

---

[6] Jewish Press, 17 June 1994, p. II.

his mission. When the Rebbe *zatzal* [of blessed memory] was alive, Messianic claims made for him were ill-advised but well within the boundaries of normative Judaism; indeed, no serious Messianic claims have ever been set forth for a more qualified candidate. But the persistence of such a claim after his death is beyond the pale of Judaism. If it is allowed to survive within Habad even as a minority view, the movement will destroy its legitimacy as a form of Orthodox Judaism. Not only will it forfeit its claim to financial support; the most serious questions will arise about the permissibility of *davening* [praying] in a Habad synagogue and even about the acceptance of a Habad *hashgachah* [supervision of kosher food]. The belief in a dead Messiah cannot be allowed a shred of legitimacy within Judaism. It must be extirpated in its infancy.

The assumption that the withholding of Lubavitch communal resources from messianists was a realistic possibility is striking testimony to my staggering naivety regarding the standing of this belief within the movement. Gradually, step by painful step, I was to learn the full dimensions of my error.

The *Jewish Press* published several letters in response elaborating upon the sources that were to become the stock in trade of messianists defending a kosher-style Second Coming, and we shall have occasion to look at those sources presently. In early July, a Hebrew announcement appeared in the Lubavitch-oriented Yiddish weekly the *Algemeiner Journal* signed by ten leading Chabad rabbis which impelled me to write yet another naive letter, this time to Rabbi Israel Meir Lau, the Ashkenazi chief rabbi of Israel.

The announcement propounded fifteen directives to help hasidim cope with the terrible crisis. The thirteenth forbade posters in the public arena proclaiming the *Yeḥi* ('May our Master . . . the King Messiah live . . .?') because of concern about the reaction of readers and went on to say that the question of reciting the verbal declaration was to be decided by Chabad rabbis in individual localities, whose followers are obligated to obey them 'without convoluted argument' (*beli pilpulim*). At the time, I did not recognize the names of any of the signatories, who hailed from the United States, Canada, England, Australia, and Israel. I now know that several are prominent messianists. Ironically, however, the name, or more precisely, the title which aroused my immediate concern was that of a rabbi who has since pursued a courageous anti-messianist policy: Rabbi Levi Bistritsky, chief rabbi of Safed. In those days, I was staggered to see the name of a man holding such a position on a document that tolerated, even—in some circumstances—required, the recitation of a formula declaring that a rabbi who had just been buried in Queens was the Messiah.

And so I wrote a Hebrew letter to Rabbi Lau:

Honoured Rabbi:

In the last few weeks, we have been witnessing a frightening phenomenon that touches the core of Judaism.

I enclose a letter which I wrote to the *Jewish Press* three weeks ago along with a notice that appeared in the *Algemeiner Journal* last week. Since one of the signatories on that notice is the chief rabbi of Safed, I feel an obligation to bring the matter to the Rabbi's[7] attention.

Paragraphs 13–15 require Chabad hasidim in certain places to continue to declare, 'May our Master, Teacher, and Rabbi, the King Messiah, live for ever.' (A week ago, some of my family members heard a group of children in a Chabad summer camp reciting Grace after Meals with the petition, 'May the Merciful One bless our Master, Teacher, and Rabbi, the King Messiah'.)

I am as removed from zealotry as east is from west, but we are dealing here with a fundamental deviation from one of the basic principles of Judaism as that principle has been understood by the Jewish People as a whole for millennia . . .

There is not a modicum of doubt in my mind that the Rabbinate has a clear and urgent obligation to remove Rabbi Bistritsky from his position if he does not declare unequivocally that it is forbidden to proclaim the *Yeḥi* and that he utterly rejects the belief that the Rebbe of blessed memory is Messiah son of David.

Even in those early, naive days, I don't suppose that I expected Rabbi Lau to fire the chief rabbi of Safed forthwith. In late November, a rabbi working in Rabbi Lau's office sent me a copy of a brief letter that he had mailed to Rabbi Bistritsky asking him to respond to me directly. Needless to say, I heard nothing more.

In the meantime, my sense of puzzlement, bewilderment, disorientation began to grow. The world appeared surreal, as if I had been transported into Alice's Wonderland or a Jewish Twilight Zone. The rules of Judaism seemed suspended. A regular paid feature in the *Algemeiner Journal* entitled 'Torah Thoughts of the Lubavitcher Rebbe May He Live a Long Life' became 'Torah Thoughts of the Lubavitcher Rebbe the King Messiah'. My misreading of the situation was so egregious that I could not believe that an Orthodox publication, notwithstanding its Lubavitch orientation, would print this. Messianist advertisements, prayers, banners, and books persisted and proliferated. Here was a movement of posthumous false messianism self-evidently alien to Judaism that no generation of mainstream Jewish leaders would ever have countenanced even for a fleeting moment. Each day, I expected to hear that major rabbinical figures and organizations had declared this belief unaccept-

---

[7] i.e. Rabbi Lau's. In Orthodox Jewish discourse, especially when conducted in Hebrew, it is often customary to address distinguished rabbis in the third person. This convention will make its appearance periodically in the course of this book.

able in Judaism, disqualified its adherents from holding positions of religious authority, and prohibited Orthodox support for institutions espousing it. But there was nothing. Complete, deafening silence.

The first glimmer of hope came in an unlikely place and, given later developments, was marked by excruciating irony. On 2 December the English-language *Forward*, a thoroughly secular weekly newspaper, published an article reporting that 'Rabbis Blast Crown Heights Messianism'. I was one of those rabbis; the second was a long-standing critic of Lubavitch whose credentials are also essentially academic, but the third was an authority of great distinction. Rabbi Ahron Soloveichik (b. 1918), of Chicago's Yeshivas Brisk as well as of New York's Rabbi Isaac Elchanan Theological Seminary (an affiliate of Yeshiva University), where I was his student in 1962, was reported to have reacted with incredulity to reports that some hasidim continue to believe that the Rebbe is the Messiah: 'I don't believe it. I don't believe it. It is incredible . . . There is no possibility whatsoever' that the Rebbe would emerge from the dead to be the Messiah. 'That could be possible in the Christian faith but not in Judaism.' The very suggestion is 'repugnant to everything Judaism represents'.

Two weeks later, on 23 December, the *Forward* published a letter from Rabbi Soloveichik expressing concern about the earlier report not because of its depiction of his substantive position but because it implied that he considered the belief in the messiahship of the deceased Rebbe characteristic of Lubavitch as a whole:

Everything [your] correspondent wrote in my name is fairly accurate. However, the context in which she wrote it tends to give the impression that I too consider the Lubavitch movement as a cultist movement whose followers are convinced that the late Lubavitcher Rebbe will be resurrected shortly and that he will redeem the Jewish people from exile. Such a notion . . . is the antithesis of the truth.

Your distinguished correspondent quotes me correctly: The late Rebbe . . . 'can't be the Messiah—he is not living—a Messiah has to [be] living—a living Messiah, not a dead Messiah'. All the words of this quotation are perfectly accurate. . . . My complaint consists in the fact that the tone of the article implies that . . . the Lubavitch movement is a cultist movement. This is despicable. . . . My intention was to relate my understanding that the overwhelming majority of the Lubavitcher Chasidim do not [sub]scribe to the notion that the Rebbe will be resurrected as the Messiah.

The letter concluded with a passionate encomium of the late Rebbe and the Lubavitch movement for their remarkable achievements in spreading Judaism to unaffiliated Jews throughout the world.

While I knew even by this juncture that the factual assertion about the overwhelming majority of hasidim was incorrect, my concern was with the issue of principle, and here Rabbi Soloveichik had expressed himself with vigour and without a scintilla of equivocation. A group affirming the messiahship of the Rebbe would be a cult maintaining a belief possible in Christianity but not in Judaism and repugnant to everything Judaism represents. Still, it was clear from his letter that he would not pursue efforts to address an issue which he thought confined to a tiny number of marginal individuals, and the *Forward* article had no discernible effect on the standing of messianist rabbis, educators, or institutions in the larger Orthodox world. As it turned out, Rabbi Soloveichik's profound sympathy for Lubavitch was to lead to unfortunate consequences a year and a half later, but let us, pursuant to a rabbinic dictum, leave this tribulation to its own time.

One response to the *Forward* report came in a letter to the English section of the *Algemeiner Journal* by Zushe Silberstein,[8] the Lubavitch rabbi of the Young Israel of Val Royal, a small synagogue in Montreal. Either unaware or wilfully oblivious of Rabbi Soloveichik's letter, Rabbi Silberstein suggested that the reporter must have misunderstood the statements of the 'renowned scholar' or taken them out of context. Criticism of the messianists, he went on, is merely a resumption of years of misguided attacks on the Rebbe's projects; various sources validate belief in the messiahship of a deceased figure, and one suspects that critics are motivated by scepticism about the dogma of resurrection itself.

In response, I denounced the last assertion as libellous, made a few remarks about the key messianist prooftext (Babylonian Talmud, *Sanhedrin* 98*b*), and noted that even the tiny number of sources that may toy with the possibility that the Messiah could return from the dead 'do not suggest that [he] may die and be buried in the midst of his redemptive mission and then rise up to redeem the world'.[9] Beyond the substance of Rabbi Silberstein's letter, I was deeply troubled by the fact that a spokesman for a movement of false messianism could serve as the rabbi of a synagogue affiliated with the Young Israel movement, a major network of mostly Modern Orthodox synagogues standing near the centre of North American Orthodoxy. By this time, however, my eyes were sufficiently open to reality that I recognized the futility of contacting the National Council of Young Israel to ask how this could be possible.

In the wake of this exchange, I received a curious phone call in my Brooklyn College office. The caller would not say who he was or why he wanted to speak to me but urged me to agree to see him. When it turned out

[8] 3 Feb. 1995.   [9] *Algemeiner Journal*, 24 Feb. 1995.

that the most convenient place to meet would be in my office at Yeshiva University, where I teach a course once a week, I told him that he would probably have to wait at the guard's desk in the lobby, at which point I could be called and would come down to pick him up. 'How will I recognize you?' I asked. 'I'll be the one who looks Jewish', he replied. Although this is arguably not a very useful criterion at Yeshiva University, I left it at that.

Once he had identified himself at our meeting, it turned out that he was a Chabad rabbi of considerable learning who held a position in a non-Chabad synagogue. Distressed to distraction over the transformation of much of his movement into a messianist cult, he had read my letter and came under the cover of anonymity to see if we could think of a way to rescue the situation. Though I could not conjure up a cooperative venture that might easily be pursued with an anonymous collaborator, the meeting was highly informative.

It became painfully evident that the messianist element in Chabad was extremely numerous and powerful, to the point where an uncompromising anti-messianist like my new acquaintance was afraid of identifying himself, where finding like-minded marriage partners for his children was a challenge, and where he had to compromise by putting a mild messianist message into a wedding invitation. In the summer of 1995, I was sent a copy of a bar mitzvah invitation that announced the date as 'the Yartzeit [the anniversary of the death] of HaRav [Rabbi] Levi Yitzchok Schneerson who rests in Eden, father of the Rebbe, King Moshiach, who lives forever with no interruption, who has already been revealed and brought us the Redemption and will immediately bring it to completion with the building of the 3rd Beis HaMikdosh [Temple] and the holy city of Jerusalem. . . . May the king live!'[10] Some time later, another anti-messianist hasid told me that he had to accept a son-in-law who said the *Yeḥi* but at least did so only once a day. Thus, when I was told by friends close to Lubavitch leaders that their sources informed them that the messianists constituted about 5 per cent of the movement, I had no difficulty recognizing self-serving misinformation.

As time passed, it became clearer and clearer that Orthodox Jewish leadership throughout the world was evincing no interest whatever in curbing the messianist belief and that people could openly declare their faith in the Rebbe as the messianic king without incurring any serious consequences in the larger community. I lay awake for many hours asking myself how this was possible, whether the stand of generations of Jewish polemicists against

---

[10] I have reproduced the English side of the invitation but added the phrase 'with no interruption', which appears only in the Hebrew.

Christianity was being summarily discarded, and whether a more ambitious effort on my part to do something would be quixotic and redolent of hubris.

As I agonized over these questions, two phone calls from journal editors aroused me from my non-slumber. Neal Kozodoy, an old classmate from Columbia Graduate School, had recently become editor of *Commentary*. He called to ask if I would review the autobiography of a distinguished Jewish historian, and in the course of our conversation I mentioned my interest in Lubavitch messianism. What emerged from this discussion was the first version of the article ultimately entitled 'The New Messianism', which needed some revision for a *Commentary* audience. I had decidedly mixed feelings about publishing an attack on a group of hasidim in a non-Orthodox journal, and while mulling over the question of making the requisite revisions, I was called on a different matter by Matis Greenblatt, the literary editor of *Jewish Action*, the official journal of the Union of Orthodox Jewish Congregations of America, to whom I had never spoken before. This seemed like the perfect vehicle for such a piece, and I used the opportunity to broach the subject.

For the very reason that I wanted to publish in *Jewish Action* the decision was an exceedingly sensitive one for both the journal and its sponsoring organization. Lubavitch is a major force on the Orthodox scene, and the decision to publish an article attacking a significant segment of the movement was not taken lightly. My misperception that the non-messianists in Chabad would welcome the piece may have been shared by some decision-makers in the Orthodox Union. Every effort was made to avoid the slightest offence to this group. *Jewish Action* highlighted a sentence which called upon Jews to make non-messianist Lubavitch institutions a philanthropic priority, and I was successfully urged to change the assertion that the Rebbe 'strongly implied that he was the redeemer' to 'strongly implied that he *might* be the redeemer'. Each member of the editorial board, several additional rabbis, and a number of lay leaders in the Orthodox Union were asked to read the article. The board was unanimous, and in late spring the article was accepted for publication in the Fall issue.

As the weeks passed, I kept wondering whether the piece would have to be withdrawn because major rabbinical groups would make a declaration that would render its argument moot. After all, the first anniversary of the Rebbe's death would arrive on 1 July, and I had been told by self-styled experts that the rabbis were probably waiting till then to allow the hasidim to overcome their grief. In the light of what I now know about the readiness of rabbinical leaders to speak out on this matter, my expectations were so ludicrous as to be embarrassing. Nothing impeded publication. The article appeared, and I had crossed my personal Rubicon into an explosive public controversy.

TWO

The New Messianism: Passing Phenomenon or Turning Point in the History of Judaism?

I believe with complete faith in the coming of the Messiah, and even though he may tarry I await him each day, hoping that he will come.

THIS VERSION of Rambam's twelfth principle of Judaism has served as a source of faith and consolation for generations of Jews, and, in Christian countries, as a central affirmation of resistance to belief in the messiahship of Jesus. During the past year, we have witnessed a profound transformation in the understanding of this principle by a major movement located well within the parameters of Orthodox Judaism. This may be a passing phenomenon, but it may also mark a significant moment in the history of the Jewish religion. The more convinced Jews are that it is the former, the more likely it is to become the latter.

I

Classical Judaism provides remarkably few normative details about the unfolding of the messianic process and the nature of the end of days. The uncontroversial content of the traditional messianic faith can be compressed into a single sentence: a king from the House of David will arise who will preside over a peaceful, prosperous, monotheistic world with the Temple rebuilt and the Jewish people—including at some point its resurrected dead—returned to its land.

These are hardly trivial assertions, but they left believing Jews in frustrated ignorance about so much that they wanted to know. When will the end arrive? Will it come after a lengthy, perhaps even naturalistic messianic process or burst upon us without the slightest warning? Once the Messiah's reign is in place, are we to expect fundamental changes in the natural order or

Originally published in *Jewish Action* (Fall 1995), 35–44, 88. Reprinted by permission.

a familiar world distinguished only by the absence of political oppression? Perhaps we can expect both, as one redemptive period gives way to another. What is the place of the Torah and the commandments in the age of redemption, particularly in its second phase? At what point can we expect the resurrection? Is it inclusive or highly restrictive? What is the fate of Gentiles to be in the new order? And on and on.

These questions and so many more were disputed by scholars and visionaries, while in the popular imagination their ramifications remained obscure or riddled with contradictions. I think it is fair to say that most Jews envisioned an unending messianic age in which the resurrected dead along with the generation alive at the time of redemption would populate a peaceful, monotheistic world where the Torah is in full force. This perception took little account of the Maimonidean position that resurrection is a temporary state, of the conviction that the world would eventually end, or of the widely held view that the second stage of the redeemed world is one without eating, drinking, or sexual relations (with all that this implies for full observance of the commandments). Jews through the ages have believed in the Messiah, but the precise contours of that faith remained exceptionally fluid.

While it was surely desirable to know the details of the messianic scenario, there was special urgency to the question of when the process would begin. With respect to both points, Rambam turned ignorance into a virtue:

As to all these matters . . . no one knows how they will happen until they happen, because they are impenetrable matters among the prophets. The Sages too had no tradition about these issues; rather, they weighed the scriptural evidence, and that is why they differed about these matters. In any event, neither the order in which these events will take place nor their details are fundamental to the faith, so that no one should . . . spend an inordinate amount of time studying rabbinic statements about these issues . . . nor should one calculate the end; indeed, the rabbis said, 'Blasted be those who calculate the end.' Rather, one should wait and believe in the general doctrine as we have explained. (*Mishneh torah*, Laws of Kings 12: 2)

Nevertheless, the desire to know could be overwhelming, and Jewish literature both before and after Rambam is replete with messianic calculations. The same page of the Talmud which records the curse against calculators provides messianic dates. And Ramban (Nahmanides, 1194–1270), writing less than a century after Rambam's reiteration of the talmudic warning, explained that the talmudic rabbis' concern need not prevent him from calculating. They may have meant their strictures to apply only at a time when the messianic age was still very far off or only to people who proffer their calculations with certitude. Moreover, if I understand him correctly, he provides a particularly sharp argument that stands the rabbinic admonition on its head: the Sages were explicitly motivated by concern that Jews will abandon the messianic faith if a proposed date passes without redemption. But now various messianic calculations are already on the table; if Ramban puts forth a later one and the earlier dates then pass uneventfully, he will have sustained belief in the Messiah by providing a time to which people can still look forward. It is precisely by his silence that he would contribute to undermining the faith.[1]

Not only was Rambam's opposition to messianic calculations often ignored; his assertion that rabbinic statements about the end of days may be unreliable led to a profoundly ironic consequence. His intention was to discourage excessive attention to messianic texts, thereby preventing the heightened expectations that this pursuit could arouse. But if one takes his statement about the potential unreliability of rabbinic information concerning the Messiah and transfers it into an age when a major messianic movement already exists, something extraordinary happens: Rambam provides the most effective defence available against the critics of a messianic pretender.

Though this point has gone unnoticed, it is really quite straightforward. If a messianic claimant is neither a heretic nor an ignoramus, there is only one way to refute his pretensions decisively during his lifetime. The critic must point to specific events that should have taken place at this point in the messianic process which have in fact not occurred. But the only source of such information is precisely the rabbinic material which Rambam has declared unreliable! Thus, the scepticism and messianic caution of the great rationalist backfired, and the supporters of the seventeenth-century Messiah Shabetai Tzevi utilized Rambam's invocation of ignorance to defend the most successful and frenzied messianic movement in the history of the Jewish exile.[2]

II

And so we come to messianic movements.

They are remarkably few. Indeed, a good case can be made that between the Bar Kokhba revolt in second-century Israel and the Sabbatian movement of the seventeenth century, not a single significant movement was generated. This is not to deny that historians can point to two dozen or so messianic figures or precursors during that period, but we ought to have standards when we use the term 'messianic movement'.

---

[1] *Sefer hageulah*, in *Kitvei ramban*, i, ed. Chaim Dov Chavel (Jerusalem, 1963), 290.

[2] I noted and analysed this phenomenon in 'Some Ironic Consequences of Maimonides' Rationalistic Messianism'.

In some cases, as in early Muslim Persia, the messianic ingredient was less than central; in others, we know a name and little more. For more than two decades, a fellow named Norman Bloom stalked the universities of New York and New Jersey, handing out voluminous messianic literature, eventually signing it 'I am the Lord your God Nachum Bloom', and even eliciting a written response from Carl Sagan. Depending on the vagaries of historical preservation, one can easily imagine some future historian writing a study of the Bloomian messianic movement in the north-eastern United States during the latter part of the twentieth century. Even when we can identify a significant following, medieval movements dissipate in extremely short order.

The reason that such movements do not last goes to one of the most fundamental messianic convictions in Judaism: failure is failure. Although Rambam spoke of our ignorance of the details of redemption, his uncertainty stopped at the water's edge:

If a king arises from the House of David who studies the Torah and pursues the commandments like his ancestor David in accordance with the written and oral law, and he compels all Israel to follow and strengthen it and fights the wars of the Lord—this man enjoys the presumption of being the Messiah. If he proceeds successfully, builds the Temple in its place, and gathers the dispersed of Israel, then he is surely the Messiah. He will perfect the entire world so that its inhabitants will serve God together, as it is written, 'For then I will make the peoples pure of speech, so that they all invoke the Lord by name and serve Him with one accord.' But if he does not succeed to this extent, or is killed, it is evident that he is not the one whom the Torah promised; he is, rather, like all the complete and righteous kings of Israel who have died. (*Mishneh torah*, Laws of Kings 11: 4, in the uncensored version.) [I have provided a better, fuller version of the uncensored passage, where the penultimate sentence appears later, in Appendix I.]

There were, of course, two messianic movements in Jewish history which survived the death of their founders: Christianity and Sabbatianism. These movements, which were quickly separated from the mainstream of Judaism, have now been joined by a third group of believers undeterred by the evidence of history: the messianists in Lubavitch, or Chabad, hasidism who continued to affirm the messiahship of the Rebbe after the summer of 1994.

The conditions that produced the extraordinary messianic fervour within Lubavitch during the last decade will no doubt be the subject of much scholarly investigation. These surely include the persecution of the movement in the Soviet Union, the trauma of the Holocaust, and the emphasis placed upon imminent redemption in the writings and discourses of the last two Rebbes.

In some sense, Lubavitch messianism has not been alone. The events of the mid- and late twentieth century have also spawned another form of atypical messianism—religious Zionism's affirmation of an incipient messianic era still lacking an identifiable Messiah. In its more extreme manifestations, this is a genuine messianic movement. It too can be vulnerable to untoward historical developments—the return of parts of the land of Israel to non-Jewish rule, for example—but it is not endangered by the death of a particular mortal. Chabad, however, specifically rules out any messianic significance in the establishment of the State of Israel, which it sees as a purely exilic phenomenon. Nonetheless, for the messianists in Lubavitch, imminent redemption is a certainty, and the redeemer is Rabbi Menachem Mendel Schneerson.

Even during the latter years of the Rebbe's life, Chabad messianism was *sui generis*. With the possible exception of Bar Kokhba, about whom we know very little, Judaism has never had a serious messianic candidate with the *curriculum vitae* of the Rebbe *zt"l* [of blessed memory]. Virtually all the accolades heaped upon him by the messianists are true: he established a worldwide empire of followers, spread Orthodox Judaism to places where it had never been known, energized Jewish education, led substantial numbers of irreligious Jews to observance, and much more.

These exceptional credentials enabled the believers to proffer an argument which is, to my knowledge, unique in the history of Jewish messianism: anyone, they said, who rejects the determination that the Rebbe is the Messiah designated for this generation must identify a superior candidate. Since the position that every generation must have a potential redeemer seems to follow from the widely held belief that sufficient merit can bring the Messiah instantaneously, this challenge carried significant weight.

Thus far, however, we had only a Messiah *in potentia*. The messianists, therefore, reinforced this consideration with two complementary assertions. First, the Rebbe had declared this to be the generation of the redemption. Second, he was said to have fulfilled all the criteria for a presumptive Messiah detailed in the first sentence of the Maimonidean passage quoted above. It is true that this required reinterpreting four words ('king', 'compels', 'all', and 'wars') in the space of a single sentence, but the Rebbe's genuine achievements enabled many Chabad rabbinical courts in the nineties to issue what was labelled a legal ruling that he had met the Maimonidean criteria. So we began to see massive signs on homes and highways, full-page advertisements in the Jewish and general press, and a wave of leaflets and booklets hailing the Rebbe as Messiah.

And then he was felled by a stroke.

Before his illness, the Rebbe appears to have sent out mixed signals regarding his identification as the Messiah. He vigorously proclaimed the imminence of the redemption, encouraged the cry, 'We want Moshiach now', strongly implied that he might be the redeemer, and certainly did not stop the messianist campaign.[3] At the same time, he refrained from any open, explicit proclamation of his own messianic identity, taught that public relations must be conducted in a manner that would win acceptance, and continued to encourage leadership roles for people who were known to oppose the messianists.

Rather than temper messianic enthusiasm, the Rebbe's incapacity fanned its flames. Cryptic gestures could be interpreted as encouragement of the most explicit messianic propaganda, and the illness itself was invested with redemptive significance. Thus, the suffering servant of Isaiah 53, who plays a critical role in Christian theology and anti-Jewish polemic, was mobilized by the believers, so that the passage's complex history was further enriched: it now referred to the suffering of the Jewish people in exile (mainstream medieval Jewish exegesis), or the crucifixion, or the spiritual agonies of Shabetai Tzevi after his forced apostasy, or the stroke of the Lubavitcher Rebbe.

That stroke, however, would not, could not, be fatal. The Rebbe, after all, was the designated Messiah of this generation, which is the generation of the redemption. Not only would the Rebbe not die of this illness; he would not die at all. Rambam wrote of the death of the Messiah at some point after the completion of his mission; the messianists within Lubavitch, however, endorsed other strands of the tradition and popularized a chant that was meant to be taken quite literally: 'May our Master, Teacher, and Rabbi, the King Messiah, live for ever!'

III

And then he passed away.

At this point, everything in Jewish tradition cried out for the need to face reality. But this was not to be.

Days after the Rebbe's death, a messianist newspaper in Israel compared non-believers to the worshippers of the golden calf who lost faith because Moses was absent one day longer than had been anticipated. '[The Rebbe]

---

[3] For a collection of relevant statements compiled by the messianists but containing references to sources which can generally be checked, see *Vehu yigalenu* (Brooklyn, NY, 1994), 17–28, published in English as *And He Will Redeem Us* (Brooklyn, NY, 1994), 29–45.

will appear with literal immediacy and redeem Israel.[4] Five months later, a more moderate publication of Israeli believers pointed to Rambam, who had, after all, set forth 'a great principle, that with respect to these matters, no one knows how they will happen until they happen'.[5] The point, of course, is not to cast doubt on the Rebbe's messiahship but to blunt the force of his death. Shabetai Tzevi's prophet had cited the same Maimonidean passage after his hero's apostasy; once again, the great medieval rationalist was mobilized to defend a failed messianic mission.

Needless to say, the Rebbe's death did create an intellectual and emotional crisis. The primary arguments for the Rebbe as Messiah had manifestly collapsed. If each generation must have its Messiah, this presumably means that he must be among the living, and any appeal to Maimonides' criteria seemed clearly impossible. But no one should underestimate the power of faith.

Within a few months of the tragedy, two stunningly produced volumes appeared, the first in Hebrew and the second in English, explaining the grounds for continued faith (*Vehu Yigalenu*; *And He Will Redeem Us*).[6] The Rebbe's strongest assertion of the imminence of redemption was now understood as a literal prophecy. When a prophet has spoken, no further evidence is necessary, and all contrary evidence is null and void. Two thousand years of messianic literature was scoured to find a handful of broadly relevant, though inapplicable, quotations (and several more irrelevant ones) to demonstrate that Judaism may countenance the belief in a Messiah who returns from the dead.[7] Besides, the Rebbe is expected to return so soon that he remains the

---

[4] *Hageulah ha'amitit vehashelemah*, 38 (6 Tammuz 5754).

[5] *Sihat hashavua*, ed. Menahem Brod (Merkaz Tze'irei Agudat Ḥabad), *Parashat* 'Vayigash', 6 Tevet 5755 (9 Sept. 1994), 3.   [6] See above, n. 3.

[7] Anyone impressed by the citations and arguments in these volumes and in other messianist works such as Shalom Dov Wolpo's *The Last Trial* (Heb.) (Kiryat Gat, 1994) should consider the following brief observations, which assume familiarity with those arguments:

1. Transmigration of souls is not resurrection.

2. 'Concealment' (see *Bamidbar Rabba* 11: 3 and parallels), transferral to the lower Gan Eden (Garden of Eden), or elevation to a heavenly location à la Moses or Elijah are not the same as death and burial. (Some messianists who recognize this assert, as we shall soon see, that the Rebbe never died. The tomb is empty.)

3. With respect to *Sanhedrin* 98*b*: according to the second interpretation in Rashi (there is actually some question about the authorship of the 'Rashi' commentary on this chapter of *Sanhedrin*, *Ḥelek*), the text is irrelevant to our issue. Even according to the first, which was surely a minority reading and is not presented as Rashi's own belief, one talmudic sage asserted that if the Messiah will come from the dead, he will be Daniel, not someone like Daniel. (For some minimal elaboration on the problems with the first interpretation, see my letter to the *Algemeiner Journal*, 24 Feb. 1995, English section, p. B2 (where I wrote the following: 'The first interpretation is problematic not only because it must neutralize the word "like" in the talmudic passage, but also because it produces the assertion that if the Messiah will come from the living he will be R. Judah

Messiah of this generation. Finally, a number of disturbing statements that he himself had issued after his predecessor's death completed the argument.

As the months passed, even this position did not suffice, and a growing number of messianists have begun to make the remarkable assertion that the Rebbe never died, that he remains alive in the full sense of the word. The Rebbe 'is absolutely not dead like other people are'.[8] What happened on 3 Tammuz 5754 was an illusion, analogous to Satan's stratagem before the sin of the golden calf when he showed the Jewish people what appeared to be the coffin of Moses. The Rebbe's funeral, like Moses' coffin, was a

'test for carnal eyes'. . . . In truth, there was no passing away or leavetaking at all, God forbid. . . . What is special about the Prince of the generation is precisely that he is a human being *in a physical body* which must be a part of *the world*, and that is how he unites the world with the Godhead. We cannot say, we do not wish to say, it is entirely impossible to say that there was any 'passing away', God forbid. The Rebbe lives and exists [*ḥai vekayam*] among us now exactly as he did before, literally, literally [*mamash, mamash*].[9]

In many Chabad circles, then, 'moderation' has become the belief that the Messiah really died in 1994 and will soon arise to redeem us.

While the intellectual superstructure is necessary to establish legitimacy, the driving force of faith in the messiahship of the Rebbe has little to do with the interpretation of texts. A remarkable movement had been led for decades by a brilliant leader who prepared no successor. Many hasidim would lose their moorings if they faced the death of their spiritual anchor

the Prince, who maintained, according to the Jerusalem Talmud, that he was of Davidic descent only through his maternal line. See JT *Kilayim* 9: 3.' For a reiteration of this point, a presentation of the letter's reinforcing argument from Tosafot on *Sanhedrin 5a*, and an explanation of my view that the first interpretation was a minority opinion, see Ch. 4 n. 5.)

4. A small minority of Jews believed that King David will return as the Messiah, but this meant King David himself, not one of his descendants.

5. Even Jews who believed that King David would be the Messiah (or the vanishingly tiny number who may have left open the possibility that Daniel might be) did not believe that a Davidic figure born (or reborn) during or after their lifetime would begin the redemptive process only to die and be buried before its completion. Such a position is utterly alien to the most basic messianic posture of all non-Sabbatian Jews through the ages.

[8] R. Shmuel Butman, a major organizer of the Moshiach campaign, as quoted by Debra Nussbaum Cohen, 'One Year after Rebbe's Death, Lubavitcher Soul Burns Bright', *JTA Daily News Bulletin*, 73: 121 (27 July 1995).

[9] R. Levi Yitzchak Ginsberg, 'Thoughts before the Yartzeit of our King Messiah—The Holy Day 3 Tammuz' (Heb.), *Beis Moshiach*, 41 (9 June 1995), 13. Emphasis in the original. The stunning speed with which this belief has spread in the absence of a scintilla of evidence should capture the attention of all historians who have struggled to explain and reconstruct the development of the early Christian belief in the resurrection and the empty tomb.

with unflinching realism, and a French Chabad publication candidly affirmed that without the Rebbe life would be bereft of meaning.

Because all of this seems so strange to outsiders, many observers cannot bring themselves to see the truth: the dominant elements among hasidim in the major Lubavitch population centres of Crown Heights in Brooklyn and Kfar Chabad in Israel—perfectly normal people representing a highly successful, very important Jewish movement—believe that Rabbi Menachem Mendel Schneerson will return from the dead (or from his place of concealment) and lead the world to redemption. With rare, courageous exceptions, the hasidim who do not believe this, among them some impressive intellectuals and communal leaders, remain publicly silent in the face of social pressures that are very difficult to resist. Both the silent and the outspoken members of this valiant, beleaguered group need our help, and I can testify to the fact that they seek it. Thus far, we have failed them.

IV

What, then, has been the reaction from the outside?

The general Jewish community is amused by what it sees as a curiosity. But the future of this belief will not be determined by secular, Reform, or Conservative Jews. There are prices to be paid for religious reform. Once you deny the essentials of a particular doctrine, you lose your standing in a debate about its details. Most Conservative and all Reform Jews have long ago relinquished the belief in a personal Messiah; such Jews cannot readily insist that he must come from the living. Moreover, non-Orthodox Jewry lacks institutional leverage in dealing with hasidim of any variety.

There is, however, one area where this Jewry retains leverage. The power of the purse is no small matter. A significant number of non-Orthodox Jews provide financial support to Orthodox institutions for a variety of perfectly good reasons: nostalgia, a sense that this is after all the most authentic version of historic Judaism, and the conviction that Orthodoxy is the firmest guarantor of a Jewish future.

In a recent issue of the messianist weekly *Beis Moshiach*, a prominent activist indicates that after the Rebbe's death he prayed at the grave for a sign that would determine whether or not he should continue his role in the Moshiach campaign. 'I decided the sign would be simple. If I was able to procure *all* [emphasis in the original] the funds necessary, I would continue. Needless to say, within 24 hours I had been given several tens of thousands of dollars in cash, the entire amount I needed.'[10]

[10] *Beis Moshiach*, 31 (17 Mar. 1995), 67.

The source of these funds is unspecified, but if the donors believed, as they must have, that they were in fact supporting an authentic expression of historic Judaism, they were tragically mistaken. Their contributions buttressed a profound distortion of a classic Jewish belief and helped to undermine the first line of defence against Christian missionizing, which has always been that Judaism cannot accept a Messiah who dies in the midst of his redemptive mission. Ultimately, recognition of this last point may well serve to diminish support from non-Orthodox Jews who are not concerned with the messianic faith *per se* but instinctively recoil from beliefs that smack of Christology. On the other hand, a Lubavitch institution led by someone who rejects the new belief without equivocation could—and should—become a philanthropic priority.

Orthodox Jewry has a particularly large stake in this development. While I was not entirely surprised by the belief that the resurrected Rebbe would return as the Messiah—indeed, I indicated the possibility of such a belief in public lectures—I have been astonished by the tepid reaction in Orthodox circles. Fund-raisers continue to be held, charity boxes proliferate, messianist literature circulates unimpeded in non-Lubavitch synagogues, openly messianist rabbis retain positions in such synagogues and serve in a variety of posts supervised by the Israeli rabbinate.

Numerous factors have come together to bring about this de facto legitimation. Unlike earlier messianic movements, Chabad hasidism has a historical identity and legitimacy which is independent of its messianic message. This makes it possible to hope for the survival of the movement purged of the new belief, but it can also lead to the toleration of the messianic element because of other, attractive characteristics. At the height of the Sabbatian movement in 1666, the spread of mass repentance in expectation of imminent redemption served to mute potential opposition; similarly, Chabad's peerless achievement in attracting *ba'alei teshuvah* [Jews who return to religious observance] throughout the world generates reluctance to disown the movement. In the United States, empathy with a community recently victimized by a pogrom reinforces this reluctance. Consequently, most Orthodox Jews refuse to believe the true dimensions of the messianist takeover and tell themselves that ignoring it will make it go away. On the other hand, some segments of extremely orthodox Judaism broke so decisively with Lubavitch even before the Rebbe's death that they see little need to denounce a movement which they have already placed beyond the pale.

Finally, contemporary Chabad messianism differs from earlier messianic movements because it has arisen in a pluralistic environment. Modern Orthodox Jews have long endorsed the ideal of toleration, and in many contexts they cooperate with secular, Reform, and Conservative Jews whose ideological distance from them is greater than that of the Chabad messianists. In this instance, of course, the level of cooperation is far more intimate and the degree of legitimation far greater. As for the so-called ultra-Orthodox, even they have become accustomed to living with religious variation in a larger Jewish community; at worst, Lubavitch would be another group of inauthentic Jews. In all circles, pluralism moderates the intensity of the reaction.

V

With the exception of Sabbatianism, Lubavitch messianists have already generated the largest and most long-lived messianic movement in Jewish history since antiquity. Along with Sabbatianism and Christianity, this movement has survived the death of its Messiah. Although it has much in common with its two predecessors, it is also significantly different, and some of the differences, particularly Chabad's commitment to observing all the mitzvot and the character of its messianic figure, still entitle us to use the term *lehavdil* in comparing these movements. At the same time, the similarities are so striking and the issue so critical that we have no right to mince words in drawing analogies. A summary comparison, then, should provide a useful overview.

Among the similarities:

- The creation of new grounds for belief in response to apparent failure.
- Faith in an immediate return which is then postponed.
- The citation of evidence from biblical verses, and, in the case of Sabbatianism and Lubavitch, from rabbinic literature as well.
- The appeal by Sabbatians and Lubavitch hasidim to Rambam's affirmation of ignorance regarding the details of the messianic process.
- The belief (held by some but not all Lubavitch messianists) that the messianic figure is not really dead at all.

Among the differences:

- The exceptional qualifications of the Rebbe.
- The argument before the Rebbe's death, and in some circles even after it, that the sceptic is obligated to provide a superior candidate.
- The movement's viability in the absence of its messianic component.
- The belief in a Messiah who, unlike Shabetai Tzevi and perhaps unlike

Jesus, never made a formal, explicit declaration of his messiahship. Hence—a movement that might be described as false messianism without a false Messiah.

- The commitment to the full observance of Jewish law.
- The availability of a vast library of videotapes which can preserve a sense of the departed Messiah's physical presence.
- The pluralistic environment.

VI

What is the likely future of this belief?

Confidence that it will disappear because outsiders consider it irrational is profoundly misplaced. The belief that the Rebbe is the Messiah is no more irrational than the belief that Jesus of Nazareth was resurrected, ascended bodily to heaven, and will one day return to redeem the world. It is true that the 'logic' of the position that the Rebbe is the Messiah of this generation requires abandonment of the faith after the passage of time, but it is no less true that the logic of the argument for his messiahship during his lifetime required abandonment of the faith after his death. Sufficiently motivated believers could readily construct an argument to avoid this unwanted conclusion; indeed, for believers that the immortal Rebbe is currently alive and that his lifetime defines the generation, the argument has already been constructed. As I write, thousands of Jewish children are being taught to chant 'May our Master, Teacher, and Rabbi, the King Messiah, live for ever' with reference to a man who was buried last summer [1994]. Anyone who thinks that it will be easy to uproot such a faith, let alone that it will soon evaporate of its own accord, is engaging in self-deception.

Should the belief survive for any length of time, how is it likely to evolve? One Lubavitch hasid who opposes this development but is resigned to its success has consoled himself with the hope that the messianic description of the Rebbe will become an empty title. Lubavitch has 'the old Rebbe', 'the middle Rebbe', and 'the prior Rebbe'; now it will add 'the Rebbe, the King Messiah'. This is not impossible, but a look at Christianity and Sabbatianism raises the spectre of something far more serious.

The radicalization of those earlier movements was no accident. There is a logic immanent in the belief in a deceased Messiah which pushes the faithful in a disturbing direction. Once the redeemer can come from among the dead, he must compete for his crown with a stellar list of all the scions of the

House of David who ever lived. In the Rebbe's lifetime, messianists already applied to him a favorite *midrash* [rabbinic homily] of medieval Christian polemicists which described the Messiah as greater than Moses and the ministering angels, while others occasionally described him as 'the essence of the Infinite in physical garb'.[11] The growing conviction that his physical existence has continued without interruption strongly underscores this uniqueness. A believer has recently asked me, 'Who disseminated more Torah? Moshe Rabbenu [Moses our Rabbi, i.e. Moses of the Bible] or the Rebbe?' As for full-fledged incarnationist rhetoric, I do not believe that it is yet pervasive, but at least one disturbing report has come to my attention, and I do not hesitate to say that there is cause for grave concern.

At this point, the messianists can still finesse the other radicalizing force in posthumous messianic movements—the need to explain the purpose of the first Coming. Since the Rebbe's return is believed to be imminent, this remains a unitary messianic career. But at some point the question will rear its head, and the answers provided by Christians and Sabbatians are not reassuring.

We stand at the beginning of a remarkable and intriguing phenomenon. After two thousand years of Jewish confrontation with Christianity, a significant group of Orthodox Jews is prepared to affirm belief in a Messiah who was laid to rest in the summer of 1994. It is not yet clear if we are dealing with a transient development or with a faith which can be sustained. It may still be that vigorous opposition from the outside, the cessation of financial support, and internal dissent will succeed in aborting this belief. It may also be that the belief will survive, perhaps in radicalized form, and that Chabad will consequently be marked as a pariah movement in Judaism. A profound, tragic irony would follow: through the misguided efforts of his own followers, one of the great leaders of twentieth-century Jewry would be remembered primarily as a failed Messiah.

But it may also be that we shall continue to see a situation that I should never have thought possible a year ago. There will be no further radicalization, at least in the short run. The widely held belief among Lubavitch hasidim that the Rebbe is the Messiah will persist with undiminished fervour. Yet the bearers of this faith will remain an accepted part of Orthodox Judaism

[11] See e.g. M. Zeligzon (ed.), *A Voice Announcing and Saying: Anthology of New Torah Interpretations. The King Messiah and the Final Redemption* (Heb.) (1983), 32, 48–9. See also Shalom Dov Wolpo, 'Comfort Ye, Comfort Ye, My People—Double Comfort' (Heb.), *Kfar ḥabad*, 106 (5743), 6–7. (I am grateful to Zalman Alpert of the Mendel Gottesman Library of Yeshiva University for bringing R. Wolpo's article to my attention.)

because a bemused/sympathetic/tolerant/self-deceiving/indifferent/distract-ed/contemptuous leadership does nothing to delegitimate them.

Should this situation continue, the fluidity of the Jewish messianic idea will have proven to be greater than our ancestors could have imagined, our children will no longer be able to tell Christian missionaries that the Jewish faith does not countenance belief in a Messiah whose mission is interrupted by death, and one of the defining characteristics of Judaism in a Christian world will have been erased.

There is no greater responsibility for any generation of Jews—and all the more so for its rabbinic leadership—than to serve as faithful guardians of the basic contours of the faith, so that we transmit the essentials of Judaism to our children the way we received them from our parents. We are in the process of betraying this fundamental trust. The issue is not whether we our-selves believe that the Rebbe is the Messiah. When a leading messianist is appointed rabbi of a neighbourhood in Jerusalem, when a synagogue rabbi can proclaim the messiahship of the Rebbe without jeopardizing either his position or his synagogue's affiliation with a mainstream Orthodox move-ment, when rabbis raise funds for open messianists and treat them as Ortho-dox Jews in good standing, we thereby affirm the full legitimacy of this belief. We award victory to Christianity in a crucial aspect of its millennial debate with Judaism. We accept a fundamental revision of a cardinal principle of the faith. We must tremble before the judgement of God and history.

THREE

Aborted Initiatives and Sustained Attacks

REACTION to the article was swift, widespread, and varied. A leading Orthodox commentator and communal figure called *Jewish Action* to say that this was the most important piece they had ever published. The late Rabbi Shmuel Yaakov Weinberg, head of Yeshiva Ner Israel of Baltimore, told a member of the editorial board that publishing it was an act of great merit (*mitzvah gedolah*). Rabbi Chaim Dov Keller of the Telshe Yeshiva in Chicago, who had written a critical article about Lubavitch during the Rebbe's lifetime, called to express his congratulations. A prominent spokesman for Satmar hasidim, who represent a very different element in the Traditionalist Orthodox spectrum and whose long-standing hostility to Lubavitch I have already noted, did the same. There was even one call of unmitigated support from a Lubavitch emissary in New Jersey.

Nonetheless, the dominant reaction from ostensibly anti-messianist Lubavitch circles shattered yet another of my naive expectations. Despite the article's careful focus on the messianist group, Chabad solidarity prevailed, and the Orthodox Union (OU) was accused of having authorized an attack on Lubavitch as a whole. The non-messianists, I was told, were taking care of the matter internally, and external criticism would only complicate their task. A columnist for the *Algemeiner Journal* suggested that the OU might have published the article because it saw itself as 'the potential economic beneficiary of the hit that David Berger suggests the rest of the Orthodox community deliver to Lubavitch'.[1]

While I was gratified by the many private expressions of support and disappointed by the reaction within the movement, my primary concern was to turn this article into a vehicle for meaningful statements by groups and individuals whose views would really count. And so I sent copies along with

[1] Larry Gordon, 'Has Moshiach Lost the OU?', *Algemeiner Journal*, 3 Nov. 1995, English section, p. B3. Gordon was so enamoured of his insight that he published a similar observation more than two years later (*Algemeiner Journal*, 20 Feb. 1998, p. B3).

covering letters to several major rabbinic figures and organizations, including the Rabbinical Council of America (RCA), which represents the Modern Orthodox rabbinate in North America, the Council of Torah Sages (Moetzes Gedolei Hatorah), which is the governing body of the Traditionalist Orthodox Agudath Israel of America, Rabbi Aharon Lichtenstein of Yeshivat Har Etzion in Israel, one of the greatest rabbinical figures in contemporary Modern Orthodoxy, and Chief Rabbi Jonathan Sacks of England.[2]

To the RCA:

. . . Enclosed [is] a proposed resolution that I urge the RCA to adopt.

I have spent a significant part of my professional career studying the Jewish–Christian debate as well as Jewish messianism. If this article and [this letter] achieve nothing else, they should at least enable me to tell the *beit din shel ma'alah* [the heavenly court], *Yadi lo hayetah bama'al hazeh* ['My hand has not been in this betrayal[3]']. It is my fervent hope that every member of the RCA will be able to do the same.

Proposed Resolution

The Rabbinical Council of America declares that the belief that the late Lubavitcher Rebbe *zt"l* [of blessed memory] is the Messiah has no place in Judaism. No one affirming this belief should be permitted to serve in a rabbinical position or exercise any rabbinic function. At the same time, the RCA urges Jews to extend support to Lubavitch institutions whose leaders are prepared to reject this belief publicly and without any equivocation.

To the Council of Torah Sages:[4]

. . . The phenomenon addressed in the [enclosed] article touches the core of Judaism, and I stand bewildered at the absence of a reaction from the sages of Israel. Is it imaginable even for a fleeting moment that the Hazon Ish [Rabbi Abraham Karelitz, 1878–1953, leader of Traditionalist Orthodoxy in pre-state Israel] or Rabbi Aharon Kotler would have remained silent in the face of a movement of false messianism commanding the loyalty of thousands of observant Jews? In light of these new developments, even one who identified with Rabbi Schach's sharp criticism during the Rebbe's lifetime may not in my view rely on that criticism and remain silent in this hour.

For a millennium and more, the first Jewish response to Christian missionaries was that Judaism rejects the belief in a Messiah who dies and is buried in the midst of his mission. It is perfectly clear that this answer was not simply a polemical tactic; it reflected the sincere, profound belief of the Jewish people. If we do not immediately declare that a believer in the messiahship of the Rebbe stands outside the boundaries of authentic Judaism, we annul the central messianic stance of our fathers and

---

[2] I also wrote letters that I have not reproduced here to R. Norman Lamm, President of Yeshiva University, and the chief rabbis of Israel.   [3] Cf. Ezra 9: 2.   [4] Translated from Hebrew.

forefathers, treating it as the dust of the earth, and we transmit to our descendants a Judaism that differs from the Judaism of all generations on a point of the most profound importance. It seems to me that a declaration like the one that I proposed to my RCA colleagues in the enclosed letter is the most minimal step that will enable our children to point to a *fundamental* rejection of this new belief by the rabbis of our generation.

Every one of us stands as a guardian of the faith of Israel. If the current silence continues, I am profoundly concerned that our descendants will remember us as the generation that declared false messianism kosher and blurred the boundary between Judaism and Christianity for untold generations to come.

Who knows if it was not for such an occasion that you attained to royal position? [Esther 4: 14]

To Rabbi Lichtenstein:

. . . I admire the Rebbe *zt"l* enormously. The steps I am recommending are not only consistent with such admiration; they may well be necessary to prevent his going down in history as a false Messiah. (In the article, I used the more appropriate phrase 'failed Messiah', but in the real world such subtle distinctions will surely be lost.[5])

My main concern, however, is not for the Rebbe's place in history; it is for the preservation of an uncorrupted messianic faith. I am not exactly a prototypical *kano'i* [zealot], and I share the Modern Orthodox community's discomfort with steps that smack of intolerance. But the highest value in Judaism is not tolerance. The highest value in Judaism is Judaism. . . .

The blithe acceptance of this development over the last year has left me in stunned disbelief, and the notion of becoming the *Defensor Fidei* [Defender of the Faith] seems like some surreal fantasy. The time has come for people with genuine qualifications to assume this task.

To Rabbi Sacks:

. . . I hope somewhat wistfully that this article will accomplish something, but the last year has taught me that all my instincts about what Orthodox Jews will and will not accept are thoroughly unreliable . . .

---

[5] The term 'failed messiah' is borrowed from a highly controversial article by Irving Greenberg, in which he suggested that it be used for a figure who is mistaken about his messianic status but puts forth a message reflecting the right values. 'False messiah' should be restricted, he said, to figures whose teachings were intrinsically harmful. See his 'The Relationship of Judaism and Christianity: Toward a New Organic Model', in Eugene Fisher, A. James Rudin, and Marc H. Tanenbaum (eds.), *Twenty Years of Jewish–Catholic Relations* (New York and Mahwah, NJ, 1986), 191–211. Greenberg is well aware that Jews have been accustomed to use the expression 'false messiah' about all messianic pretenders; as Yosef Hayim Yerushalmi of Columbia once put it in an oral presentation, 'A false messiah is a messiah who fails.' The controversiality of Greenberg's proposal lay in its context: he proposed that the new term be used about Jesus. Whatever one's view of its applicability in that instance, the neologism seemed perfect for my purposes here.

Maybe I react so strongly because of a personal *negi'ah* [special interest]. You once wrote some very kind things about *Jews and Jewish Christianity*. The chapter I wrote for that book called 'Jesus and the Messiah' used to be one of my hopes for a *ḥelek la'o-lam haba* [a portion in the world to come]. If Lubavitch messianists continue to be accepted as Orthodox Jews and even as Orthodox rabbis, the central argument of that chapter will be null and void, and I will have to pursue the standard, far more difficult path to eternal felicity.

Of all these letters, the one which I followed up with alacrity was the proposal to the RCA. The response was: 'Do you want us to start a fight with Lubavitch?' In discussions with various knowledgeable individuals, many of them sympathetic, the unanimous consensus was that no such resolution would ever be adopted. Lubavitch was too powerful and the RCA too involved with all segments of Orthodoxy to allow a divisive declaration of this sort. I would simply have to forget about it.

My other letters also failed to elicit useful results, and I was compelled to turn my attention to another, inevitable consequence of the article. *Jewish Action* began to receive written responses, some laudatory, some critical, some carefully reasoned, some sarcastic and denunciatory. One of my reservations about writing the article (and this book) stemmed from reluctance to publicize the messianists' interpretation of the handful of rabbinic sources that they cite to buttress their doctrine. Some readers insufficiently anchored in a millennial Jewish consensus might, I feared, lose their moorings and conclude that belief in the Second Coming of the Rebbe is after all an acceptable option in Judaism. It was for this reason that I buried my response to those citations in a footnote encapsulating the key points and kept it brief, almost cryptic. Nonetheless, I understood perfectly well that if the article would elicit the expected stormy reaction, the effort to restrict myself to a brief refutation would fail, and I would be forced to confront the issue at greater length.

Though the editors of *Jewish Action* sent me all the letters that they received, they chose to publish only four. The first, by Zalman Alpert, spoke of the importance of appointing a successor to the Rebbe and required no response. The second, by Jena Morris Breningstall, argued briefly that though much of what I wrote was regrettably true, I did not distinguish sharply enough between the messianists and their opponents. The latter, she said, who head 'the *official* Lubavitch institutions', have publicly distanced themselves from the messianists and are deserving of an apology.

The next two letters were very lengthy and very critical. One, by Rabbi

Isser Zalman Weisberg of Toronto, was virtually as long as the original article, and offered a point-by-point refutation of my key arguments. The other, sharper and more personal, came from Rabbi Shmuel Butman, head of the Lubavitch Youth Organization and the most visible advocate of the messianist position, who signed his letter, 'Chairman, International Campaign to Bring Moshiach'. It is difficult not to smile at the name of this organization, which is paralleled by an Israeli 'Committee for the True and Complete Redemption', but when the smile has faded away, there are serious issues to confront.

Before proceeding to summarize the arguments levelled against my article, I should like to inoculate readers by reproducing the two messianist propositions formulated in the introduction to this volume:

1. A specific descendant of King David may be identified with certainty as the Messiah even though he died in an unredeemed world. The criteria always deemed necessary for a confident identification of the Messiah—the temporal redemption of the Jewish people, a rebuilt Temple, peace and prosperity, the universal recognition of the God of Israel—are null and void.

2. The messianic faith of Judaism allows for the following scenario: God will finally send the true Messiah to embark upon his redemptive mission. The long-awaited redeemer will declare that all preparations for the redemption have been completed and announce without qualification that the fulfilment is absolutely imminent. He will begin the process of gathering the dispersed of Israel to the Holy Land. He will proclaim himself a prophet, point clearly to his messianic status, and declare that the only remaining task is to greet him as Messiah. And then he will die and be buried without having redeemed the world. To put the matter more succinctly, the true Messiah's redemptive mission, publicly proclaimed and vigorously pursued, will be interrupted by death and burial and then consummated through a Second Coming,

The few genuinely relevant sources cited by my critics purportedly demonstrate the presence in Jewish thought of a theoretical possibility that the Messiah can come from the dead. None of them even begins to demonstrate that either of the above propositions has ever been affirmed by any mainstream Jew.

Let us turn, then, to a summary of the criticisms themselves.

Rabbi Weisberg:

A number of sources indicate the legitimacy of the belief in a Messiah who comes from the dead. First, the Talmud in *Sanhedrin* 98*b* quotes the sage Rav as follows: 'If [the Messiah] is of the living, he is like our holy rabbi [i.e. Rabbi Judah the Prince]; if he is from the dead, he is like Daniel.' [The commentary generally ascribed to Rashi (1040–1105) provides two explanations: (1) if the Messiah will be from the living, then he will be Rabbi Judah, who is marked by both suffering and absolute piety; if from the dead, he will be the biblical Daniel, who combined the same two traits. The word 'like' in the talmudic statement must be elided; (2) if a *model* for the Messiah can be found among the living, it would be Rabbi Judah; if from the dead, it would be Daniel.] The remark in the article that only 'a vanishingly tiny number' of Jews may have left open the possibility that Daniel would be the Messiah is unsupported by even a scintilla of evidence. Rabbi Isaac Abarbanel, in his late fifteenth-century work *Yeshuot meshiḥo*, also indicates that belief in a resurrected Messiah is acceptable [when he cites this talmudic passage as evidence that one should not be surprised by such a rabbinic opinion]. Moreover, the Jerusalem Talmud (*Berakhot* 2: 4) says, 'if the messianic king is from the living, his name is David; if from the dead, his name is David.' Though some take this to mean that a spark of King David's soul will be in the Messiah, others refer it to David himself. Finally, the article's 'assertion that all the sources are inapplicable and irrelevant'[6] is further undermined by passages that may indeed not refer to the Messiah's death and resurrection but predict his bodily ascent to heaven or his appearance, disappearance, and reappearance.

The interpretation of the sources is in any event not central. When confronting difficult questions, Jews are required by the biblical precept of *lo tasur*, i.e. do not stray from the instruction of rabbinic authorities, to follow the opinion of their *rav muvhak* (their principal teacher). Since the Lubavitcher Rebbe stated that those who believed in the messiahship of his father-in-law need not abandon this belief even after the latter's death,[7] Lubavitch hasidim are obligated by the Torah to accept his view. While it is true that there is some debate within the movement as to the Rebbe's position, this is an internal matter of no concern to anyone outside that community.

As for Maimonides, he indeed asserted that if a person presumed to be the Messiah dies, it is clear that he is in fact not the Messiah. All this means, however, is that he has lost the legal presumption. Once he is resurrected he could certainly regain his lost status. One would hardly object to the belief that a distinguished rabbi of the past will be resurrected as high priest or head of the

---

[6] My actual words were 'a handful of broadly relevant, though inapplicable, quotations (and several more irrelevant ones)'.

[7] For example, his talk on 13 Shevat 5711 (20 Jan. 1951), printed in *Likutei siḥot*, vol. ii, p. 517.

rabbinical court. Moreover, in the light of a later formulation unknown to Maimonides that a resurrection of the very righteous will surely take place shortly before the redemption,[8] the presumption may never be lost at all. In any event, the Lubavitch conviction that the Rebbe is the Messiah rests not on this Maimonidean presumption but on the movement's tradition 'that the *Tzaddik* [the most righteous leader] of the generation is also the potential *Mashiach* of the generation. . . . Until another *tzaddik* with the proper credentials is crowned as the new Rebbe (which, for several reasons, will not happen), Hasidim will continue to consider the Rebbe as the *Mashiach* of this generation.'

There may, in fact, be an additional dimension that can further enrich our understanding of the Rebbe's messianic role. Jewish tradition speaks of a *mashiaḥ ben yosef* (Messiah son of Joseph) who, despite his title, is of Davidic descent.[9] He dies before completing the redemption and is ultimately resurrected by Messiah son of David. Since some sources suggest that these two figures are in fact the same person,[10] who knows if the Rebbe may not be Messiah son of Joseph or even the two messiahs in one?

However that may be, the motive for the messianists' faith is crystal clear. Though one of the main points of the article is that the conditions that produced the messianic fervour in Lubavitch 'will no doubt be the subject of much scholarly investigation', little investigation is needed. The fervour results solely from the words of the Rebbe, who said that the Messiah is already here and that the process of redemption is beginning to unfold.[11] It is hardly surprising that the hasidim believed him. In the event that the Messiah does not arrive in the near future, the Rebbe's reputation will be no more affected than that of Nahmanides was when the latter's predicted messianic date came and went uneventfully.

Finally, the article vastly exaggerates the threat of this belief, which in fact poses not the slightest danger to Judaism. Parallels to Christianity are irrelevant since many Jewish beliefs are also affirmed by Christians. As to the polemical issue, 'a simple examination of the major debates between great Torah scholars and Christians throughout the ages will reveal that [the] argument [against 'a Mashiach who dies'] plays no role at all'. Indeed, when the

---

[8]   R. David ibn Abi Zimra (Radbaz, 1480–1574), *Responsa* (Heb.), vol. iii, no. 1069.

[9]   Ben Yehoyada on *Sanhedrin* 98*b* and additional sources cited in Reuben Margaliot, *Margaliyot hayam* (Jerusalem, 1958) on *Sanhedrin* 94*a*, no. 4. This evidence, as we shall see, is questionable.

[10]   Nathan Sternhartz, *Biography of R. Naḥman of Bratslav* (Heb.) (Bratslav, 1875), 13, and *Ramatayim tzofim* (R. Shmuel of Sieniawa, 1881) on *Eliyahu zuta*, 20. Here too we shall see that the evidence is less than compelling. (I have not reproduced two additional citations that are somewhat peripheral.)   [11]   Talk on *Parashat* 'Mishpatim' 5752 (1 Feb. 1992) and elsewhere.

apostate who confronted Nahmanides at the Barcelona disputation of 1263 cited a rabbinic passage 'to prove that *Mashiach* was born long ago and passed away', the response was not 'that the belief in a *Mashiach* who passes away is alien to Judaism but rather, that the fact that the Midrash groups *Mashiach* with several other individuals who are in Gan Eden [paradise] proves that *Mashiach* is human, not divine'. While recent works directed against the Christian mission (like the book I wrote with Michael Wyschogrod) make the argument against a Messiah who dies without completing the redemption, and the need to abandon it may consequently cause some difficulties for 'modern day anti-missionary activists', these are insufficient grounds for penalizing believers in 'a legitimate Torah view'. The genuine, classic Jewish argument was that Jesus (and Shabetai Tzevi) did nothing to prove their messianic role; on the contrary, rather than strengthen Torah, they strove to change it. Even more fundamentally, the primary Christian deviation from Judaism lay in the concept of the Trinity and the attribution of divinity to a human being.

In the final analysis, while messianist publicity is undesirable, we must avoid any steps that would hamper the crucial work of Lubavitch 'in all corners of the world'.

A reasoned, vigorous argument.

Rabbi Butman:

Rabbi Butman began his letter with the assertion that my 'writings on Lubavitch and the belief in Moshiach claim to be scholarly while only rehashing the same old apologist propaganda' of anti-Lubavitch circles since the 1950s. Other than Maimonides, I quote no traditional sources to support my position, and the Maimonidean reference to the Messiah's 'failing or being killed' is clearly inapplicable to the Rebbe, whose emissaries continue the effort to bring the redemption to this day. In a passage that Rabbi Butman deleted in response to an editorial request that he compress his reply, he cited a talk by the Rebbe to buttress a remarkable assertion: Maimonides' requirement that the Messiah build the Temple in its place really means, at least in the initial stage, 'in *his* place' and was consequently met by the renovation of 770 Eastern Parkway (the headquarters of the Lubavitch movement). As to the ingathering of the exiles, this had already begun with the exodus of Soviet Jews to Israel.

The letter goes on to cite the rabbinic statements and the remark by Abarbanel noted by Rabbi Weisberg and adds a passage by the Sedei Hemed (as R. Hayim Hezekiah Medini (1832–1904) is known, after the title of his encyclopedic work) quoting a letter sent to him by another rabbi indicating that in the light of *Sanhedrin* 98*b*, it is remotely possible that the Messiah will come from the dead. Thus, both Abarbanel and the Sedei Hemed regard this possibility as a 'practical likelihood'.

Moreover, says Rabbi Butman, though I concede the importance of the Lubavitch movement's activities, I am in effect arguing with the Rebbe himself. It was he who declared in 1951 that his deceased predecessor 'will redeem us'; it was he who encouraged the singing of 'Long live the Rebbe, King Moshiach' in 1991 and thereafter 'even as he was aware of the events that would transpire between that time and the present'. Finally, my criticism of Jewish leaders for failure to act is misplaced and pompous. There is no reason to believe 'that their motivation for not speaking out with Berger's venom is for any reason other than that they do not share his ignorance and lack of tolerance'.

Though *Jewish Action* sent me the initial versions of Rabbi Weisberg's and Rabbi Butman's responses in a timely fashion, the editors indicated that both would undergo revision at the authors' hands. I was thus able to fill a letter-size piece of paper with scribbled comments but could not actually sit down to write a careful rejoinder. By the time Rabbi Weisberg's final text arrived, I had one full day to begin and complete the job. Though I had thought very hard about the issues for many months, this remained a daunting challenge, and there are two omissions that I continue to regret. I did not point out that the Sedei Hemed was reproducing a lengthy letter that he had received from an obscure rabbi; the passage at issue consists of a few lines in the middle of an extensive document. While it is reasonable to argue that he would not have reproduced that passage had he considered it fundamentally at odds with Judaism, there is no basis for concluding that he agreed with it. More importantly, I did not explicitly make the point about the inapplicability of the messianists' sources to a movement that *confidently* identifies a specific deceased descendant of David as the Messiah, thus abolishing entirely the classical criteria for an unequivocal identification of the redeemer. The rejoinder reprinted in Chapter 4, then, was the result of an exhausting day and evening that would, I imagined, bring my involvement in this matter to its end.

FOUR

The Second Coming: A Rejoinder

O N 1 7 J U N E 1994, five days after the *petirah* (passing) of the Lubavitcher Rebbe *zt"l*, an advertisement appeared in the *Jewish Press* declaring that he would be resurrected as the Messiah. At that point, I wrote a letter containing the following assertion: 'There is no more fundamental messianic belief in Judaism than the conviction that the Davidic Messiah who appears at the end of days will not die before completing his mission' [*Jewish Press*, 1 July 1994; see above, Ch. 1].

In my article in *Jewish Action* [see Ch. 2], I formulated the point as follows: 'Even [the small minority of] Jews who believed that King David would be the Messiah (or the vanishingly tiny number who may have left open the possibility that Daniel might be) did not believe that a Davidic figure born (or reborn) during or after their lifetime would begin the redemptive process only to die and be buried before its completion. Such a position is utterly alien to the most basic messianic posture of all non-Sabbatian Jews through the ages.'

I repeat these formulations here because their key point has apparently been missed by both Rabbi Butman and Rabbi Weisberg. Although, as we shall see, I regard the belief that Mashiach ben David (Messiah son of David) can come from the dead as a rejected position (a *shitah dehuyah*), the core of my argument does not depend on this conviction. Whoever the Messiah might be, once he begins his messianic activities, there is no dispute as to the certainty that he sees the process to its completion without an intervening death, burial, and resurrection.

Jews have written numerous works through the ages describing the career of the Messiah. In some cases, we find only highlights of the unfolding messianic drama, in others, painstaking accounts of every stage. Differences abound. Alternative scenarios are proposed. But nowhere—nowhere—does Messiah son of David appear on the eschatological stage only to die and be

Originally published in *Jewish Action* (Winter 5756/1995), 65–8. Reprinted by permission.

buried before the end of the final act—not in the *Bavli* [Babylonian Talmud] not in the *Yerushalmi* [Jerusalem Talmud], not in the Zohar [the major work of Jewish mysticism], not in the standard midrashim [rabbinic exegetical and homiletical works], not in the *pesiktot* [a genre of midrashic literature], not in the apocalyptic midrashim (*Sefer zerubavel*, *Sefer eliyahu*, *Otot hamashiah*, *Nistarot derabbi shimon bar yoḥai*, and many more), not in the letter of Rabbi Hai Gaon (939–1038) [a work describing the messianic process], not in the treatise of Rabbi Sa'adiah Gaon (882–942) [a section on the messianic age of *The Book of Beliefs and Opinions*], not in the *Sefer hage'ulah* [Book of the Redemption] of Ramban [Nahmanides], not in the messianic works of Abarbanel—not anywhere.

This is no ordinary argument from silence. The notion that this option existed but was not mentioned in any of the texts whose fundamental purpose was to describe the unfolding of the messianic age defies reason. Since the essence of Lubavitch messianism rests on the claim that the Rebbe had begun the process of redemption and would soon return to complete it, there can be no question that we are dealing with a belief utterly rejected by every generation of Jews before the summer of 1994.[1]

Are there sources which make this rejection explicit? Aside from Rambam [Maimonides], whom we shall revisit later, Jews repeatedly and vigorously rejected such a belief precisely where we would expect them to do so—in confrontations with representatives of a dominant faith which was partly defined by that very belief.

Rabbi Weisberg makes the remarkable assertion that 'a simple examination' of the major Jewish polemics shows that the argument that the Messiah will not die before completing his mission 'plays no role at all'. Let us begin, then, with selections from a famous passage in the *Vikuaḥ haramban* [The Disputation of Nahmanides, or Barcelona Disputation].

I cannot believe in [Jesus'] messiahship, for . . . the prophet said that in the time of the Messiah, 'No longer will they need to teach one another and say to one another, "Know the Lord", for all of them shall know me etc.' And it says, 'For the earth shall be filled with knowledge of the Lord, as water covers the sea.' And it says, 'They shall beat their swords into plowshares. . . . Nation shall not take up sword against nation; they shall never again know war.' And from the days of Jesus till today the entire world is full of pillaging and robbery . . . indeed, how difficult it would be for you, my lord the king, and for your knights, if they would never again know war.

---

[1] This point has now been made in a book by a Lubavitch rabbi in Israel which appeared after my *Jewish Action* piece. See Rabbi Yehezkel Sofer, *Matters Will Be Purified and Clarified* (Heb.) (Beer Sheva, 1995), 67, 71. More on this book later.

Furthermore, the prophet says concerning the Messiah, 'He shall strike down a land with the rod of his mouth.' The *aggadah* explains . . . 'If the messianic king is told, "This nation has rebelled against you", he will say, "Let the locust come and destroy it" . . .', and this was not true of Jesus.[2]

The argument that Jesus cannot be the Messiah because the prophecies of the messianic age have not been fulfilled, an argument which in its very essence denies that a messianic career can be interrupted by death, is ubiquitous in Jewish polemical literature. It appears in the *Vikuaḥ hameyuḥas laradak* (ed. Talmage, pp. 85–6), Jacob ben Reuben's *Milḥamot hashem* (ed. Rosenthal, p. 78), Rabbi Meir ben Simeon Hame'ili of Narbonne's *Milḥemet mitzvah* (Parma MS, fos. 31ᵛ–32ʳ, 44ʳ⁻ᵛ and elsewhere), Solomon de' Rossi's *Edut hashem ne'emanah* (Rosenthal's *Meḥkarim*, i. 390), Mordecai of Avignon's *Maḥazik emunah* (Vatican MS, fos. 9ᵛ–11ʳ), *Sefer nitzaḥon yashan* (my edition, pp. 107–8), Rabbi Moses Hakohen's *Ezer ha'emunah* (ed. Shamir, pp. 64–5), Rabbi Yom Tov Lipmann Muehlhausen's *Sefer nitzaḥon* (sect. 279), Yair ben Shabtai da Correggio's *Ḥerev pifiyot* (ed. Rosenthal, pp. 77–8) and elsewhere, not to speak of a slew of Christian polemics which quote this Jewish argument.[3] The famous story in which Rabbi Chaim Soloveitchik of Brisk confounded a missionary by manoeuvering him into saying that Bar Kokhba could not have been the Messiah because he was killed before the redemption gains its power not from its innovative content but from the clever way in which it expresses the consensus of *kelal yisra'el* [the Jewish people as a whole]. Neither Michael Wyschogrod nor I nor any other 'modern day antimissionary activist' invented this argument.

These passages and others like them certainly reject the position that the Messiah can die in the midst of his mission, but it is difficult to read them in that limited a fashion; they almost surely deny altogether the option of a Messiah who returns from the grave. Moreover, these denials come in a context which refuses any Jewish legitimacy to the alternative position. This is not an ordinary *machlokes* [disagreement]; it is an assertion of what the Jewish religion believes as a defining element of the faith.

What, then, of the sources cited by Rabbi Butman and, more fully, by Rabbi Weisberg? The statements of *Ḥazal* [the talmudic Sages] about David and Daniel can easily be understood, as Rabbi Weisberg himself indicates, in a manner which lends no support to the belief in the option of a Messiah

---

[2] Nahmanides, *Works* (Heb.), ed. C. D. Chavel (Jerusalem, 1963), 311.

[3] For some of the Christian citations and several more Jewish ones, see my book *The Jewish–Christian Debate in the High Middle Ages* (Philadelphia, 1979; repr. Jason Aronson, Northvale, NJ and London, 1996), 271, 279.

who comes from the dead. The issue before us, then, is the later authorities who interpreted these texts to allow for this option.

Let me begin with a methodological point. A commentator explicating a text will sometimes explain the meaning of that text without endorsing its validity. In the case of a traditional commentator on the Talmud, this may be so when the opinion in the text itself is one of several views and when the commentator presents more than one interpretation. Thus, when I wrote that the first interpretation in Rashi on *Sanhedrin* 98*b* (the Daniel passage) is 'not presented as Rashi's own belief', I meant simply that we cannot know from here that Rashi—assuming that this is Rashi's commentary—endorsed the view that the Messiah might come from the dead.[4]

Why did I write that a 'vanishingly tiny number' of Jews may have held open the possibility that Daniel would be the Messiah? The reason is the absence of virtually any reference to this option in Jewish works outside of a few commentaries to this passage in *Sanhedrin*. We have already had some taste of the vastness of Jewish messianic literature. The possibility that the Messiah will be a renowned figure of the past hardly seems like a trivial matter that would leave all messianic authors through the ages so unimpressed that they would ignore it completely. Yet the year-long labours of Lubavitch messianists appear to have produced precisely two passages which raise this possibility as what Rabbi Butman calls 'a practical likelihood'. (He means, or should mean, 'possibility'.)[5]

---

[4] For both sides of the scholarly controversy on the ascription of this commentary to Rashi, see the references in Avraham Grossman, *The Early Sages of France* (Heb.) (Jerusalem, 1995), 217 n. 278.

[5] The virtual silence of the sources regarding the Messiah's return from the dead is also the key factor in persuading me that Rashi's first interpretation was a minority reading. It appears clear that this option played no role in the Jewish messianic consciousness. We could explain this by assuming that most Jews attributed this view to Rav but dismissed it out of hand; this, however, hardly seems like an explanation of choice. It seems far more likely that Jews ignored this option because they did not think that any rabbi had proposed it.

 This conclusion is reinforced by the internal difficulties that appear to beset the first interpretation. According to this interpretation, Rav said that if the Messiah is from the living, he is Rabbi Judah the Prince (not someone like him); if he is from the dead, he is Daniel (not someone like him). There is good reason for Rashi's decision to neutralize the word 'like' in the talmudic passage (though this step in itself is a serious obstacle for this interpretation). If the Messiah is only *like* Daniel, why can't he be from the living? The reading that he is only like Daniel would slide so close to Rashi's second interpretation (that if the *model* of the Messiah is to be sought among the dead, then that model is Daniel) that it is hard to see the point of proposing it. However, once the word 'like' is neutralized, we are left with the troubling assertion that R. Judah the Prince could be the Messiah despite his own assertion reported in JT *Kilayim* 9: 3 that he is of Davidic descent only through his maternal line. The tosafists' endorsement of that JT passage (*Tosafot, Sanhedrin* 5*a*, s.v *dehakha shevet*), constitutes powerful, if indirect, evidence that they follow Rashi's second interpretation here. See too the references cited in the commentary *Yefeh einayim* on *Sanhedrin* 5*a*. (I made some of these points in a letter to the *Algemeiner Journal*, 24 Feb. 1995.)

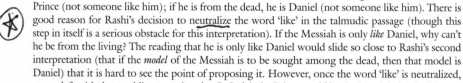

" neutralize "

In fact, only one of these citations—that of the Sedei Hemed—really qualifies. This was one of the passages that I had in mind when I wrote of 'a handful of broadly relevant, though inapplicable quotations'.[6] The Sedei Hemed does understand the *gemara* [the talmudic passage] to raise the possibility that the Messiah will come from the dead. He makes it unmistakably clear that he regards this option as far less likely than the alternative and says that it will take place only if the generation has 'great merit'. It is also evident that unlike Lubavitch messianists, the Sedei Hemed believed that once the Messiah appeared in his redemptive capacity, he would see the redemption through to its conclusion without an intervening death.

In general, I do not believe that an isolated passage, even by a great rabbi, automatically legitimates a theological position against the weight of overwhelming contrary opinion. Even with respect to issues of full-fledged heresy, one can point to isolated statements by distinguished Jews which differ from the Jewish consensus. This is true of anthropomorphism and even of certain issues touching on the composition of the Torah.[7] These statements do not mean that an Orthodox Jew is permitted to entertain the belief in a corporeal God or to be open to revisionist views about the Mosaic authorship of any part of the Torah. The position of the Sedei Hemed is, I believe, invalidated by the weight of the entire Jewish polemical tradition, a tradition which surely reflects the genuine belief of *gedolei yisra'el* [leading rabbinic figures] through the ages. However that may be, even the Sedei Hemed's position lends no support to the current belief of Lubavitch messianists.

The passage in Abarbanel's *Yeshuot meshiho*, which is also cited by Rabbi Weisberg, is Rabbi Butman's second example of a statement that presents the scenario of a resurrected Messiah as a 'practical likelihood'. This passage deserves some careful attention.

We will recall that Rabbi Weisberg cited a discussion in the *Vikuah haramban* in which the Christian quoted a *midrash* that speaks of the Messiah's birth on the day of the destruction of the Temple to prove that he has already come (not, as Rabbi Weisberg says, that he 'was born long ago and passed away'). Notwithstanding Rabbi Weisberg's inexplicable misrepresentation of Ramban's reply, the actual response was twofold. First, Ramban said that he does not believe this *midrash*, an assertion which has generated an entire

[6] R. Weisberg's long footnote about the sources he says I called irrelevant is revealing. I never specified which sources I considered irrelevant and which I considered merely inapplicable. He no doubt senses—quite correctly—the weakness of those arguments and consequently assumes, more or less correctly, that I regarded the sources upon which they are based as, strictly speaking, irrelevant.

[7] See some of the citations in Marc B. Shapiro, 'The Last Word in Jewish Theology? Maimonides' Thirteen Principles', *Torah U-Madda Journal*, 4 (1993), 187–242.

literature but need not detain us here. Second, he said that he will accept it at face value for the sake of argument because it proves that Jesus, who was not born on the day of the destruction, is not the Messiah. When asked how the Messiah could be living for more than a thousand years, he replied that this was entirely possible in the case of a man who would ultimately inaugurate an age in which the effects of the first sin would be undone. What Ramban does not say is that the Messiah may have since died but will be resurrected to redeem the world.

In *Yeshu'ot meshiḥo*, Abarbanel addresses the Christian argument from this *midrash*. He says that if we are to take the *midrash* literally, we could say, as Ramban did, that the Messiah has been living, presumably in the lower Gan Eden [Garden of Eden, or paradise] for well over a thousand years. But, he adds, if we indeed take the *midrash* literally, *which he does not*, he would prefer to understand it in the light of the view, based on *Sanhedrin 98b*, that the Messiah could have died in his youth and will return at the end of days. Abarbanel clearly excludes the option that the Messiah's redemptive career will begin before his death, and he goes on to explain how he understands the *midrash* in non-literal fashion. Thus, like the Sedei Hemed, Abarbanel does understand the *gemara* to present the option of a resurrected Messiah, but because he rejects the literal meaning of this *midrash* altogether, we have no basis for saying that he regarded this scenario as a practical possibility. Indeed, in discussing the 'servant' figure in Isaiah 53, he refutes the *rabbinic* view—he had earlier disposed of the Christian view—that this is the Messiah by citing, among other arguments, the verse that says 'He was cut off from the land of the living.'[8]

At this point, we can turn to Rambam's decisive invalidation of the messianists' belief. At the beginning of *Ma'amar teḥiyat hametim* [Treatise on the Resurrection], Rambam shares his frustration over accusations that he denied the belief in resurrection. He had, after all, expressed his affirmation of this belief in the clearest possible language. Even this, however, could not stop people from attributing to him a view which he explicitly rejected. He goes on, however, to seek consolation in the fact that God himself could not avoid this problem. He wrote in the Torah, 'Hear, O Israel, the Lord is our God, the Lord is one', and Christians took the three divine names as evidence of the Trinity.

Once more, Rambam is being subjected to the same indignity. He is no longer here to defend himself, and so the task falls to us. In the clearest

---

[8] *Perush al nevi'im aḥaronim* [Commentary on the Later Prophets] (Jerusalem, 5716), 243, bottom of col. 2.

imaginable language, Rambam writes that if a Davidic king compels all Israel to follow the Torah and fights the wars of the Lord, he enjoys the presumption of being the Messiah. 'If he proceeds successfully, builds the Temple in its place, and gathers the dispersed of Israel, then he is surely the Messiah. . . . But if he does not succeed to this extent or is killed, *it is evident* (literally, 'known') *that he is not the one whom the Torah promised*.' In effect, Rabbi Weisberg makes this last phrase mean, 'It remains entirely possible that he will be the Messiah.' Rabbi Butman obscures the point by taking what he calls the Messiah's 'failing' out of its clear context, which refers to a failure to build the Temple and gather the dispersed of Israel. Some messianists in Rabbi Butman's circle have extended and, in my view, misapplied a homily of the Rebbe and argued that the Maimonidean reference to building the Temple refers to 770 Eastern Parkway. Thus, one fulfils a key requirement for moving from presumptive Messiah to definite Messiah by building a large synagogue in Brooklyn.

All of this is nothing less than an affront to Rambam. We plunge into a surreal world in which words have no meaning and all rational discourse is impossible. The belief of Lubavitch messianists is flatly incompatible with Rambam, who rules as he does despite his full awareness, in a passage noted by Rabbi Weisberg himself, that the resurrection may precede the coming of the Messiah.[9] The fact that the Rebbe declared the *Mishneh torah*'s discussion of the messianic process to be halakhically binding makes the messianists' predicament all the more uncomfortable,[10] but the dilemma is of their own making.

Before turning to the large question of how dangerous all this really is, let me deal briefly with several matters of detail.

1. In a very brief paragraph, I made the passing remark that the conditions producing the messianic fervour in Lubavitch will no doubt be the subject of scholarly investigation. Rabbi Weisberg's characterization of this peripheral comment as one of the three 'main points' of the article is exceedingly strange.

2. Rabbi Weisberg argues that Lubavitch hasidim who believe that the Rebbe declared himself the Messiah are duty-bound to maintain this belief on pain of violating a biblical prohibition. Internal debates about the Rebbe's intentions are 'not the concern of the non-Lubavitch community'.

There are several problems with this analysis. First, if an authoritative figure says something which appears to contradict a deeply held Jewish belief,

---

[9] Abraham Halkin and David Hartman, *Epistles of Maimonides* (Philadelphia, 1985), 222.
[10] See Sofer, *Matters Will Be Purified and Clarified*, 20.

every effort should be made to explain that statement in a way that removes the contradiction. This is precisely what Rabbi Yehezkel Sofer, a Lubavitch thinker who is the rabbi of Ben Gurion University in Beersheba, has just done in his new book.[11] Second, even if we extend the prohibition of *lo tasur* ['Do not stray'] to the leaders of each generation and add to this the general obligation to follow one's *rav muvhak* [principal teacher], it is difficult to understand the suggestion that endorsing a position held by every single *gadol* [great rabbi] of your generation other than your *rav muvhak* is a violation of this prohibition. Finally, the commandment applies by definition to the leaders of your generation; the suggestion that following the view of all *gedolei hador* [major rabbinic leaders] against that of your *deceased* leader violates *lo tasur* staggers the imagination.

As to the argument that outsiders should not interfere in the internal affairs of Lubavitch, I am reminded of a comment by a former neighbour who expressed distress over a controversial theological position held by another Jew. When I responded that he must at least admit that the concept is fascinating, he replied, 'Yes, but that's my religion he's talking about.'

3. For the most part, Rabbi Weisberg's discussion of Messiah son of Joseph has no bearing on my article. I should, however, point out that his assertion that 'the general picture which emerges from primary sources' depicts this Messiah as a 'scion of the Davidic dynasty' is highly misleading. There is not a whisper of a suggestion in *Ḥazal* or the *rishonim* [medieval rabbinic authorities] that this Messiah is anything but a physical descendant of Joseph and a member of the tribe of Ephraim, and some sources assert this with a clarity that makes any other interpretation impossible. Later, we begin to find suggestions that he *might* be of Davidic descent,[12] and finally, a few sources actually regard this as likely.

With respect to our issue, the only passages which appear, at least superficially, to be germane are two nineteenth-century remarks which allegedly assert that the two Messiahs are the same person. One of those, in *Ramatayim tzofim*, almost surely means that the two Messiahs are united by belonging to the Davidic family, not by sharing the same body. The second, ascribed to Rabbi Nahman of Bratslav, may signify more than that, but even this probably means that some element of the second Messiah's soul exists in the first

---

[11] See above, n. 1.

[12] This is the most that is said in the sources cited by R. Weisberg in the footnote allegedly documenting his assertion. Ben Yehoyada does not even say this much but speaks of a 'spark' of Messiah son of Joseph in Messiah son of David.

Messiah. Equally important, by the nineteenth century there was a widespread tradition that Messiah son of Joseph would not have to die after all, and so even if one person were literally both Messiahs, this would not require him to die and then be resurrected as Messiah son of David.[13]

4. Rabbi Weisberg suggests that the messianists pose no danger to the ultimate reputation of the Rebbe even if the Messiah's arrival is delayed. After all, did not Ramban also provide a messianic date which went unfulfilled?

The difference, of course, is that Ramban explicitly declared that he proffers his statement without certainty (*divrei shema ve'efshar*); the messianists maintain that the Rebbe issued a 'clear prophecy' that the redemption is imminent. What a delay would do to the Rebbe's reputation if this assertion is believed is too terrible to write and too obvious to have to write.[14]

5. Both Rabbi Butman and Rabbi Weisberg make the unimpeachable point that Jews should not abandon authentic Jewish beliefs simply because they were borrowed by Christianity. Of course not. But Jews should also not adopt *alien* beliefs which they have been denouncing for untold generations in their debates with Christians.

6. Rabbi Butman begins his letter by asserting that my article 'claim[s] to be scholarly while only rehashing the same old apologist propaganda'. I did not make such a claim. My contribution to *Jewish Action* was not intended as a scholarly article but as a popular one, though it rested, I hope, on the foundation of good scholarship. In this response, the need to discuss the sources in some detail has forced me into a more scholarly mode, though even here I have tried to keep scholarly jargon and apparatus to a minimum. (I was helped by the fact that the pressure of the journal's deadline forced me to write this response quickly.) Since the article addressed the *posthumous* belief in the Rebbe, I wonder how old its apologist propaganda could be.

As for 'rehashing' old material, I was more than a little amused to notice

[13] On the sources for Messiah son of Joseph, see Menahem Kasher, *The Great Era: The Voice of the Turtledove* (Heb.) (Jerusalem, 1969), 421–8. On the view that he need not die, see pp. 428–31. On R. Nahman's comment, see the later Bratslaver work which explains that 'even though the soul of ben David was also in him, he was primarily from the side of Messiah ben Joseph' (quoted in Arthur Green, *Tormented Master: A Life of Rabbi Nahman of Bratslav* (Tuscaloosa, Ala., 1979), 194). [Marc Shapiro has since called my attention to a remarkable assertion by Joseph Levenstein in *Hapeles*, 3 (1903), 47, that he was the real author of *Ramatayim tzofim* (purportedly written by R. Shmuel of Sieniawa) but concealed his authorship for a 'hidden reason'. I have not seen the article and am not qualified to evaluate this assertion.]

[14] See Sofer, *Matters Will Be Purified and Clarified*, 83–8, for a vigorous argument that the Rebbe never issued such a prophecy. R. Sofer's book also addresses the Rebbe's statements about his predecessor as well as the other arguments which R. Butman makes based on the Rebbe's teachings through the years.

that Rabbi Butman's aversion to this practice appears to have dissipated with startling rapidity. Five of the eight sentences in the third and fourth paragraphs of his letter correspond almost word for word to a letter by Rabbi Zushe Silberstein that appeared in the *Algemeiner Journal* on 3 February 1995 and was later reprinted in *Beis Moshiach*.

7. I not only agree with Rabbi Butman that Lubavitch has done exceedingly important work; I even agree that the Messiah campaign has had a salutary effect in enhancing awareness and understanding of the messianic faith. My efforts to combat the religious catastrophe that we have allowed to develop in the wake of the Rebbe's *petirah* [passing] have made me realize to what degree the messianic instincts of knowledgeable Jews have atrophied because of the withering of a meaningful Christian threat. The instinctive horror that our ancestors would have felt at the belief in a Messiah who was just buried has waned and, in some cases, virtually disappeared. Perhaps this exchange will help reawaken it.

At the same time, this potential good is balanced, even outweighed, by an evil. Because of the indelicate, propagandistic character of the Messiah campaign even in the last years of the Rebbe's life, the messianic faith itself came to be approached with wariness or, worse, amusement even by observant Jews. The problem has worsened now that the Rebbe is gone. Jews are more aware of the belief in Mashiach, but that awareness is tinged with irreverence. *Yatza sekharenu behefsedenu* [Our benefit has been neutralized by our loss].

8. Jena Morris Breningstall takes me to task for failure to credit sufficiently the forces within Lubavitch who are attempting to combat the messianists. While it is difficult for an outsider (and, I have discovered, even for insiders) to have a clear picture of the current situation, I do have a better sense now of the position of the anti-messianist group. In many respects they have shown significant courage, sometimes even physical courage, in preventing messianist takeovers of events and institutions. International Habad organizations have, I think, remained largely resistant to messianist forces, and they deserve great credit for this.

At the same time, I cannot agree with the dominant position in these circles that one must work quietly to undermine the messianists. On 10 September of this year [1995], schoolchildren in Crown Heights were bussed to Avery Fisher Hall in Manhattan for an event *lekabalat penei meshiah tzidkenu* [to welcome our Messiah] clearly identified as the Rebbe. Lubavitch hasidism is suffering from acute danger to its soul. We need to hear a very simple sentence from the non-messianist group. It must be said in public and without equivocation. 'The Rebbe *zt"l* is not the Messiah.' Not 'he is probably the Messiah but it is improper to announce this'. Not even 'he may or may not be the Messiah'. 'He is not the Messiah.' As long as this sentence sticks in the throat of the non-messianist group, the danger to the movement—and to Judaism—will remain.

And so we finally arrive at Rabbi Weisberg's concluding point, which must be taken very seriously indeed. Is this a benign error or is it a threat which must be confronted and either quarantined or defeated?

This is a question that needs to be addressed on two levels: theological and historical. On the theological level, Rabbi Weisberg and I disagree about the fundamental issue. In my view, the belief that Mashiach ben David [Messiah son of David] can die in the middle of his unfulfilled mission is antithetical to the deepest messianic convictions of all our ancestors. There is no source in all of Jewish literature that supports it. Our ancestors rejected it in a context that often led to Kiddush Hashem [martyrdom]. The major halakhic source dealing with the Messiah rejects it explicitly and firmly. Metaphorically, it can be said that the denial of this belief is a *ma'aseh rav shel kelal yisra'el* ['the act of an authoritative figure' performed by the Jewish people as a whole] which has firmly closed the door on messianic claimants after their death. Without this denial, there can be no closure, and one wonders how Rabbi Weisberg knows that Bar Kokhba was indeed not the Messiah. On a purely religious level, what does it mean to say that such a belief is benign?

Historically, the assertion that this is a benign error flies in the face of Jewish experience. History does not have to repeat itself, but we ignore it at our peril. One reason for the historical framework of my article was to underscore the dangers of posthumous messianic movements, one of which has been the transformation of the messianic figure into something more than a human being.

Rabbi Weisberg maintains that Christianity's most serious deviation from Judaism was attributing divinity to a human being, and in this he is surely correct. In my article, I attempted to raise this issue as briefly and delicately as I could. At this point, I have to be slightly more forceful. The term 'Essence of the Infinite' (*atzmut einsof*) was used for a short time to describe the Rebbe during his lifetime. Examples of this terminology have apparently surfaced again since the Rebbe's death, when history indicates that they can become especially dangerous.[15]

---

[15] See *Or torah* (Nisan, 5755) 572–3 (called to my attention by Prof. Marc Shapiro) for a letter criticizing this usage, which appeared according to the letter writer in *Siḥat hashavua*, 'Parashat Koraḥ' 5754 and 'Parashat Vayeshev' 5755. My effort to obtain these issues has been unsuccessful.

The article also made a fleeting, cryptic reference to a 'disturbing report' of 'full-fledged incarnationist rhetoric'. A friend in Israel whose reliability is beyond question told me that some time ago—he thinks it was while the Rebbe was still alive—he was listening to a call-in radio programme which featured a fairly prominent Lubavitch guest. A caller reported that while working in a Lubavitch institution in the United States, he had heard staff members tell children that the Rebbe is the Ribbono shel Olam [Master of the Universe]. The guest's reaction was not outraged denial; rather, he replied, 'There are certain things one does not discuss on the radio.'

Let me emphasize that I am not suggesting that this is a widespread belief even among the messianists; what I am saying is that this story underscores my conviction that confident, relaxed equanimity about a belief which has shown so much explosive potential in the past is unwise and irresponsible. The identity of the eschatological *kohen gadol* [High Priest] or head of the Sanhedrin [High Court] is not bound up with an article of faith, nor has it been associated, even indirectly, with Jewish martyrdom, nor has it torn the Jewish people apart. We have no right to stand by quietly as a belief standing at the core of Judaism is radically transformed.

Let us imagine that many thousands of observant Jews had launched a movement declaring a recently deceased rabbi as the Messiah in the generation of the Hazon Ish and Rav Aharon Kotler. Of the Hafetz Hayim and R. Hayim Ozer [leaders of early twentieth-century European Orthodoxy]. Of the Hatam Sofer [an early eighteenth-century rabbinic figure]. Is it conceivable that they would have refrained from proclaiming its illegitimacy?

And so I turn to the religious leaders of our generation and ask you to consider Rabbi Butman's challenge to me. If you are silent, he says, it must be because you 'do not share [my] ignorance', that is, because you maintain that there is nothing objectionable about the belief that Mashiach ben David was buried in the summer of 1994. If this is not your position, he implicitly asks, why then do you not speak out? Why indeed?

FIVE

Revisiting the Second Coming

A T T H I S P O I N T, the imperative of thematic coherence compels me to interrupt the chronology of the narrative by turning to a critical article that appeared more than two years after this rejoinder. Jacob Immanuel Schochet, a Lubavitch rabbi and academic who has written widely on theological topics, responded not to my arguments but to an essay by Rabbi Chaim Dov Keller that I will have occasion to discuss in its proper time.[1] Rabbi Schochet is a non-messianist who nonetheless affirms the essential legitimacy of the messianist position; precisely because he is not a believer himself, the messianists take special satisfaction in his arguments. Some of those arguments are familiar, but others raise new issues that require us to extend our discussion of the return of a resurrected Messiah from a redemptive mission interrupted by an untimely death.

Rabbi Schochet vehemently criticized Rabbi Keller for 'an obscene analogy' between the belief that the resurrected Rebbe will be the Messiah and the similar Christian belief in a dead and risen redeemer. The critique included the standard argument that belief in a resurrected Messiah 'does not violate normative Judaism or valid Halachah one iota' since this possibility is estalished by such sources as *Sanhedrin* 98b and Abarbanel as well as an additional text that we shall examine in due course. But there is also a more original slant. We are presented with a somewhat ambiguous formulation distinguishing Christian and Sabbatian doctrine from that of Lubavitch messianists by the degree of fulfilment allegedly achieved by the interrupted messianic mission.

'Christians (as well as the Sabbateans)', writes Rabbi Schochet, differ from the messianists because

they believe that their savior was already the Messiah in actu, and that the Messianic redemption is already an established fact, though yet to move to a new stage with the 'second coming'. This is not a matter of semantics but fraught with practical

[1] See the end of Ch. 10. Rabbi Schochet's article, 'G-d-Centered or Machloket-Centered: Which is Normative Judaism? A Response to Rabbi Chaim Dov Keller of Chicago', appeared in *Algemeiner Journal*, 27 Mar. 1998, English section, pp. B3–B4.

implications: that belief caused them to abrogate Torah and mitzvot (even as the Sabbateans too changed Halachah because of their belief).

Messianists, however, remain punctiliously observant.

Let us try to unpack this argument. Rabbi Schochet apparently maintains that Judaism has no objection to the belief that the Messiah will appear on what I called 'the eschatological stage'[2] and die before completing his mission. It is entirely possible that he will announce himself, initiate a redemptive campaign, unequivocally predict imminent fulfilment, and then die before that fulfilment. According to Rabbi Schochet, we may embrace this scenario as perfectly consistent with normative Judaism even though no Jewish source ever envisages it, many clearly reject it, and the abandonment of faith in deceased messianic figures throughout history rested on this rejection. It is presumably Rabbi Schochet's understanding that when Jews argued against the messiahship of Jesus on the grounds that he did not effect a true redemption, they meant to demonstrate only that he was not already the Messiah *in actu*. Whatever other reasons they had for rejecting his status as ultimate redeemer, they did not intend this argument to rule out the possibility that he could still turn out to be the Messiah. I do not believe that any careful reader of Jewish polemical works or of the selected extracts in Appendix I will come away with this impression.

Beyond its inconsistency with numerous sources, this position is further complicated by the critically important fact that most if not all Lubavitch messianists do believe that to a very significant degree the redemption has already been realized. The task of completing the invisible, cosmic redemptive process (*avodat haberurim*) has been achieved; consequently, 'We are already in the Days of Moshiach.'[3] (This was the very doctrine that persuaded Sabbatians that the redemption was an established fact.) The Messiah 'has already come'. He has brought together the dispersed of Israel through his purportedly central role in rescuing much of Soviet Jewry. He has presided over the downfall of the Evil Empire and the dawn of universal peace. All that is left is for us to greet him. In post-1994 terminology, all that is left is for him to reveal himself 'to eyes of flesh'. Since these oft-repeated assertions rest for the most part on statements of the Rebbe himself, their centrality to the messianist position is beyond question. Of course there is still a further stage, but this is true in Sabbatianism and Christianity as well.

---

[2] See Ch. 4, p. 41.

[3] So Simon Jacobson, author of a widely read work on the Rebbe's teachings, in an interview entitled 'The Service of Refining the World has been Completed—That's a Fact', *Beis Moshiach*, 267 (25 Feb. 2000).

Fully aware of this unacknowledged set of messianist beliefs, Rabbi Schochet mobilizes the issue of the law in order to rescue his distinction. He initially appears to maintain that Judaism denies that the Messiah can effect a redemption deserving of the status of 'an established fact' and then die before completing it, but in the final analysis he virtually defines such an 'established' redemption in terms of the abrogation of the Torah. Judaism rejects only the sort of incomplete messianic mission that nonetheless achieves the annulment of the Torah. Otherwise the difference between the Christian and Sabbatian redemption and that of Lubavitch messianists blurs to the point of vanishing, and the 'obscene analogy' re-emerges, as it should, in all its disturbing validity.

One problem with this desperate strategy is that in Judaism, even the ultimate, fully established redemption can take place without any fundamental change in the Torah; indeed, this is precisely the standard position of most Jews through the ages. Consequently, when Jews disqualified messianic figures for failure to effect a complete redemption they did so irrespective of the question of the law. Many Sabbatians remained observant. In theory at least, there are 'Torah-observant messianics' in our own day who believe, or say they believe, that the Torah remains in force even after the coming of Jesus. The status of the Torah in the messianic age was an issue of the first importance in the classic Jewish–Christian debate, but the rejection of a Messiah who undertakes a messianic mission and dies without completing it did not rest upon the Christian belief that Jesus had annulled the law.

For Rabbi Schochet, who is not a messianist, the assertion that belief in a resurrected Messiah does not violate any valid halakhah one iota simply means that such a Messiah is a possibility, but his assertion here defends the religious legitimacy of the full messianist position. By doing so, he trivializes important distinctions. We have already seen that none of the sources cited by the messianists—not *Sanhedrin 98b*, not Abarbanel, not the Sedei Hemed—allows us to ignore the classical criteria of a realized messianic age in making a *confident* identification of the Messiah, and none of them allows a scenario in which the Messiah announces imminent redemption and then dies in an unredeemed world. In my view, the fact that the Rebbe did announce imminent redemption, spearheaded a messianic campaign, and then died before its fulfilment disqualifies him as the Messiah even if one concedes a theoretical possibility that God might choose a deceased redeemer. Judaism denies that God would play such cruel games with the Jewish people.

As to the issue of confident identification, the messianists proffer various approaches. In November 1997, six Lubavitch rabbis of considerable distinction issued a *pesak din*, or legal ruling, that Jewish law requires belief in the Rebbe's messiahship. Cleverly sidestepping the classical Jewish criteria for identifying the Messiah, they argued that the Rebbe had established himself as a prophet and had—for anyone with eyes to see—declared himself the Messiah. Since it is obligatory to obey the words of a prophet, the inexorable, obvious conclusion follows. The signatories were the head of the Crown Heights Rabbinical Court, the rabbi of Kfar Chabad (the largest Lubavitch community in Israel), the vice-chair of Agudat Harabbanim (a once prominent organization of Orthodox rabbis), the rabbi of the Chabad community of the Israeli city of Lod, the head of a rabbinical court in Haifa, and a Montreal rabbi who would be appointed as head of its rabbinical court several months later.

To assess its quite remarkable argument, we need to examine the document in its entirety. The text that follows is a not particularly felicitous translation of the Hebrew original, but I reproduce it verbatim from a Chabad source.

In the *Sichas Kodesh* [holy discourse] of *Parshas Shoftim* [Deut. 16: 18–21: 9], the Lubavitcher Rebbe established as *halacha* [Jewish law] the fact that this generation has a prophet and we must listen to him, as codified in the Rambam [Maimonides' code], *Hilchos Yesodei HaTorah* [Laws of the Foundations of the Torah], chapter 7.

These are the Rebbe's holy words: We must publicize to all people of the generation that we have merited to have *Hashem* [God] select and appoint someone with the power of free choice, who is personally incomparably greater than the people of his generation,[4] to be the 'your judges' and the 'your advisers' [Isa. 1: 26] and the prophet of the generation, to give directives and give advice regarding the service of all the Jewish people . . . including the main prophecy—the prophecy of 'immediately to Redemption' and immediately 'behold this (*Moshiach*) comes'.

The Rebbe said in the *sicha of Parshas VaYeira* [Gen. 18–22], 5752 . . . all obstacles and hindrances have been nullified in our days etc. Since this is so, there is (not only the reality of *Moshiach*, but) also *Moshiach*'s revelation, and now we must only greet *Moshiach Tzidkeinu* [our righteous Messiah] in actuality.

In the *sicha* of *Parshas Mishpatim* [Exod. 21–4], 5752, the Rebbe says, 'This is the *psak din* [ruling] of the *Rabbanim* [rabbis] and teachers of Yisroel [Israel] that the time of redemption has arrived, "a king has arrived from the house of David etc., *be'chezkas* [with the presumption] that he is *Moshiach*"',[5] and the Rebbe added these

---

[4] A straightforward reading of this discourse identifies this figure as the Rebbe's deceased father-in-law. For many of the hasidim, however, the real referent was the Rebbe himself, who was thought to share the soul of his predecessor.

[5] The reference is to the ruling to which I alluded in 'The New Messianism' (see Ch. 2), where the Rebbe was declared to have met Maimonides' criteria for presumptive Messiah.

words to this *psak din*, 'to the state of "this is certainly Moshiach"'. Moreover, in this *sicha* the Rebbe clearly hinted to his being *Melech HaMoshiach* [the King Messiah].

We (the undersigned) are establishing in this *psak halacha* according to the *halacha* of our holy Torah—based on the *halacha* in the Rambam, Chapter 7, *Hilchos Yesodei HaTorah, Halacha* 1; Chapter 9, *Halacha* 2; and Chapter 10, *Halacha* 1—that the Rebbe *Melech HaMoshiach* has the halachic status of a prophet, and it is explicit in the holy *sichos* that he alludes to his being a prophet (and it is understood from his *sichos* that he is *Melech HaMoshiach*, and he encouraged the singing of '*Yechi Admur MH"M L'Olam Va'ed*' [May our Master, Teacher, and Rabbi, the King Messiah, live for ever']), and he already predicted, before all Jews and before the entire world, things that have come to pass in their entirety during the Six-Day War, the Gulf War, etc.

Therefore, we are obligated to listen to everything we are told (by the Rebbe) as an obligation to listen to a prophet, including the fact that the Rebbe is *Melech HaMoshiach* and will immediately be revealed to us.[6]

The Rebbe's predictions are critical to this ruling since it is those predictions that constitute the sign required by Maimonides for the verification of a prophetic claim. However, the context of Maimonides' discussion, its biblical source, and elementary logic indicate that the sign must be provided in the context of demonstrating prophetic status; hence, the existence of previous correct predictions unconnected with such a claim is simply irrelevant. The messianist ruling does not even require an investigation of the possibility of prior error, so that any learned and pious Jew who ever made a correct prediction could later demand our assent to his prophetic claims. I do not doubt, moreover, that in the course of his lifetime the Rebbe did make erroneous predictions. The Chabad rabbi who approached me after my first letter to the *Algemeiner Journal* expressed his exasperation at the official line that the Rebbe never erred. Though he insisted that the track record was remarkable, he spoke of an unnamed Lubavitch leader who knew of mistakes but nonetheless publicly affirmed the inerrancy of all the Rebbe's pronouncements.

To make matters worse, the plain meaning of the Rebbe's predictions of redemption strongly implies that the messianic age should already have arrived, so that the insistence that they were meant as prophecies would, as I have already implied, turn him into a false prophet. This is surely how Maimonides would have classified anyone who issued an explicit prophecy that he was the Messiah and then died in an unredeemed world.[7] The Rebbe

---

[6] This translation appeared in a full-page advertisement with many signatories beyond the original six in the *Jewish Tribune* (Toronto), 10 Dec. 1998, p. 33.

[7] Cf. my remarks in 'Religion, Nationalism, and Historiography: Yehezkel Kaufmann's Account of Jesus and Early Christianity', in Leo Landman (ed.), *Scholars and Scholarship in Jewish History* (New York, 1990), 149–68 at 167.

does not fall into this category precisely because he did not issue such a prophecy. It is an intellectual as well as a religious scandal that this preposterous ruling has not only failed to die but, as we shall see, has gained endorsements with the passing years.

Other messianists justify their confidence by continuing to appeal to the Maimonidean category of presumptive Messiah (*ḥezkat mashiaḥ*). We will recall first of all that the assertion that the Rebbe met the criteria for presumptive Messiah is itself utterly without reasonable foundation.[8] Still, the messianists take it for granted that he attained that status and proceed with a creative elaboration. Since the redeemer, in their view, can be a resurrected figure, the presumption has not been undermined by the Rebbe's death. It is true that the redemption is not completed, and so this presumptive Messiah has not yet achieved the *legal status* of 'certain Messiah'; nevertheless, he is certainly the Messiah. (I am tempted to formulate this utilizing the Hebrew terms: The Rebbe is not *mashiaḥ vadai* but is nonetheless *bevadai mashiaḥ*.) A rabbi in the New York area asked me to comment after a congregant of his received a letter from the local Lubavitch emissary affirming that the Rebbe remains presumptive Messiah and underscoring the absence of any halakhah standing in the way of this belief. I was not in a particularly charitable frame of mind and responded in a strongly worded letter:

The notion that someone who achieves [the] status [of presumptive Messiah] and then dies in an unredeemed world can retain it after his death is so absurd that one does not know whether to cry or laugh. (Actually, I do know. I cry.) The category was established by Maimonides. It is because the term appears in the *Mishneh torah* that the author of the letter uses the terminology of *halakhah* here. Anyone who can read will see that this is a temporary status to be verified or disconfirmed by the later career of the Messianic candidate. If he proceeds successfully, builds the Temple in its place, and gathers the dispersed of Israel, his status is confirmed. If he does not succeed to this extent (as the first sentence in the censored passage continues), 'it is known' (*beyadua*) that he is not the one whom the Torah promised. If we use the term *halakhah* (I prefer something like 'required belief'), then it is unambiguously the halakhic ruling of the Rambam that one who dies in an unredeemed world not only loses the standing of *ḥezkat mashiaḥ* but is flatly ruled out as the Messiah. The notion that the [correspondent of the] Sedei Hemed, who speaks of a remote possibility that a highly meritorious generation might find itself with a Messiah who comes from the dead, would countenance the notion that a dead man is *beḥezkat mashiaḥ* is beyond nonsensical.

The confident identification of the deceased Rebbe as the Messiah is especially problematic since he now must overcome not the feeble competition of

---

8   See Ch. 1, p. 9.

his contemporaries but the far more daunting competition of a stellar array of departed Jewish notables. The usual messianist response is that the Messiah needs to be—or to have been—the leader of the generation of the redemption, and this remains true of the recently deceased Rebbe. This response, however, falls victim to a deeply ironic difficulty. The only legitimation for the belief in a resurrected Messiah comes from one or two rabbinic sources as interpreted by some authorities. Those sources speak of figures—David, Daniel, Abarbanel's hypothetical short-lived, unknown individual born on the day of the destruction of the Temple—who lived long before the people who identified them or, in the last case, was never a leader at all. Thus, the very sources that supposedly grant this position legitimacy directly contradict the assertion that the deceased Messiah must have led the current generation—or even that such a figure receives preference. The Rebbe's formidable competitors cannot be swept aside.

Rabbi Schochet agrees that confident, public assertions of the Rebbe's messiahship are arrogant and inappropriate, but he does not see that they amount to an abolition of Judaism's criteria for identifying the Messiah. His failure to realize the gravity of this matter may result from a source he cites that played no role in the earlier discussion. He tells us that an important hasidic rabbi, Rabbi Menahem Nahum of Chernobyl (1730–87), 'stated his conviction that the resurrected Ba'al Shem Tov will be Moshiach'. Although Schochet goes on to distinguish between a private conviction and a 'categorical imperative', he may see this report as evidence that Rabbi Menahem Nahum was fully convinced of this identification.

In fact, we do not have remotely sufficient evidence to draw a firm conclusion that Rabbi Menahem Nahum said anything of this sort, confidently or otherwise. Rabbi Schochet as well as a recent messianist book cite a collection of material about the Ba'al Shem Tov that partially reproduces a story in a 1903 work entitled *Precious Stories and Discourses*.[9] According to this story, which is to the best of my knowledge unattested before the 1903 book, the rabbi of Chernobyl made a cryptic remark to two students in a private conversation held during the lifetime of Rabbi Dov Baer of Mezhirech, who died in 1772. An unknown party told the author of the book that this story was told by a grandson of Rabbi Menahem Nahum who was born seven years after his grandfather's death and hence would have heard it from an earlier unknown party.

[9] Yeshaya Wolf Tzikernik, *Precious Stories and Discourses* (Heb.) (Zhitomir, 1903), repr. in *Sefer sipurim uma'amarim yekarim* (Shikun Skvere, 1994), 100. The messianist book is *The Era and Redemption in the Teachings of the Lubavitcher Rebbe* (Heb.) (Kefar Chabad, 1999), where the point is made at p. 53 n. 8, and p. 126 n. 5.

The Rabbi of Chernobyl was alleged to have said that normally the leader of a generation is replaced by an equivalent leader in the following generation. However, there never was nor will there ever be anyone like the Ba'al Shem Tov until the advent of the redeemer, and 'when the Messiah comes he will be' (*kesheyovo hamoshiaḥ vet er zayn*). This can mean that he will be present in that generation, it can mean that his soul, or a 'spark' of his soul, will be in the Messiah (an attested concept in hasidic writings), and it can mean that he will simply be the Messiah, which was the grandson's interpretation according to the author's unknown informant. What is far more likely than all these possibilities is that this 1903 book, with its uncertain chain of transmission and its many other questionable narratives, provides nothing resembling a reliable record of what Rabbi Menahem Nahum said to two people more than 130 years earlier, so that any effort to parse these words is futile, almost comical. There is no legitimate way that such a book and such a story can be used to demonstrate that the rabbi of Chernobyl believed that the Messiah might come from the dead, let alone that he was firmly convinced of the messiahship of the Ba'al Shem Tov. Indeed, as Rabbi Schochet himself observes, he surely did not believe that one could make such an assertion with the certainty necessary for public affirmation. The need to resort to such a story is itself striking evidence of the desperate measures required of those desiring to legitimate the messianist position.

Let us now step back and take stock of the large picture. A few medieval authorities believed that the Talmud recorded a view that the Messiah could come from the dead, though they did not affirm their endorsement of this position. Maimonides unequivocally disqualified any candidate who does not complete the process of redemption during his lifetime. Numerous sources, some of which I have translated in Appendix I, vigorously concur. The overwhelming consensus affirming this understanding of the Messiah's mission has significant bearing on practical issues of Jewish law ranging from the determination of one's attitude towards the contemporary messianist *pesak din* to one's obligation to obey the injunctions of a deceased messianic claimant. Both as a matter of halakhah and as a belief repeatedly formulated as a defining element of Judaism, this Maimonidean ruling sets forth the established contours of Judaism's messianic faith.

Moreover, as I have repeatedly stressed, the delegitimation of Lubavitch messianism does not depend upon this position. What we confront today is not merely an affirmation that a deceased individual might theoretically be resurrected as the redeemer. By confidently identifying a presumed descendant of David as the Messiah despite his death in an unredeemed world,

Lubavitch messianists invalidate Judaism's bedrock requirements for making such an identification. To make matters worse, this individual asserted that the cosmic process necessary for redemption has already been completed and all that is left is to welcome the Messiah. The record in such a case leaves no room for a scintilla of ambiguity. Judaism absolutely rejects the belief that God will send the real Messiah to preach that the redemption is arriving 'right away' (as the Rebbe certainly did), let alone to identify himself unequivocally as the redeemer (as the messianists believe he did), and then have him die before the fulfilment. Jewish tradition has unambiguous criteria for evaluating such a claim, criteria rooted in the biblical prophecies that define the messianic faith itself. To affirm the messiahship of the deceased Rebbe is to undermine a foundational belief of the Jewish religion.

SIX

The Rabbinical Council of America Resolution

LET US RETURN, then, to our story. The most gratifying reaction to the exchange in *Jewish Action* came in a brief conversation with Isadore Twersky, who followed up with an even briefer letter. Twersky, who passed away in 1998, was an unusual figure: Professor of Jewish History and Literature at Harvard, hasidic rebbe, expert on Maimonides, and son-in-law of Rabbi Joseph B. Soloveitchik, one of the leading rabbinic figures of the century and pre-eminent expositor of the decidedly non-hasidic talmudic tradition of a family marked by exceptional genius. In his oral reaction, Twersky articulated his pleasure at the manner in which the article had mobilized history for a religious purpose and expressed surprise that rabbinic leaders had not declared meat ritually slaughtered by messianists to be forbidden. In the letter, he wrote: 'excellent, compelling use of scholarship. . . . As I told you, the silence of rabbinic groups is astounding. Many contexts show that *dor yasom* [orphaned generation] is indeed an apt characterization. Your voice is heard. I mentioned to you my dissociation from the messianism over the years.'

At the same time, a distinguished rabbi in the Traditionalist Orthodox community contacted me to express his long-standing hostility towards Lubavitch. This was my first direct, personal experience of the scathing, sweeping, almost breathtaking denunciation of the movement in some quarters. The Rebbe, I was told, had regularly visited his father-in-law's grave so that it should already be established as a shrine when he himself would be buried nearby. He had his followers construct and display giant menorahs of an atypical sort, insisting on the view that the spokes of the original menorah were straight rather than curved, 'because every new religion needs a symbol'. I did not quite know how to react and eventually came to realize that for all his sympathy to my argument, this rabbi saw nothing significantly new in the latest developments. To him, Chabad had long been a species of religion clearly outside the boundaries of Judaism.

In the early months of 1996, the little tempest that I had created spent itself, and Chabad's position in Jewish life continued much as it had before. Every once in a while, a messianist advertisement would arouse a flurry of discussion, the word 'crazy' would be flung about, and all would return to what passes for normalcy in the Jewish community. There were in any event more momentous concerns to address. The Oslo agreement had launched a peace process in the Middle East that aroused intense concern in the Orthodox community. Debate swirled around the permissibility or prohibition of returning any part of the Land of Israel to non-Jews, and the spectre of such a return plunged a sector of religious Zionism into ideological crisis. To concentrate on the foibles of a few purportedly unbalanced hasidim was itself to court the suspicion of harbouring an obsessive disorder. I saw no evident avenue to pursue on the Chabad front and turned to other matters.

In short order, however, I came to realize that I could not make peace even with the most benign legitimation of messianists. A fund-raising breakfast is held in my neighbourhood annually for an organization that arranges for the circumcision and religious education of Soviet Jews who have come to the United States. In itself, this is a cause that any observant Jew would embrace with alacrity and enthusiasm. To me, it is especially poignant. I vividly recall a scene during those memorable few weeks in Moscow as I sat at a Sabbath meal across from a student in his twenties, a talented mathematician enrolled full time in the new yeshiva, and listened to an account of his relatively recent, illegal circumcision.

It was winter. Sunset was approximately 4 p.m. The *mohel*, the man scheduled to perform the clandestine operation, was detained as a result of a traffic accident. Jewish law requires that circumcision be performed during the day, and rescheduling the procedure was fraught with complications. Finally, the *mohel* arrived. With insufficient time for the anaesthetic to take full effect and with bystanders regularly calling the phone number that provides the exact time, the patient was entered into the covenant of Abraham. Stifling tears, I turned to the faculty member—a Lubavitch hasid—who was sitting next to me and said, 'If we succeed in living a long life as very good Jews, there is a remote possibility that we will merit a place close enough to the front of Gan Eden that we will be able vaguely to make out the backs of the students in this yeshiva.'

A year or so after returning from Moscow, I received a letter from a different student, who had attended only part-time. He sent me a picture of a little hut that he had built himself for the festival of Sukkot at a school where he was studying and added that he had finally screwed up the courage to be circumcised. Until now, he wrote, he could not bring himself to recite the phrase in the Grace after Meals which thanks God for 'the covenant which you have sealed into our flesh'; finally he had begun to say it. This time, the tears were not contained.

For me, then, the association of circumcision and Russian Jews evokes emotions that beggar description. But there was a rub. Several Lubavitch-run organizations are devoted to this and similar objectives, and the beneficiary of this event is one of them. Shortly before the 1995 breakfast, I had called to speak to one of the directors. In a conversation made all the more moving by his request that we speak in Yiddish, I asked apologetically if the heads of the organization believe in the messiahship of the Rebbe. The softspoken but unequivocal answer was, 'I spent many years in the Soviet Union as a Marrano observing Judaism in secret, and I will not live as a Marrano here. I indeed believe that the Rebbe is the Messiah.' One could not help but admire the courage and tenacity of this man's faith, while simultaneously reflecting on the bitterest of ironies: he clung to Judaism heroically through the hell of Soviet oppression so that he might emerge to declare his belief in a deceased Messiah.

I decided not to attend the breakfast. Looking at the issue narrowly, I certainly prefer a circumcised, observant messianist to an uncircumcised Jew entirely alienated from the tradition. This breakfast, however, sponsored by almost every one of the multitude of Orthodox synagogues in central Queens, was unquestionably an implicit assertion of the Orthodox legitimacy of this organization and the theological orientation of its leadership. There is not the slightest doubt that these synagogues would not have sponsored an event supporting an organization led by Conservative rabbis that provided circumcision to Russian Jews even if the *mohel* were unimpeachably Orthodox. Such a breakfast, then, could only be seen as another step in the process of embracing the belief in a deceased Messiah as an acceptable option within the Orthodox fold, thus driving another nail into the coffin of Judaism's messianic faith.

From this perspective, the question is no longer the choice presented at the outset of the previous paragraph. Rather, the alternatives need to be framed in far broader terms. You can gain ten thousand (or one hundred thousand, or one million) additional observant Jews at the price of accepting a fundamental change in a core belief of Judaism. Are you prepared to pay that price? Posed in the abstract to an Orthodox audience, this should be a rhetorical question. The challenge is to persuade people with compelling emotional motives to resist that it is the right question.

When the invitation to the 1996 breakfast arrived complete with its imposing array of sponsors, I was surprised by the degree to which it shook me. Surely I had no doubt that it would be forthcoming and that even rabbis who had agreed with my article would not abandon their sponsorship. Still, as the previous year's conversation rang in my ears and synagogue after synagogue, rabbi after rabbi, passed before my eyes, I realized that my article may have elicited compliments but had accomplished very little. If my efforts were to mean anything, I would have to take the next step, quixotic though it might be. And so, despite my abortive earlier approach, I turned once again to the Rabbinical Council of America.

On 12 April, the day after Passover, I wrote a letter to Rabbi Steven Dworken, executive vice-president of the RCA:

Dear Rabbi Dworken,

After considerable deliberation, I have decided that I would still like to propose a resolution about Messianism at the RCA conference. The text, however, is more focused and no longer speaks of practical steps to be taken beyond the resolution itself.

The new proposal reads as follows:

'In light of disturbing developments which have arisen following the passing of the Lubavitcher Rebbe *zt"l*, the Rabbinical Council of America declares that there is no place in Orthodox Judaism for the belief that Mashiach ben David [Messiah son of David] will begin his Messianic mission only to experience death, burial and resurrection before completing it.' . . .

About two weeks later, I sent an additional letter to the scores of RCA members with whom I was personally acquainted:

Enclosed please find a letter to Rabbi Steven Dworken outlining a resolution that I hope to propose at the RCA convention in response to recent developments in Habad. I have taken this highly uncharacteristic step because I am convinced that a core belief of Judaism is in grave jeopardy.

Many Orthodox rabbis appear to have concluded that support for the valuable activities of Lubavitch messianists is so important that it should impel us to risk the long-lasting deformation of a fundamental principle of the Jewish religion and to concede that Christians may well have been correct in rejecting a central argument against the Messiahship of Jesus put forth by innumerable Jews from the Ramban to R. Chaim [Soloveitchik].

Needless to say, few if any rabbis have knowingly and intentionally embraced these conclusions. In most cases, they have either not thought the matter through or have persuaded themselves, on grounds which elude me, that there is no meaningful

risk. What is certain is that they do not actually want these consequences to material-
ize. A resolution of this sort is the only way I can see to put the Orthodox Rabbinate
on record, so that our children will not have to say that we acquiesced in legitimating
the belief in a Second Coming as an authentic variant of Orthodox Judaism.

Severe damage has already been done. Messianists argue persuasively that our
silence has already established the Second Coming as an acceptable Orthodox Jewish
doctrine. We can still reply that we have not spoken out until now because we
thought this belief would dissipate after the initial period of mourning, because our
attention was captured by momentous events of critical importance in Israel, or
because we simply did not take the entire matter seriously. After two years, these
arguments are beginning to ring hollow. If we wait much longer, they will lose all
credibility, and we will face a condition of *me'uvat lo yukhal litkon* ['a twisted thing
that cannot be made straight'—Eccles. 1: 15]. Judaism will have been transformed on
our watch.

I appeal to you not to let this happen. If it is even remotely possible for you to
support this resolution in person, I beg you *bekhol lashon shel bakashah* [in every manner of request] to do so. A trip to the convention is a small price to pay to preserve the
messianic faith of the Jewish people in its full integrity.

My sense of what to expect from Jewish leaders had been so shattered
during the two years since the Rebbe's death that I wrote these letters without the slightest premonition as to the likely outcome. Would the ideal of
unity impel the RCA leadership to prevent such a resolution from being proposed? If proposed, would it be thoroughly defeated? Would it defy the predictions of the previous year and pass? Would it, as I believed it should, pass
almost unanimously? Faced with possibilities ranging across so wide a spectrum, I had absolutely no idea of the reaction that would prevail.

The conference was scheduled to begin on 10 June, just six weeks or so
after my second letter. Encouraging signs began to appear. One rabbi wrote
that he wished the resolution would be longer and stronger; another, unable
to come in from Israel, commended 'the historic step'; a third forwarded a letter he had sent to Rabbi Dworken expressing 'clear and unequivocal support'.
I met with Rabbi Norman Lamm, president of Yeshiva University, who
would not be at the vote but expressed his support of the resolution. Within a
few weeks, I knew of approximately twenty rabbis who had reacted favour-
ably and none who were unequivocally opposed. Shortly after the conference,
I received a letter from Lord Jakobovits, the former chief rabbi of Britain,
indicating that he had just returned from a long trip to Australia and New
Zealand. 'I am fully in accord', he wrote, 'with the sentiments expressed in
your letter. . . . I share your fear that if this is not contained and reversed great
damage may be done, as history proves only too tragically.'

Further encouragement came in early May when Rabbi Barry Freundel of Washington, DC, chair of the RCA Resolutions Committee, called with a request that I reformulate the resolution to include some positive statements about the Lubavitch movement and the Rebbe. I was happy to comply, and so the text that I presented to the membership on 12 June 1996 read as follows:

In light of disturbing developments which have arisen following the passing of the Lubavitcher Rebbe *zt"l*, the Rabbinical Council of America

1. expresses its anguish over the void created in the Jewish world by the loss of this extraordinary leader,

2. underscores its admiration for the important work that Habad has done for Judaism and the Jewish community over the years, and

3. declares that there is no place in Orthodox Judaism for the belief that Mashiach ben David [Messiah son of David] will begin his Messianic mission only to experience death, burial and resurrection before completing it.

Though my aggressiveness in pursuing this objective may seem inconsistent with shyness, I am very uncomfortable about confronting people on an individual level. I hesitate endlessly before picking up the phone to ask someone to serve on a committee or to do me the smallest favour. Consequently, although I had been at the conference for two and a half days before the vote and the text of the resolution was available in a booklet distributed to all participants, I did not raise the matter with anyone and had precious few conversations about it. In short, I rose to address the session on resolutions with cautious optimism but with no assurance as to the outcome. The text of that brief address follows.

It is my deep conviction that at this hour, in this room, we stand at an important moment in the history of the Jewish religion.

I take for granted the truth of the operative clause in this resolution. A distinguished Rabbi who supports the resolution told me several days ago that it represents the proverbial 'motherhood and apple pie'. For anyone who needed convincing, I discussed the sources at length in the Winter 1995 issue of *Jewish Action* and cannot revisit them here.

The question is: why is this resolution necessary?

The tragic answer is that during the last two years—through sins of omission and commission—we have helped to undermine a fundamental element of Judaism's messianic faith.

First—a word about the importance of the belief in the Rebbe's Messiahship within Lubavitch itself. I am no enemy of Lubavitch, and this resolution certainly expresses no such enmity. . . . But we must be aware of the fact that right now, *Yeḥi Adonenu morenu verabenu melekh hamashiaḥ le'olam va'ed* ['May our Master, Teacher, and Rabbi, the King Messiah, live for ever'] is recited aloud and in unison, by men and by women, three times, at both the Friday night and Saturday morning service in the main synagogue at 770 Eastern Parkway [the main headquarters of Lubavitch].[1] The educational system is in the hands of messianists.[2] This is no marginal belief. Not every Lubavitcher hasid—thank God—is a messianist, but the movement has been compromised at its core.

Even more important, we have been treating open messianists as Orthodox Rabbis in good standing. . . . The message, though unintentional, is simply unmistakable: the belief that Mashiach ben David [Messiah son of David] began his messianic mission in the 1950s, was buried in 1994, and will soon return to complete his task is an acceptable option within Orthodox Judaism.

My own position is that we should not engage in any activity with or on behalf of messianists that a liberal, Modern Orthodox Rabbi would not pursue with or on behalf of Conservative Rabbis or institutions. This resolution, however, does not require such a conclusion. On the contrary, anyone who believes that close cooperation with messianists should continue is all the more obligated to support the resolution. Let me explain.

Those of us who participated in the Synagogue Council of America [an umbrella organization of the major Jewish religious denominations] were able to say that we had made clear in numerous ways that we did not regard Conservatism or Reform as legitimate options within Judaism. Consequently, our participation in the Synagogue Council could not be misconstrued. It is only by supporting this resolution that people who will continue a relationship with messianists in Orthodox contexts will have some basis for asserting that this relationship cannot be taken as a legitimation of belief in a Second Coming.

We have allowed a seismic shift in Judaism—and in the public perception of Judaism—to begin. I was reliably informed that in a private conversation, Senator Moynihan of New York made a telling remark. 'It took centuries', he said, 'for Christians to accept the fact that Jews reject the Messiahship of Jesus because they cannot recognize a Messiah who did not bring the redemption. Now,' he concluded, 'we are beginning to think that we've been had.'

Before hearing this, I was concerned by what we would tell the Ramban [Nahmanides] when he asks us why we allowed his most famous argument against the Messiahship of Jesus to be thrown into the wastebasket. Now I must wonder what we can tell Daniel Patrick Moynihan.

It is critically important that this resolution pass, that it pass with a minimum of

---

[1] Messianists routinely recite the *Yeḥi* at every prayer service. These remarks reflected the information available to me at the time.

[2] Although this is largely true, it is too sweeping, and I shall qualify it to a moderate degree later in the book.

dissent, and that it be publicized as widely as possible. At that point, we will be able to face Senator Moynihan; we will, if we merit it, be able to face the Ramban; and, most important of all, we will be able to face the Ribbono shel Olam [the Master of the Universe].

In the ensuing discussion, fewer than a handful of participants expressed any substantive reservations; those that did were concerned either by the spectre of friction with Lubavitch or by technical concerns. A rabbi from Texas argued against delay by noting his direct experience that 'we are already losing people' to missionaries because of Chabad messianism. Surprisingly, it was the added, laudatory material that provoked substantial opposition, largely because of a preference for a spare, unencumbered text. I myself argued for the longer version, but the advocates of brevity prevailed.

Finally, the word 'Orthodox' was dropped. My reason for incorporating it was perhaps excessively subtle: though I do not regard Reform Judaism as an authentic version of the historic faith, I—and most members of the RCA—do describe it as a denomination of 'Judaism'. The assertion that there was no room for Lubavitch messianism in 'Judaism' might put the organization in the questionable position of defending the proposition that belief in a dying and resurrected Messiah is worse than a denial that the laws of the Torah are binding at all. Nonetheless, since the whole point of my campaign was to exclude this belief from authentic Judaism, I expressed no resistance to the amendment. The final resolution, then, which passed with an insignificant number of negative votes, read as follows:

In light of disturbing developments which have recently arisen in the Jewish community, the Rabbinical Council of America in convention assembled declares that there is not and never has been a place in Judaism for the belief that Mashiach ben David will begin his Messianic mission only to experience death, burial and resurrection before completing it.

The purportedly impossible had been achieved with no formal campaign, no personal lobbying. The world's largest Orthodox rabbinical organization was on record.

I was naturally deeply gratified, but the inevitable attacks as well as a wholly unexpected thunderbolt were not long in coming.

The resolution evoked substantial coverage in the Jewish media. The *Jewish Press* published my speech to the Conference.[3] Other newspapers in the United States as well as *Ha'aretz* in Israel ran stories about the resolution. Interest was enhanced in some circles by the coincidental decision by the

---

[3] 21 June 1996, p. 42.

Southern Baptist Convention, which met in the same week as the RCA, to institute formal efforts to convert Jews to Christianity. Since I had been told by several critics that my concern about Lubavitch messianism was over-drawn because of the waning of a Christian threat, I found the very strong reaction to the Baptist decision instructive. Jews can still be jolted by Christian missionary campaigns, but they find it difficult to understand that accepting the legitimacy of a dead and resurrected Messiah is exponentially more dangerous to the Jewish defence against missionizing than any short-term or even long-term proselytizing initiative by American Baptists. This is a classic case of seeing trees and missing the forest.

And then the thunderbolt struck. On 28 June, several Jewish newspapers published a shocking public statement over the signature of Rabbi Ahron Soloveichik directly contradicting the unequivocal position that he had expressed less than two years earlier. The key sentences of this declaration read as follows:

Insofar as the belief held by many in Lubavitch, based in part on similar statements made by the Rebbe himself concernimg his predecessor the Previous Rebbe—including prominent Rabbonim and Roshei Yeshivah, that the Rebbe can still be Moshiach, in light of the Gemara in Sanhedrin, the Zohar, Abarbanel, Kisvei HaArizal, Sdei Chemed and other sources, it cannot be dismissed as a belief that is outside the pale of Orthodoxy. Any cynical attempt at utilizing a legitimate disagreement of interpretation concerning this matter, to besmirch and to damage the Lubavitch movement—that was, and, continues to be, in the forefront of those who are battling the Missionaries, assimilation and indifference—can only contribute to the regrettable discord that already plagues the Jewish and, particularly, Torah community.[4]

Many indications revealed to the discerning reader that Rabbi Soloveichik had not actually composed this letter. His command of English is far too good to have produced such an awkward document; two of the sources need to be so egregiously misinterpreted to make them relevant that they are not even cited by self-respecting messianists;[5] the statement appears oblivious of the resolution's careful reference to a messiah who dies in the midst of his mission; and the characterization of the vote, without a modicum of evidence, as a cynical effort to besmirch Lubavitch is utterly uncharacteristic of a man of

---

[4] Reproduced precisely as published in the *Algemeiner Journal*, 28 June 1996, English section, p. B2.

[5] The passage from the Zohar cited by irresponsible messianists ('Balak' 203, a reference supplied in the *Jewish Press*'s footnotes to the letter) refers to the death of Messiah son of Joseph, not Messiah son of David. The passage from *Kisvei HaArizal* (i.e. the works of the eminent 16th-c. mystic R. Isaac Luria, or, more precisely, the works of his most famous student) does not speak of the Messiah's death, burial, or resurrection at all.

the highest ethical sensitivity. Nonetheless, I initially, perhaps unforgivably, assumed that he had probably read the final text at least cursorily before allowing his deep sympathy for Lubavitch to impel him to authorize its release.

To my relief, I subsequently learned from impeccable sources with an intimate knowledge of the chain of events that the document contains substantive assertions that the rabbi did not authorize at all. He had agreed to a statement opposing denunciation of Lubavitch and trusted the individual who had approached him to formulate the language.[6] Though this trust was betrayed, Rabbi Soloveichik's commitment to amity would not allow him to say so sharply and explicitly. Instead, he issued a clarification the following week that was couched in such gentle and ambiguous terms that it left room for messianists to continue citing the first declaration to this day. The second statement reads as follows:

I recently lent my name to a statement deploring attacks on the Lubavitch movement which has done so much for the Jewish people through the years. I regret that some may interpret my statement in a way that suggests that I was endorsing specific views or claims concerning *Mashiach* instead of regretting attacks against Orthodox Jews who might hold these views. I have great respect for the Lubavitcher Rebbe's living legacy and continue to believe that Jewish unity and communal comity is poorly served by our attacking each other in public.

Since no one had suggested that Rabbi Soloveichik believed that the deceased Rebbe was the Messiah, the only misinterpretation that could have motivated this declaration was the understanding that he regards such a belief as legitimate. The difficulty is that the first statement declared the belief legitimate in so many words, so that the real problem he faced was not misinterpretation but misrepresentation. Since he did not want to say this explicitly, a terrible misimpression remained. Those with a correct understanding of his position could not adequately explain the weak formulation of the second statement; messianists could not explain why he issued it at all. When Jews for Jesus

---

[6] The rabbi's infirmity no doubt played a significant role in preventing him from overseeing the process with the vigour and thoroughness that he would have evinced in earlier years. A stronger letter with a similar point was issued a year later by R. Pinchas Hirshprung of Montreal, a venerable rabbinic scholar with long-standing connections to Lubavitch, several months before his passing; see the *Algemeiner Journal*, 20 June 1997. It is the unequivocal view of Montreal residents who knew and admired the rabbi that at that point in his life he was in no condition to resist pressures and that his signature on this document is consequently bereft of meaning. Many Orthodox Jews recoil instinctively from such an assertion because it appears disrespectful. In fact, precisely the opposite is true. It is the refusal to acknowledge what everyone knows to be the case that defames a learned rabbi by falsely describing an acutely embarrassing declaration as the product of his considered judgement and asking history to remember him as a defender of false messianism.

predictably released a document to the press on 9 July expressing their satisfaction with 'the Tzaddik [righteous man] from Chicago', Dr David Luchins, a former student maintaining a close relationship with the rabbi, consulted with him and wrote a letter published in both the English *Forward* and the *Jewish Week* affirming that Rabbi Soloveichik opposed attacks on Lubavitch but stood by his earlier teachings on the substantive issue.[7] We have already encountered those teachings: a belief 'possible in the Christian faith, but not in Judaism' and 'repugnant to everything Judaism represents'.

Since the RCA resolution was not formulated as an attack against Lubavitch and addressed the messianist belief in language milder than that used by Rabbi Soloveichik himself, it appears clear that its content was initially misrepresented to him by his informant, who proceeded to produce a largely unauthorized statement, enmeshing the rabbi in a wrenching controversy that did him a tragic disservice. For the most part, the offences of messianists are theological and in no way diminish their standing as decent human beings; this one is ethical and much more difficult to forgive. I hope that this account will help to set the record straight.

In the meantime, some Lubavitch hasidim levelled strong attacks against the RCA and even stronger attacks against me. I had 'managed to hijack' the convention in a manner that is 'still a mystery';[8] I am blinded by 'hatred based on jealousy';[9] I incited the RCA to issue a baseless libel as a result of hatred that has distorted my judgement.[10] In the *Jewish Press*,[11] my long-standing critic Rabbi Isser Zalman Weisberg revisited aspects of our earlier exchange on both a substantive and personal level.

Addressing the Jewish polemical sources, he argued that they 'imply the exact opposite' of my position. They '[do] not state or imply that J[esus] cannot be Mashiach because he died before completing the "messianic process", but rather because J[esus] accomplished *absolutely nothing* of Messianic nature, *he did not begin anything* of Messianic proportions, and therefore there is absolutely no reason to assume that he will return to complete that which he did *not* begin'. In fact, many of the polemicists decidedly say that any messianic figure who dies in a unredeemed world is not the Messiah. Moreover, the argument he attributes to them could elicit a disconcerting counter-argument from a Christian. Maimonides, after all, maintained that

[7] English *Forward*, 12 July 1996; *Jewish Week*, 12 July 1996.

[8] Larry Gordon in the *Algemeiner Journal* of 28 June, p. B3.

[9] Rabbi Zushe Silberstein in the *Algemeiner Journal* of 5 July, p. B4, and in the *Jewish Press* of the same date, p. 50.

[10] A statement by seven distinguished Lubavitch rabbis from the United States, Canada, France, Australia, and Israel, *Algemeiner Journal*, 5 July, p. 3.   [11] 5 July 1996, pp. 50, 62.

Christianity is part of a divine plan to prepare the world for the Messiah by spreading knowledge of the Torah.[12] In addition, despite profound Jewish objections to trinitarian and incarnationist theology, it cannot be denied that the religion set in motion by Jesus' career erased pagan-style polytheism from vast sections of the earth. I should hate to depend on an argument that Jesus did *absolutely nothing* of a messianic nature. The classical Jewish stance makes greater, quite specific demands of the Messiah that Jesus did not meet.

Rabbi Weisberg went on to level an *ad hominem* attack contrasting my deficient religiosity with the devotion of Lubavitch hasidim to the observance of Jewish law. Rabbinic law prohibits using *ḥalav akum* (milk produced by non-Jews without Jewish supervision) lest it turn out to come from a non-kosher animal. Though many Orthodox Jews rely on government supervision in this matter, Lubavitch hasidim are especially punctilious about maintaining the requirement. 'It would take less', writes Rabbi Weisberg, 'to cause Dr. Berger and a thousand like him to convert to Christianity than it would take to cause one Lubavitcher to eat *Chalav Akum*!'

This comment elicited a gratifying reaction in a twenty-page document by a vigorously anti-messianist Lubavitch hasid. Moshe Friedman had spent much of the previous two decades translating and publicizing the Rebbe's teachings. Deeply distressed by what he saw as a profound distortion of the Rebbe's words, he called his work *A Good Resolution about Moshiach: Many Lubavitchers Thank the RCA*.[13] Near the end of his detailed analysis of the issues, he describes Rabbi Weisberg's remark as revolting and adds, 'Dr. Berger and his *thousand thousands*, who would surely rather die than convert, G-d forbid, are unquestionably due an immediate apology.' I hope, of course, that this assessment will never be tested. In any case, the booklet as a whole provided some fleeting grounds for optimism that meaningful, unqualified opposition would arise within the movement itself.

Another Lubavitch hasid, a talented young scholar named Shaul Shimon Deutsch, left the community entirely because of the extreme manifestations of messianism and set up a synagogue in Boro Park where he established himself as a rebbe. He has so far written two volumes of a biography of the Rebbe,[14] sections of which have aroused lively controversy. Rabbi Deutsch's

---

[12] See Appendix I, no. 3.

[13] Published by Friedman's 'Chassidus Unlimited', then at 733 Eastern Parkway, Brooklyn, NY 11213, and now at 1571 45th Street, Brooklyn, NY 11219. (The change of address from Crown Heights to Boro Park is not insignificant.) As of December 2000 the booklet may be read on Friedman's website: <http://hudson.idt.net/~mf733>.

[14] *Larger Than Life*, i (New York, 1995); ii (New York, 1997). I was surprised and grateful to discover that the second volume, which begins with a reproduction of my speech to the RCA as pub-

activities continue to attract sporadic media attention that can be very useful in stimulating public scrutiny of this issue, and I wish him every success. Nonetheless, because he now functions outside the organized Lubavitch community, he cannot affect its destiny directly.

At the height of the uproar following the RCA resolution, the editor of the *Algemeiner Journal* invited me to an interview that was ultimately not published. Nonetheless, one personal question posed during the interview forced me to think harder about a puzzle that I had considered sporadically over the previous months. Why, the editor wanted to know, was I so much more concerned about this issue than almost anyone else? In responding, I came to realize that, for better or for worse, a nearly unique set of characteristics converged in me.

First, I actually believe in the traditional messianic faith of Judaism. Anyone who does not, however much he or she may be disturbed by the Christianization of that faith, cannot generate the same level of concern about its deformation.

Second, I have spent much of my professional life studying the history of both the Jewish–Christian debate and Jewish messianism. In dealing with issues of such sensitivity, there is a tense, complex interplay between personal commitment and disinterested scholarship that cannot help but leave a mark on my response to the announcement of a Jewish Second Coming. Seeing this development through a historical prism has alerted me to its capacity to refashion the parameters of Judaism. What others see as an episode, I see as a watershed. During a later lecture on the Jews who were killed or committed suicide to avoid conversion in the course of the first Crusade, I told a synagogue audience, 'I have spent a significant segment of my professional life with the victims of 1096; it is not surprising that I react strongly to the effective declaration by Orthodox Jewry that on a matter of fundamental principle our martyred ancestors were wrong and their Christian murderers were right.'

Third, on one formal occasion I crossed the line from academic study to religious apologetics when I acceded to the Jewish Community Relations Council of New York's request to join Michael Wyschogrod in writing *Jews and Jewish Christianity*'. I have already alluded to my concern that one of the key chapters—reproduced in Appendix I—would have to be discarded (along with much additional anti-missionary literature) if Lubavitch messianism became an acceptable variant of Orthodox Judaism.

lished in the *Jewish Press*, is 'dedicated to Dr. David Berger for his tremendous courage in standing against the Messianic campaign'.

Finally, I came to this development as an admirer of Lubavitch. Unlike some other Jews, I did not dismiss it as an irrelevant or already discredited movement.

In mid-July, the RCA sent its members a two-page summary of the issues that I prepared in the wake of the controversy, and with that, the matter receded once again from public attention. For all the declarations and denunciations, the resolution stands: there is no place in Judaism for this belief.

SEVEN

The Council of Torah Sages

IN THE WORLD of Modern Orthodoxy exemplified by the Rabbinical Council of America, I have friends, acquaintances, former students, and a modicum of standing, so that I could accomplish something from within. The leaders of Traditionalist Orthodoxy, marked by greater insularity and profound reservations about higher secular education, are far less accessible to me, though I have relatives and acquaintances within that community as well. Committed to the authority of *da'at torah*, or 'the opinion of the Torah', the Traditionalist Orthodox Agudath Israel has set up a group of distinguished rabbis (*gedolim*) empowered to decide issues of both Jewish law and public policy. This Council of Torah Sages (Moetzes Gedolei Hatorah) and its equivalent bodies in Israel hold a position of unparalleled influence in a major segment of Orthodoxy, and the leading authorities in that community command great respect among Modern Orthodox Jews as well.

I have already alluded to an early letter that I wrote to the Council immediately after publication of 'The New Messianism' (see Chapter 3 above). At some point, I was able to meet with one of the members, who expressed sympathy but provided an unequivocally discouraging assessment of the prospects that a public statement would be issued. As events unfolded, I sent the rabbis copies of the exchange in *Jewish Action*, my letter to the RCA, and two additional letters commenting on the RCA resolution and the controversy over Rabbi Soloveichik's statements. In the absence of any response, I had no way of assessing the reaction.

The status quo at the end of July 1996 was fraught with irony. The RCA, many of whose members are deeply sympathetic to Lubavitch and actively supportive of its activities, had excluded belief in the messiahship of the Rebbe from Judaism. The leaders of Agudath Israel, many of whom felt long-standing, even visceral hostility towards the movement, observed this development with public equanimity. I was informed that one member of the Moetzes noted in his yeshiva that I had achieved something very positive, though its impact had been diminished by Rabbi Soloveichik's statement. Another, I was told much later, made a similarly congratulatory remark. Still, the Council itself remained utterly silent.

In late August I wrote once again:

By now, a letter with my return address no doubt elicits a groan along with the inclination to discard it unread. Nonetheless, I have just heard a report which impels me, particularly as the *yomim noraim* [the High Holidays] grow near, to try a somewhat different approach.

Thus far, my primary argument has been couched in apocalyptic language. I have argued that the silence of great *rabbonim* [rabbis] is facilitating a fundamental transformation of the Jewish religion and that the failure to utter a word of public criticism is, in the words of my letter to the RCA, a betrayal of the messianic faith by which our ancestors lived and died. I believe to the very core of my being that this assessment is correct; it appears, however, that at least some of the *gedolim* on the *Moetzes* disagree, and there is no point in my attempting to force the issue in this form.

Let me then focus on more modest concerns. What inspired me to write again was a conversation with a reporter for the *Jerusalem Post* who told me a heartbreaking story about a Lubavitcher hasid loyal to the authentic messianic faith who is struggling vainly to find a Habad-oriented school for his children.

Thousands of *tinokos shel beis rabbon* [little children] throughout the world are now being taught to embrace a movement of false messianism. This is a statement of undeniable fact with which every member of the *Moetzes* surely agrees. Despite the great importance of the RCA statement, the teachers of these children tell themselves that real *gedolim* have refrained from delegitimating this belief. While a statement by the *Moetzes* will not instantly destroy this movement, it will surely accomplish the objective of *le'afrushei me'issura* [preventing sin] for many waverers and potential waverers. It will provide enormous *chizzuk* [encouragement] for Habad hasidim engaged in an uphill struggle to preserve themselves in the face of this onslaught. What consideration can possibly provide a *hetter* [permissive ruling] not to speak out?

I have heard some people say that the belief in the Messiahship of the Rebbe will die out and that public criticism will only strengthen the messianists. To begin with, the assertion is implausible on its face. Is the influence of the *Moetzes Gedolei Hatorah* so negligible that its formal declaration that a particular belief is illegitimate would make it easier for the bearers of this belief to function within the Orthodox community? Would such a declaration make it *easier* for them to persuade wavering hasidim? Even more important, what will make this belief die out in the absence of such delegitimation? At what age will the indoctrinated children experience a revelation and say, *Sheker nochalnu mimoreinu* ['We have inherited falsehood from our teachers']? Is the power of education so slight? The current reality is that the younger generation is *more* committed to this belief than their elders. However bizarre we may find the conviction that *Mashiach ben David* [Messiah son of David] died in the middle of his mission, we must remember that every President of the United States in our lifetime has believed this. Surely we have no right to act on the *confident conviction* that this belief will disappear of its own accord. And what of our responsibility to people whom we can save right here and now?

Then, one hears the argument that *machlokes* [divisiveness] must be avoided at virtually all costs. In the face of outright false messianism, I genuinely do not understand this argument. Let us imagine the following: A Modern Orthodox institute for women begins to issue *semicha* [rabbinic ordination], and some synagogues begin to hire these *musmochos* [ordained women]. The 'Rabbis' remain on the women's side of the *mechitza* [partition], deliver sermons from a pulpit which is separated from the men's *shul* [synagogue], perform funerals and unveilings but not weddings, *pasken shayles* [rule on questions of religious law] and visit the sick. Would the *Moetzes Gedolei Hatorah* and the Agudah refrain from expressing a single word of public criticism because of fear of *machlokes* with Jews who are *shomrei Torah umitzvos* [observant of the Torah and the commandments]? The question answers itself. The bulk of the Torah community—Modern and Traditionalist alike—would properly raise its voice in no uncertain terms. And yet the scenario I have outlined—even if we hold that it violates an *issur* [prohibition] against *serarah* [some types of positions of authority] for women and compromises standards of *tznius* [modesty], not to speak of the larger implications—is *far* less serious than kissing the picture of a dead man, declaring him *Moshiach ben Dovid*, and transmitting this belief to thousands of little children.

Ofor ani tachas kappos raglei hageonim hatzaddikim [I am as dust beneath the feet of the erudite and pious rabbis]. I do not have the standing to issue even the gentlest *tokhachah* [rebuke], surely not to *gedolei hador* [the great rabbis of the generation]. And yet, I must confess my perplexity as to how the members of the *Moetzes*, who serve as guardians of the *massorah* [tradition], can face the Ribbono shel Olam [the Master of the Universe] on *yom hadin* [the Day of Judgement, i.e. the High Holidays] and explain their silence.

At this time of year, I ask *mechilah* [forgiveness] for anything I may have written in this or earlier letters which might be seen as inappropriate temerity in addressing *gedolei yisroel* [the great rabbis of Israel]. My only intention is to undo what I perceive as a religious catastrophe that has befallen us, *veHashem hatov yekhapper* [and may the benevolent Lord provide atonement].

During the course of the controversy, a non-practising rabbi with connections in both the Agudath Israel environment and Lubavitch had called to express his solidarity with my position and to search for ways to strengthen the anti-messianist position within the Lubavitch community. A week or so after I wrote this letter, he arranged a meeting in Crown Heights in which he and I spoke with two hasidim opposed to the messianist position. His objective was to set up a private conversation between anti-messianist figures of genuine stature within Lubavitch and counterparts on the Council. It ultimately turned out that the hasidim were unable to provide such participants, but the conversation was instructive and disturbing. In its wake, I wrote another letter to the Council just one day after the Jewish New Year:

Please forgive me, but significant new information impels me to write once again.

Very recently, an individual who shares my concerns arranged a meeting in which the two of us spoke to two anti-messianist Lubavitcher hasidim in Crown Heights. One of them is open in his opposition, while the other is fearful of expressing his views publicly. The latter, who holds a position of authority in a Habad school, made two observations of great relevance to the issue before us.

First, he said that many messianists explicitly rely on the silence of *gedolei yisroel* as evidence that their position cannot be fundamentally objectionable.

Second, he told the following story:

Not long ago, he noticed that a picture of the Rebbe had been placed on the *mizrach* [eastern] wall of a classroom in which students *daven* [pray].[1] When he indicated to a student that it is halakhically problematic to *daven* while facing a picture, the response was that the picture had been moved to that wall pursuant to a specific directive from one of the *mashpi'im* [religious guides], who explained that this should be done because the Rebbe is *'elokus bilevush gashmi'* [Divinity in physical garb]. (My informant hastened to add that he can explain this expression. In other words, it does not mean that the Rebbe is literally God, though the subtle distinctions are surely lost on the majority of students.) When the Rabbi confronted the *mashpia*, the latter stood his ground, and the picture remained.

It is true that *davening* in the direction of a picture is in and of itself a relatively minor infraction which can be remedied by closing one's eyes, but bowing down toward a picture *for this reason* raises questions which can hardly be set down on paper without a trembling hand. . . . It seems difficult to avoid the conclusion that [this is] a literal, not merely metaphorical, act of idolatry.

If this is so, then all sorts of corollary questions arise which I do not need to spell out. But more important than *shayles* [questions] about wine and shechitah [ritual slaughter][2] is the fact that if we are to take my informant's first statement seriously, innocent Jewish children are engaging in what is arguably idolatry as a direct result of the silence of *gedolei yisroel*. People speak of the need for *brayte playtzes* [broad shoulders] in a *godol* [great rabbi], but no one has broad enough shoulders to bear this sort of responsibility.

One final observation. For the vast majority of Jews, the natural revulsion at identifying a recently buried individual as *Moshiach ben Dovid* was imbibed with their mother's milk; it was not formulated following a *seder* [study session] in *Hilchos Melokhim* ['The Laws of Kings' in Maimonides' *Mishneh torah*]. In other words, we

---

[1] It is customary to turn towards Jerusalem while praying.

[2] Consuming wine prepared by an idolater and meat slaughtered by one is, to put the matter mildly, problematic according to Jewish law. I shall have to revisit this issue later on.

are dealing with a profound religious instinct, not with an intellectual conclusion. I have discovered to my dismay that this instinct is vulnerable to an argument which says: 'You don't really know the sources. Did you learn the *gemoro* [talmudic passage] in [tractate] *Sanhedrin*? Are you capable of evaluating it? Your opposition is based on kindergarten knowledge. If this were really so unacceptable, there would be a clear delegitimation on the part of the greatest authorities.'

For many Jews, then, a messianic instinct which lies near the core of Judaism is already being eroded, and even some rabbis have published the assertion that they do not feel competent to make a determination. . . . What was once known to every Jewish tailor and shoemaker has, in the twinkling of an eye, become a *sofek* [matter of doubt] for Orthodox rabbis. The RCA resolution has helped considerably, but its impact has been weakened by R. Ahron Soloveichik's first statement, despite his effort at clarification. One intensely committed messianist has even told me that some non-Lubavitch rabbis have privately indicated that they consider the Rebbe [to be] the Moshiach but are afraid to say so openly. I responded that I did not believe him, but I do believe that once the key instinct erodes, there will be little to prevent the doctrine of the Rebbe's messiahship from leaking into the mainstream religious community.

To assure the preservation of a central belief of Judaism, we badly need a declaration by rabbis of unassailable stature who command respect across the broadest spectrum of Orthodoxy. There is simply no question that I have just described the *Moetzes Gedolei Hatorah*.

Within two weeks, just before the festival of Sukkot, I received a call providing the first significant indication that these letters were not disappearing into a void. Rabbi Moshe Sherer, president of Agudath Israel, was one of the most effective Jewish communal leaders of this generation. I had never spoken to him, though he had sent me a letter in late December 1995 acknowledging receipt of the exchange in *Jewish Action*, which he said he had read with great interest, and confirming that the Agudah office had forwarded the earlier article to members of the Council. This time he called with a brief, somewhat cryptic, but encouraging message. 'You have been writing to the *Moetzes*', he said, 'and have not received a reply. I want you to know that the members of the *Moetzes* are serious people who read serious material seriously.' He went on to say that the five-member Council had been expanded to eight and that he would connect me to his secretary so that she could provide me with the names and addresses of the three new members.

I reacted to this call with happiness bordering on euphoria, though I knew perfectly well that it guaranteed nothing. Then, immediately after the holiday, a remarkable sentence appeared in an Israeli publication that moved the discussion of idolatry closer to centre stage.

EIGHT

The Spectre of Idolatry

IN ORTHODOX JEWISH circles there is a widespread genre of leaflets or booklets ranging from one to six or so pages containing discussions connected to the weekly Torah reading, or *parashah*. After Sukkot, the annual reading cycle resumes with the beginning of Genesis (*Bereshit*). In that week's issue of *Siḥat hage'ulah* ['Discourse on Redemption', 11 Oct. 1996], a four-page messianist *parashah* booklet, the standard formula declaring the Rebbe's messiahship ('May our Master, Teacher, and Rabbi, the King Messiah, live for ever', often described simply as the *Yeḥi* after its first Hebrew word) appeared in a modified form. One of the regular features of *Siḥat hage'ulah* is a story of a miracle effected by the deceased Rebbe. In the account published in the *Bereshit* issue, a beneficiary of the miracle bursts out into thankful praise, declaring, 'May our Master, Teacher and *Creator* [*bore'enu*] the King Messiah live for ever'. The relevant section was reproduced in a religious newspaper called *Yom hashishi* and caused a flurry of discussion in Israel, with a number of Lubavitch rabbis expressing dismay.

At about the same time, the individual who had arranged the meeting in Crown Heights spoke to Rabbi Sherer, who told him that the Council of Torah Sages would probably not act unless some additional messianist provocation emerged. I was, of course, deeply disappointed and wrote a letter to Rabbi Sherer in which I may have allowed this disappointment to manifest itself more forcefully than I should have:

Rabbi [X] has indicated to me that in a recent conversation, you told him that the Moetzes is unlikely to issue a statement in the absence of some egregious public act by the messianists.

As you may know from the report in *Yom hashishi*, *Siḥat hage'ulah* for *parashat* 'Bereshit' has transformed *Yeḥi adonenu morenu verabenu melekh hamashiaḥ le'olam va'ed* into *Yeḥi adonenu morenu ubore'enu melekh hamashiaḥ le'olam va'ed*.

To date, the following have apparently not qualified as sufficiently public or egregious: Full-page ads in the *New York Times*; messianist mitzvah tanks [vans with religious materials used by Lubavitch for outreach]; billboards on major highways; cable TV shows; full-fledged idolatry in classrooms; the multiple recitation of 'Yeḥi etc.' as the climactic affirmation—after *Hashem hu ha'elokim* [the Lord is God]—in Ne'ilah [the final prayer of the Yom Kippur service]; missionary press releases utilizing this new belief for *shmad* [apostasy]; articles in the Jewish media by non-Lubavitch Rabbis who no longer know whether a fundamental Jewish belief is true.

Perhaps this issue of *Siḥat hage'ulah* qualifies. If not, I am at a loss to imagine what does. I fear that a statement of this sort, which repels even some messianists, will be dismissed as marginal and hence unworthy of attention, while 'normal' messianism will be insufficiently egregious. Hence, almost by definition, nothing will ever qualify, and, to borrow the newly minted phrase, Judaism will have defined deviancy down.

There has never been a generation in Jewish history in which rabbinic silence in the face of such developments would have been remotely imaginable. I realize that people speak of ours as a *dor yatom* [an orphaned generation]. Nevertheless, the stubborn reverence that I retain for *gedolei Torah* [great Torah Sages] continues to prevent me from making peace with the possibility that our orphaned state is this bleak, profound and shattering.

During the next several months, a number of Lubavitch documents containing startling formulations came to my attention. A catechism published in Safed in September 1996 reproduced a section of a work by Rabbi Levi Yitzchak Ginsberg, a *mashpia* in Yeshiva Tomchei Temimim in Kfar Chabad, the major Lubavitch centre in Israel, whose view that the Rebbe remains alive we have already encountered in my article in *Jewish Action*:

It does not matter at all if the physical pulse is active or not, and if various phenomena connected with physical life as we recognize them exist; the physical life of the Rebbe never operated in the manner familiar to us, and that true physical life continues with precisely the same force as before.

More than this: As has been explained on many occasions . . . the Rebbe is the 'master of the house' with respect to all that happens to him and all that happens in the world. Without his agreement no event can take place, and if it is his will, he can bring about anything, 'and who can tell him what to do'? It follows that if he wills it, he can at any moment cause his physical senses to act in a manner familiar to us, and his failure to do so is solely the result of the fact that it is not his will to do so. . . . In him the Holy One Blessed be He rests in all His force just as He is (because of his complete self-nullification to God, so that this becomes his entire essence).[1]

In mid-November, citing a work that we shall later have to examine more

---

[1] *Mashiaḥ akhshav*, vol. iv, quoted in *Questions and Answers about the Messiah and Redemption* (Heb.), 2nd edn. (Safed, Tishrei 5757 [Sept. 1996]), 28. On this phantom volume of *Mashiaḥ akhshav*, see pp. 98–9.

carefully, *Siḥat hage'ulah*[2] published this last formula in conjunction with the assertion that one is therefore permitted to bow down to a righteous man. In February, another Israeli publication cited the assertion that the Rebbe is 'the Holy One Blessed be He' with evident approval,[3] and an undated issue of the French-language *Activités juives* spoke of his 'apotheosis'.

The most elaborate of this spate of writings affirming the Rebbe's divinity appeared in English in an August 1996 issue of *Beis Moshiach*, a lengthy weekly journal with a substantial circulation in which mainstream messianist figures regularly participate. The author, a layman with a doctoral degree, set forth his view of Jewish theology:

A certain Lubavitcher Rov [rabbi] was chiding a certain Lubavitcher Chasid about his continuing faith in the Rebbe as Melech ha-Moshiach [the King Messiah]. The Chasid bit the bait and, in the ensuing banter, commented that if the Rebbe was wrong, then all Chasidus [hasidism] is disqualified all the way back to the Baal Shem Tov. The Rov became serious and said, 'No, my friend. All the way back to Moshe Rabbenu' [Moses our Rabbi].

So, being stuck with Moshe Rabbenu means being stuck with the Rebbe which means being stuck with the absolute truth of all their statements, including those statements about what is Rebbe. For example, that Rebbe is the 'Essence and Being [of God] enclothed in a body', that a Rebbe is by nature 'omniscient' and 'omnipotent', that all material and spiritual blessings flow from the Rebbe.

These are radical statements that many would like to sweep under the rug of normative Judaism. However, they are neither wild exaggerations nor poetic parables. Rather these ideas are facts of life which help us understand how a 'human being' like the Rebbe can foresee and control and coordinate the finest details of someone's personal life effecting his powerful blessings over many years and many miles removed. In other words, there is nothing shocking about the Rebbe's powers given that his nature is above the limitations of nature. . . . The Rebbe is, in fact, the boss over nature . . . he delivers . . . a symphony of countless harmonized details of particular divine providence and . . . has, in effect, past present and future all in his pocket. . . .

So who [is] *Elokeinu* [our God]? Who *Avinu* [our Father]? Who *Malkeinu* [our King]? Who *Moshianu* [our Redeemer]? Who *Yoshianu V'Yigaleinu Shaynis B'Karov* [will save and redeem us once again shortly]? The Rebbe, Melech HaMoshiach. That's who.[4]

Shaken by this material, I sent a letter in late December to the head of the kosher supervision division of The Union of Orthodox Jewish Congregations of America (OU), to two other kashrut organizations, and to several distinguished rabbis in Israel, expressing concern about both the fundamental

[2] *Parashat* 'Toledot' (16 Nov. 1996). [3] *Peninei ge'ulah* 42 (I Adar 5757).

[4] Aryeh A. Gotfryd, 'The Rebbe's Answer: A Dream Come True', *Beis Moshiach* (1 Elul 5756/16 Aug. 1996), 66–63 [pages numbered in reverse order].

religious issue and the acceptability of Lubavitch ritual slaughter. In a covering letter to one of the recipients, I expressed my deepest misgivings:

With the honorable exception of the RCA and, through *Jewish Action*, the OU itself, most of the world's Orthodox leadership has been indifferent to a mass movement of false messianism. It is entirely posssible that this indifference will extend to idolatry as well. Luther, who was nobody's fool, once suggested that missionaries approaching Jews should first argue for the Messiahship of Jesus and only later, when their targets have become accustomed to the first doctrine, emphasize his divinity. I wonder whether we have been similarly desensitized. Time will tell.

The one concrete result that I know was a minor one. A friend in Israel wrote me that shortly after my letter would have arrived, he saw a new sign in the yeshiva of one of the Israeli rabbis banning *Siḥat hage'ulah* 'and the like' from the study hall.

On 24 January 1997 an article in the New York *Jewish Week* on an entirely unrelated matter inaugurated a short series of events that rekindled a glimmer of hope with respect to the Council of Torah Sages. The newspaper ran a feature on smoking that included a discussion of the obstacles to a formal prohibition within the parameters of Jewish law. In response, I wrote a letter published on 14 February:

You point out quite correctly that both halakhic [legal] uncertainties and anticipated resistance from addicted smokers have made it very difficult for Orthodox Jewish authorities to ban smoking outright. There is, however, an alternative, more limited strategy that would work very well and save countless lives over the years.

The more traditional segments of Orthodoxy recognize rabbinic leaders to whom they attribute authority that goes beyond the domain of technical *halakhah* narrowly construed. For some this authority takes the form of a hasidic rebbe's power over his followers; for others it is formulated as 'the opinion of the Torah' (*da'at torah*) expressed by such organizations as the Council of Torah Sages.

Without addressing the question of an absolute halakhic prohibition, such authorities could declare that it is the opinion of the Torah that no individual who does not smoke should start. Within a generation or two, smoking in those subcommunities would be eradicated. I am unable to discern any argument against the promulgation of such a policy, which strikes me as a mitzvah [a religiously meritorious act] of the highest order.

I sent a copy of the published letter to the members of the Council with a covering note:

Remarkably, this communication is not primarily about Lubavitch.

Enclosed is a letter that I wrote to the *Jewish Week* which was published in the current issue. I believe that the proposal in that letter affords the *Moetzes Gedolei*

HaTorah an opportunity which may be unique in our history—the ability to prevent the premature, agonizing deaths of thousands of religious Jews by the mere stroke of a pen. . . . Though my efforts to persuade the *Rabbonim* [rabbis] to act on a matter of spiritual *pikuach nefesh* [danger to life] have thus far failed, I hope that I will be blessed with greater success on an issue of physical *pikuach nefesh*.

A short time later, I received a call from Rabbi Chaim Dov Keller, who is very close to several members of the Council. Rabbi Keller had called me on several previous occasions, when we had discussed the Lubavitch question at considerable length. This time he said, 'I'm calling to correct your English.' After receiving the anticipated puzzled reaction, he went on to explain that it is incorrect to say, 'My efforts have thus far failed.' The correct formulation is, 'They have thus far not succeeded.'

Although Rabbi Keller did not elaborate much on his cryptic words of encouragement, within a few days two important developments came to my attention.

First, I was informed that on Saturday, 1 March, Rabbi Elya Svei, a leading figure in the Council, had spoken at an Agudath Israel event in Los Angeles, where he commented on the sin of the golden calf recounted in that week's Torah reading. The Israelite collective, he said, was held responsible even though only three thousand had actively worshipped the calf (Exod. 32: 28). The sin of the people as a whole was their unconscionable silence. Similarly, he went on, we must beware of the consequences of the prevailing silence in the face of developments within the Lubavitch movement.

Then, on 3 March, the anti-messianist Lubavitch rabbi who had contacted me even before my *Jewish Action* piece called to ask if I knew anyone involved in the Association of Advanced Rabbinical and Talmudical Schools (AARTS), an accrediting organization whose constituents are Traditionalist Orthodox yeshivas. My informant reported that Rabbi Svei and others had launched an effort to decertify Oholei Torah/Oholei Menachem, a major Lubavitch yeshiva in which the messianist belief is proclaimed, and he hoped that as much influence as possible might be brought to bear to ensure the success of this initiative. I made a call to a person involved in the organization and sent him some material that was disseminated to the participants at the next meeting.

An individual present at that meeting told me that some of the heads of non-hasidic yeshivas in the association shrugged off a portion of the material (perhaps in a private conversation) on the grounds that hasidism in general is *avodah zarah*, the Hebrew term which literally means 'foreign worship' and is the rough equivalent of idolatry. While we shall soon have occasion to examine the considerations that could have led someone to make such a startling remark, I do not believe that it was meant literally. Thus, metaphorical *avo-dah zarah* neutralized literal *avodah zarah*. Despite this dismissive reaction by some participants, the organization apparently reached the brink of a decision to remove accreditation. In early June Lubavitch leadership launched a successful counterattack,[5] and Oholei Torah remained a member in good standing. Thus, an organization that would, I was told, unhesitatingly exclude a yeshiva that offered Talmud classes for women, even though this is permitted by some distinguished rabbis, retained an institution that is home to a movement of false messianism.

On the third anniversary of the Rebbe's death, a full-page advertisement appeared in *The New York Times* declaring that 'The third of Tammuz is not the Rebbe's yahrzeit', a word denoting the anniversary of an ordinary human being's demise. In this case, we were informed, the date marks the time when the Rebbe 'was liberated from the limitations of corporeal existence'. In the absence of such limitations, he

is accessible to all of us, everywhere, at any time. . . . Anyone, however great or humble, can turn to him with their deepest prayers. There are no barriers. There is no need to make a pilgrimage or stand on line to receive his blessing. . . . Amazing stories keep pouring in from all corners of the globe. People are experiencing miracles large and small. . . . And all this because of a personal connection to the Rebbe who is with all of us.[6]

Assertions that the Rebbe was still alive in an even more literal sense than this advertisement contemplates inevitably aroused amusement in many circles. For the most part, I strove to repress my laughter, reacting instead with grumpy humourlessness because of my feeling that the comic surrealism that characterized these pronouncements contributed significantly to the failure to appreciate their significance. At the same time, even my self-imposed barriers were not altogether impermeable. Jokesters quipped that round-the-clock guards had been posted at the Rebbe's grave in response to death threats. And at the end of May, *Siḥat hage'ulah* published a sentence not intended to be funny that made me laugh at least as hard as the intentional joke.

I had long ago become accustomed to the use of the abbreviation *shlita*, meaning 'may he live a long, good life, amen', after the deceased Rebbe's name. In some messianist circles, this ordinary acronym (generally used, needless to say, for the living) was replaced with the newly minted *shilo* (*shey-iḥyeh le'olam va'ed*), meaning 'May he live for ever'. But another standard

---

[5] See *Algemeiner Journal*, 20 June 1997.　　[6] *The New York Times*, 8 July 1997.

Hebrew acronym is sometimes used when a living and dead person appear in the same sentence. To avoid endangering the living through this juxtaposition, mention of his name is followed by the formula 'May he be distinguished [from the dead person] to merit a long life' (*yibadel leḥayim arukim*), abbreviated in writing as *yblḥ"a*.

Here, then, is *Siḥat hage'ulah*'s report on the conference of a Lubavitch institute whose mission is strange enough in itself:

The R.Y.A.L. Institute in New York is a scientific research institute on the subject of redemption and science. The Institute was established in memory of [the long-deceased] Rabbi Yisrael Aryeh Leib, brother of *yblḥ"a* the Rebbe *shlita* of Lubavitch the King Messiah.[7]

No caricaturist could have credibly created this, and yet these are deeply serious people whose beliefs are no laughing matter.

In the summer issue of the *Jewish Observer*, the official journal of Agudath Israel, Rabbi Keller placed himself on the record:

There is another movement that has enjoyed a cloak of relative silence that requires us to speak out. That is active messianism, which has lately taken a frightening turn toward *avodah zarah*. We have seen a highly respected Chassidic movement, with great accomplishments for Torah and *Yiddishkeit* [Judaism] to its credit, torn apart by a *machlokes* [dispute] that touches *ikrei emuna*—the fundamentals of our faith.

The Rebbe has progressed in the eyes of one faction within the movement from being a *navi* [prophet] to being the most likely candidate for *Moshiach* to being '*bechezkas*' *Moshiach* [presumptive Messiah], to being *Melech HaMoshiach* [the King Messiah], to being a dead *Moshiach* who has not died, to being 'omniscient', 'omnipotent' and being 'the Essence and Being [of God] enclothed in a body'! [There followed a quotation from *The New York Times* advertisement.]

The Orthodox world looks for guidance; the non-Orthodox world impugns us with guilt by association; those in Lubavitch who are opposed to all this look for support. And only recently has the silence in our camp [i.e. the Agudath Israel sector of Orthodoxy] been broken by Rabbi Elya Svei *shlita*. . . .[8]

In the face of these quotations, the Director of Lubavitch Chabad of Illinois disseminated a letter, forwarded to me by Rabbi Keller, arguing that the formulations cited in the *Observer* are 'well within the mainstream' of traditional Judaism. The evidence for this assertion was taken from a collection of quotations assembled by Avraham Baruch Pevzner, a Lubavitch rabbi in Israel, in a book entitled *Al hatzadikim* ('On the Righteous'), to which I have

---

[7] *Siḥat hage'ulah*, '*Parashat* "Beḥukotai"' (31 May 1997).
[8] Chaim Dov Keller, 'The Best of Times, the Worst of Times', *The Jewish Observer* (Summer 1997) 36–9 at 39.

devoted much of Appendix II. This letter convinced me that the theological radicalism which had surfaced since September 1996 was deeply rooted in mainstream Lubavitch circles.

In a lecture that I was asked to deliver at an Orthodox synagogue in Monsey, New York, I addressed this issue and, among other points, related the story about the Rebbe's picture on the eastern wall of the school in Crown Heights. One of the listeners, whose child (or children) attended a Crown Heights institution, reacted in outraged disbelief and demanded that I produce the name of my source. I responded that he had every right to be upset by my refusal to comply, but I could not violate the individual's request for anonymity. Within a week, an anti-messianist Lubavitch hasid who had attended the talk informed me that the father had proceeded to investigate the situation and was dismayed by what he had found.

In late 1997 I was invited to participate in a symposium on 'The Sea Change in American Orthodox Judaism' to be published in *Tradition*, the journal of the Rabbinical Council of America on whose editorial board I serve. One of the questions asked whether it was 'the deviationist religious movements or secularism' that posed the greatest threat to Orthodoxy and went on to enquire about the proper strategies 'in relating to either of them'.

Since I have often been asked how I square my insistence on delegitimating Lubavitch messianism with a policy of limited but significant cooperation with Conservative and Reform Jews, let me reproduce several paragraphs of my contribution to that symposium, which contains some of the strongest language I have used about Lubavitch along with a carefully calibrated formulation of my approach to non-Orthodox movements:

Within limits, the ideal of unity must also govern our relationship with non-Orthodox Jews. Aside from the evident political importance of mobilizing the largest possible Jewish community to support the needs of *kelal yisrael* [the Jewish collective], there are compelling religious reasons to hope that Conservatism and Reform retain their constituencies. At this point in history, these movements do not seriously threaten the loyalties of Orthodox Jews. For most Conservative and Reform Jews, the realistic alternative to their current affiliation is termination of their Jewish identity. In the absence of an acute threat, we must consider the religious preferability of a life of partial observance to one of radical estrangement; indeed, R. Moshe Feinstein [a leading rabbinic decisor] argued that people brought up as Reform Jews may well be rewarded for their *mitzvot* [the commandments they observe] while remaining free of punishment for transgressions that in the final analysis are not their fault.[9] Even the hope that non-Orthodox Jews may be won over depends on preserving their ties to

---

[9] *Igerot moshe*, 'Even ha'ezer', 4 (New York, 1985), responsum 26c, p. 54.

Judaism until they or their descendants might embrace the Torah in its fullness. For the Modern Orthodox, such Jews also provide a service we may be uncomfortable in acknowledging: a buffer against the outside world, the psychological comfort of feeling more religious than other Jews, protection against a naked encounter with a challenging environment.

The great deterrent to a policy of cooperation is the specter of legitimating deviationism. The problem is exacerbated by attacks against delegitimation from within and without. Orthodox advocates of friendship, civility, and engagement with non-Orthodox movements must liberate themselves by saying publicly, unequivocally and as often as necessary that we do delegitimate. Reform and even Conservative Judaism as currently constituted diverge in fundamental ways from Jewish belief and/or practice and are consequently not legitimate expressions of the historic faith. But they have religious value, their adherents are for the most part our fellow Jews, in their own way they care about the Torah, and their communal commitments often coincide with our own. We need not be embarrassed to embrace a policy of constructive cooperation and dialogue. As Reform Judaism expands to include a growing number of righteous Gentiles, this will become more difficult, but *dayah letzarah besha'atah* [let problems be limited to their own time].

The greatest danger to Orthodoxy, which is not likely to be mentioned in any other contribution to this symposium, comes not from the obvious 'deviationist movements' or from secularism but from a group of non-Orthodox Jews who are widely perceived as Orthodox. Precisely because most of Orthodoxy sees them as within the fold, Lubavitch messianists threaten to undermine a key element of the messianic faith of Judaism by having us recognize the Second Coming as a legitimate Jewish belief. The Rabbinical Council of America has, thank God, formally declared that this doctrine has no place in Judaism; nonetheless, should we continue to treat messianists as Orthodox Jews in good standing, late twentieth-century Jewry may well be remembered as the generation which allowed a historic transformation of the Jewish religion to take place.

A significant segment of this movement now declares openly that the Rebbe is not only the Messiah but God. In the last year and a half various Lubavitch writings have called the Rebbe 'our Creator', 'the Holy One Blessed be He', the *'ba'al habayit* [master] of all that occurs in the world', 'omnipotent', 'omniscient', 'our God', 'indistinguishable' from God, one who underwent an 'apotheosis' on 3 Tammuz 5754, whose 'entire essence is divinity' and to whom one may consequently bow in prayer. These formulations, complete with prooftexts, appear in publications in which Lubavitch educators participate and reflect views that can be found not only on the movement's periphery but also at its core. Without serious investigation, Orthodox Jews are accepting the *shechitah* [ritual slaughter] and contributing to the educational institutions of a group containing a significant segment of idolaters. The central objective of Avraham Avinu's [our patriarch Abraham's] migration from his land, his birthplace, and the home of his father is being undermined not with a bang but with a whimper.

Just as we must learn to delegitimate, we must learn to refrain from delegitimation. The effort in some circles to stigmatize Modern Orthodoxy places a central stream of Jewish thought through the ages outside the fold by ignoring or willfully distorting the views of many *gedolei yisrael* [leading rabbis] and entire communities of Jews.[10] Controversies over women's issues have lately created a particularly great danger of fragmentation, and we must beware of making disagreements which do not touch upon fundamentals of the faith the cause of schism within Modern Orthodoxy itself.[11]

This symposium contribution did not appear until late 1998, a full year after it was written. In the meantime, I was distressed not only by the deification of the Rebbe but by the appearance in November 1997 of the ruling with which we are already familiar that Jewish law requires belief in his messiahship. I felt the need to make these developments known as quickly as possible, and so I sent a strongly worded article to the New York *Jewish Week*, which had printed a piece that I had written about another contentious issue several months earlier. This time, weeks passed with no reaction. In the latter part of December I was scheduled to give a lecture in Jerusalem on the occasion of the dedication of a new building for Matan, a school of Jewish studies for women. I brought a copy of the article with me and took advantage of the flight to translate it into Hebrew. A friend at the Hebrew University put me into contact with an editor of the English section of *Ha'aretz*, with whom I left a copy of both versions.

Upon my return to New York, I confirmed that the *Jewish Week* had decided against publication, and on 11 January 1998 the article was featured in both the English and Hebrew sections of Israel's most prominent newspaper, arousing a stormy reaction among readers around the world, many of whom read it on the *Ha'aretz* website. The English editors introduced the piece with a provocative sentence: 'In an extraordinary essay, David Berger argues that the followers of the Lubavitch Rebbe revere him not just as a Messiah, but a God, thus writing themselves out of Judaism altogether.' Despite the recapitulation of some familiar material, I must present the text of that brief essay in full.

---

[10] On this issue, see Gerald Blidstein, David Berger, Shnayer Z. Leiman, and Aharon Lichtenstein, *Judaism's Encounter with Other Cultures: Rejection or Integration?*, ed. Jacob J. Schacter (Northvale, NJ and Jerusalem, 1997).   [11] *Tradition*, 32/4 (Summer 1998), 28–30.

NINE

On False Messianism, Idolatry, and Lubavitch

IN THE AUTUMN of 1995, I published an article in *Jewish Action*, the journal of the Union of Orthodox Jewish Congregations of America, which decried the silence of rabbinic leaders about the declaration on the part of many Lubavitch hasidim that the late Rebbe is the Messiah. This silence, I argued, combined with the treatment of messianists as Orthodox Jews in good standing, fundamentally transforms Judaism, betrays the messianic faith of our ancestors, and grants Christian missionaries victory with respect to a key issue in the millennial debate between Judaism and Christianity.

At its annual convention in June 1996, the Rabbinical Council of America responded to this challenge with a declaration that 'there is not and never has been a place in Judaism for the belief that Messiah son of David will begin his messianic career only to experience death, burial, and resurrection before completing it'. In the aftermath of both the article and the RCA resolution, defenders of Lubavitch presented sources which allegedly demonstrate the acceptability of this patently un-Jewish doctrine. They also circulated a letter in the name of a highly distinguished rabbi, R. Ahron Soloveichik of Chicago, which he had authorized only in part and which contains material flatly contradicting statements that he had issued several months after the Rebbe's death, when he affirmed that this belief is possible in Christianity but not in Judaism and is 'repugnant to everything Judaism represents'. In addition, they argued that Lubavitch hasidim, unlike Christians, observe Jewish law and do not regard their Messiah as the Deity. While I addressed the sources in some detail [*Jewish Action*, Winter 1995; see above, Ch. 4], I responded to the last point delicately, reluctantly, and briefly. Recent developments have made this caution obsolete and irresponsible.

Originally published in *Ha'aretz*, 11 Jan. 1998. Reprinted by permission. This is the text of the article as I submitted it, except for some minor stylistic changes in transliteration. The published version contained a few editorial changes and several typographical errors. Some of these were later corrected on the *Ha'aretz* website.

First, despite the isolated efforts of a handful of brave hasidim, the dominant institutions of the Lubavitch movement are either overtly messianist or unwilling to declare unequivocally that the Rebbe is not the Messiah. A formal legal ruling (*pesak din*) has just been issued by the head of the Crown Heights Rabbinical Court, the Rabbi of Kfar Chabad, the Lubavitch Vice-Chair of Agudat Harabbanim, and other major leaders of the movement asserting that Jewish law requires belief in the messiahship of the Rebbe.

In my view, this declaration alone is sufficient to exclude its promulgators from Orthodox Judaism; Lubavitch leaders who wish to salvage the movement's standing as an expression of authentic Judaism face the urgent obligation to repudiate the ruling publicly. Any Lubavitch institution which fulfils this obligation by assuring us of the summary dismissal of anyone who teaches the messiahship of the Rebbe will deserve to be placed at the apex of our philanthropic priorities.

Though the belief that the Rebbe is the Messiah is itself a repudiation of a fundamental Jewish doctrine, at this point it is only the beginning. We now confront an incredible reality which has surged beyond the confines of false messianism and the 'mere' affirmation of a Second Coming. A process which developed over decades, even generations, in Christianity and the seventeenth-century movement of the messianic pretender Shabetai Tzevi is unfolding with blinding speed in Lubavitch messianism. To a historian, this is a gripping drama, the opportunity not of one lifetime but of many; to a believing Jew, it is the bizarre rerun of a nightmare. The Lubavitcher Rebbe is becoming God.

In the autumn of 1996, the Israeli weekly *Siḥat hage'ulah* printed a revised version of the standard messianist slogan which read, 'May our Master, Teacher, and Creator (instead of 'Rabbi'), the King Messiah, live for ever', and a few weeks later it declared that it was permissible to bow to the Rebbe because 'his entire essence is divinity alone'.

A messianist catechism published in Safed describes the Rebbe, who is still physically alive, as in charge 'of all that happens in the world. Without his agreement no event can take place. If it is his will, he can bring about anything, "and who can tell him what to do?" . . . In him the Holy One Blessed be He rests in all His force just as He is . . . so that this becomes his entire essence.' Another Israeli publication (*Peninei ge'ulah*) reported approvingly that the Rebbe was addressed after his (apparent) death as 'Honored Rabbi, the Holy One Blessed be He (*kevod harav kudsha brikh hu*)'. In a French journal, 3 Tammuz (the date of the Rebbe's death) is described as the day of the King Messiah's 'apothéose' (i.e. apotheosis, or ascent to heaven as a divinity), while an English article in the journal *Beis Moshiach* characterized the Rebbe as the 'Essence and Being of God enclothed in a body . . . omniscient and omnipotent', and emphasized that these are 'neither wild exaggerations nor poetic parables'. It concluded, 'So who [is] *Elokeinu*? [Who is our God?] . . . The Rebbe, *Melekh HaMoshiach* [the King Messiah]. That's who.'

In the summer 1997 issue of the *Jewish Observer*, the journal of Agudath Israel in the United States, Rabbi Chaim Dov Keller of the Telshe Yeshiva in Chicago cited the references to essence, omniscience, and omnipotence in the *Beis Moshiach* article, alluded to a *New York Times* advertisement which urged that prayers be directed to the Rebbe, and spoke of a frightening turn towards *avodah zarah* [idolatry]. The director of the Chabad Regional Headquarters of Illinois, a mainstream Lubavitch organization which lists fifteen institutions including three schools and a summer camp on its letterhead, has disseminated a response which affirms that the material cited by Rabbi Keller is perfectly acceptable and that an exceedingly righteous man (a *tzaddik*) can become 'indistinguishable' from God. The evidence for this, which circulated in limited form even during the Rebbe's lifetime and has now become standard among believers in his divinity, consists of an absolutely literal understanding of citations that speak of the presence of God in rabbis and prophets (but never suggest, of course, that these rabbis are omniscient and omnipotent). Rabbi Keller was kind enough to share with me his trenchant rejoinder to this letter, which will, I hope, find its way into print.

It is evident, then, that the belief that the Rebbe is literally God and that he should be the object of prayer has entered mainstream Lubavitch. In the terminology of Jewish law, this is *avodah zarah*, or idolatry. (The dispute among rabbinic authorities as to whether or not Christianity constitutes idolatry for Gentiles has no relevance where the worshipper is a Jew.)[1] One who teaches this theology and urges that it be ritually expressed is an inciter to idolatry (*mesit umadiaḥ*), not an admirable educator or practitioner of outreach. One who supports an institution in which it is taught violates a prohibition so severe that there is a requirement to die rather than transgress. If a believer in this theology slaughters an animal ritually, it has the status of a non-kosher carcass (*nevelah*) which can undermine the kashrut of a restaurant or a home. A divorce document signed by such a believer and a Torah scroll or tefillin written by him are invalid. A non-Jew who converts to this sort of Judaism remains a non-Jew.

Despite its polemical tone, I regard this article as a vehicle for information whose implications should be beyond debate. Our ancestors gave their lives

---

[1] This sentence was deleted by *Ha'aretz* in the English but retained in the Hebrew.

rather than worship a divine Messiah. To the extent that we so much as consider the acceptance within Orthodox Judaism of people who direct prayers to a deceased rabbi perceived as the omnipotent, omniscient Deity, we launch an assault upon the very core of the Jewish religion.

TEN

Debating Avodah Zarah

IN *Ha'aretz* and in earlier correspondence, I pointedly used the provocative word idolatry. Though there is no better English translation of the Hebrew term *avodah zarah*, I have come to realize that Christians who read that Judaism regards incarnationist theology as idolatrous—even if only for Jews—see this as an offensive assertion that they worship the icons themselves as gods. Since neither Christians nor Lubavitch hasidim do this, I will henceforth use the Hebrew term, except, of course, in quotations from material written before I made this decision.

I have already noted that the literal meaning of *avodah zarah* is foreign worship, but this cannot serve as either a useful definition or a routine translation. Islam, for example, with a conception of God essentially identical to that of Judaism, is not *avodah zarah*, though its mode of worship is certainly foreign to Judaism. The best definition I can muster is 'the formal recognition or worship as God of an entity that is in fact not God'.[1] For Jews, any human being is such an entity. Even the generic worship of the Creator God with the intention of including one of these entities is *avodah zarah* when practised by a Jew, though there is surely a major distinction between pagan-style polytheism and *avodah zarah* in a monotheistic mode. A detailed discussion of the evidence for this position, which I have relegated to Appendices II and III, would unduly burden the reader at this point, when it is time to resume our narrative.

Within days of my article's appearance, *Ha'aretz* published a brief response entitled 'Al tige'u bimeshiḥai' (literally, 'Do Not Touch My Anointed Ones', a reference to Psalm 105: 15) by Rabbi Gedalyah Axelrod, one of the signatories of the ruling requiring belief in the Rebbe's messiahship and the head of a

---

[1] Ironically, an atypical mode of *avodah zarah* that Maimonides calls its root form (which is what I think *ikar* means in this context) is not covered by this definition. To Maimonides, the original form of *avodah zarah* was the worship of heavenly bodies not as divinities but as objects that God wants us to glorify in their capacity as His honoured servants. See *Mishneh torah*, 'Laws of Avodah Zarah' 1: 1. Later authorities expressed the intuitively obvious position that this is a less serious form of *avodah zarah* than the worship of such entities as deities. See *Perishah* on *Tur, Oraḥ ḥayim* 242, no. 4, s.v. *afilu*.

rabbinic court in Haifa.[2] He described the quotations about the Rebbe's divinity as 'anomalous comments which should not have been made', arguing that 'these exceptions are being taken care of by Chabad rabbis everywhere by means of education and guidance'. As for the messianist ruling,

I would like to make one thing absolutely clear to David Berger and to everyone else. There is no halakhic dispensation that will enable anyone to evade accepting the yoke of the belief in the Rebbe's messiahship, because of Maimonides' ruling that obligates all Jews to do so. . . . [Berger] is using this furious outburst to try to escape his obligations. . . .

We Jews, throughout all generations, have been willing to enter burning furnaces for our faith. We will remain strong in this mission as well. We will accept the prophet of God, the sovereignty of the Rebbe, Messiah the King, because we are thus obliged by virtue of our Judaism.

I received several supportive letters from Israel, and a friend, who wrote that the article 'is the talk of the town', added that people want to know what 'you do in communities where Chabad is the mainstay of the community in terms of kashrut, schools etc. and without them the religious community would disappear'.

I replied as follows:

To a significant degree, [this] question reflects the acuteness of the danger that we face. We are in danger of redefining the Jewish religion for reasons that boil down to serious inconvenience. In brief, then, my response is as follows: Lubavitch hasidim as a group have lost their *ḥezkas kashrus* [the presumption of being good Jews]. The majority have turned the movement into a movement of false messianism. . . . Participants in idolatrous journals continue to serve as *mashpi'im* in yeshivas . . . and that fellow from Illinois is the real authority, not just the titular head, in those fifteen institutions which include three schools and a camp. A generation of *ovdei avodah zarah* [worshippers of *avodah zarah*] is being raised while we stand by quietly. (There is not a modicum of exaggeration in any of this.)

Now, there still are good Jews in Lubavitch. If a particular school or *shul* [synagogue] is run by uncompromising, open anti-messianists, that's OK (though only very much *bedi'eved* [after the fact] as long as there is an integral connection to the rest of the movement). But if not, then you have a community without an Orthodox school or *shul*, and you must behave accordingly. Certainly no one with a modicum of *yiras shomayim* [fear of Heaven] should eat Lubavitch shechitah [ritual slaughter] unless he has personal knowledge of the beliefs of the shochet [slaughterer].

If we treat idolaters (or even people who say *yeḥi* when they *daven* [pray]) as Orthodox Jews, we transform Judaism in a fundamental way. Some of my academic

[2] *Ha'aretz*, 15 Jan. 1998. The editors entitled the English version 'The Prophet of God'.

colleagues are so caught up in their texts about *unio mystica* [mystical union with God] and *atzmus* [divine Essence] that they are prepared to say that this is no big deal, as if any Jew had ever permitted bowing and praying to a particular individual who was identified as omniscient and omnipotent and simply God in the full sense of the word. Not to speak of another, obvious point: even if—*ḥas veshalom* [God forbid]—one conceded that such belief and behaviour could theoretically be permissible, there is the 'little' question of mistaken identity. What renders worship of Jesus *avodah zarah* even according to Lubavitch idolaters is that he is in point of fact not God. Which means that even by their standards, anyone who is persuaded that the Rebbe is not in fact God must regard them as *ovdei avodah zarah* with all the consequences that flow from this.

The next several weeks generated both warm support and sharp criticism. An Israeli woman whom I do not know sent a touching handwritten note from Jerusalem reporting how encouraged she was by the article. *Hatzofeh*, which had ignored an earlier submission, published a strongly supportive piece.[3] An article in *Yated ne'eman*, without specifically mentioning my essay, maintained that the primary impediment to recognizing the validity of Rabbi Schach's original attacks on Lubavitch had been the external appearance and orthopraxy of Lubavitch hasidim. Now, however, it was evident to all that this was a heretical movement.[4]

Lubavitch reactions were varied and revealing. A sophisticated, almost certainly pseudonymous, Hebrew article in *Beis Moshiach* cited a series of mainly hasidic texts with the apparent intention of defending every one of the formulations that I quoted in *Ha'aretz*.[5] Most of these texts had been assembled earlier in Avraham Baruch Pevzner's 1991 work *Al hatzadikim* that had already served as the basis for the letter by the director of Lubavitch Chabad of Illinois asserting that a righteous man can be indistinguishable from God. This influential book, published by mainstream Chabad, demands very careful attention, and once again I must refer the interested reader to the detailed discussion in Appendix II. Nonetheless, its fundamental thesis must be set forth immediately. The Rebbe, we recall, came under attack for a controversial formulation about the presence of God in the righteous. To Pevzner, the assertion that a rebbe is 'the Essence and Being of God placed in a body' means that a supremely righteous man literally annuls his own identity so that his entire essence becomes God. One who recognizes this may then prostrate himself in worship before that righteous man.

[3] Amnon Shapira, '"Our Master, Teacher and Creator"—The Fundamental Problem' (Heb.), *Hatzofeh*, 16 Jan. 1998, p. 4.

[4] Natan Ze'ev Grossman, in the Hebrew *Yated ne'eman*, 13 Mar. 1998, pp. 15, 22.

[5] A. Avraham, 'And They Believed in God and in Moses His Servant' (Heb.), *Beis Moshiach*, 170 (17 Shevat 5758), 36–40.

The standing of this work within Chabad means that its highly problematic theology is deeply embedded among more than a few Lubavitch hasidim in the mainstream of the movement. For anyone who doubts this, let me note once again that one of the quotations in the *Ha'aretz* article, which I attributed there to a messianist booklet published in Safed, originally comes from volume iv of a book entitled *Mashiah akhshav* (Messiah Now) by Rabbi Levi Yitzchak Ginsberg, a mentor in Yeshiva Tomchei Temimim in Kfar Chabad. This was the passage asserting that the Rebbe is the master of all that happens in the world, that without his agreement no event can take place, that he can bring about anything, and that God rests in him 'in all His force just as He is (because of his complete self-nullification to God, so that this becomes his entire essence)'.[6]

The mysterious fate of this volume provides an intriguing sidebar to our discussion. The booklet identified its source as *Mashiah akhshav*, volume iv, pp. 24–8. I did not initially know the author of this work and consequently failed to identify it in *Ha'aretz*. By the time I turned to the writing of this book, I knew that Levi Yitzchak Ginsberg had written *Mashiah akhshav*, but neither I nor anyone else could locate more than three volumes, all of them published before the Rebbe's death. In desperation, a friend from Israel called the phone number of the Kfar Chabad distributor listed in the book. The response: 'There was a volume iv. There isn't one now.'

The style and format of the four pages reproduced in the booklet are the same as those of the first three volumes of *Mashiah akhshav*, and I have no reason to doubt that the attribution is accurate. Indeed, on 19 December 1997, just three weeks before the appearance of my article in *Ha'aretz*, Rabbi Ginsberg published an English piece in *Beis Moshiach* entitled 'I Don't Regard the Rebbe as a Basar V'Dam [flesh and blood]'. In this presentation, which was brought to my attention very recently, Rabbi Ginsberg cited with approval the following assessment of the Rebbe:

Yes, the Rebbe's body is composed of flesh and blood, but as far as he's concerned he is not compelled or limited by anything—not by physical limitations nor by spiritual limitations. He 'is what he is'. [We are, I assume, expected to think of the divine

---

[6] The last section of this passage, asserting that God rests in the Rebbe in all his force just as He is, reappeared almost verbatim in a book by Hayim Sasson with the striking title *I Know that my Redeemer Lives* [Job 19: 25]: *Chapters of Analysis on the Third of Tammuz from the Book* Now I Know (Heb.) (Jerusalem, 1999). The book, which argues that the Rebbe's soul has never left his body, appeared with approbations given to the larger work in 1998 by R. Gedalyah Axelrod of Haifa and Rabbi Yehudah Kalman Marlow of the Crown Heights rabbinical court. The verse from Job refers, of course, to God; here, it clearly refers to the Rebbe, whose picture appears prominently immediately beneath it.

name in Exodus 3: 14.] Even as he is enclothed in a physical body, he remains limited by nothing whatsoever and he has the ability to do everything and be everything in an unlimited manner.[7]

My best guess is that the article in *Ha'aretz* led to the hiding away or destruction of the newly published fourth volume of *Mashiah akhshav* because the official line was that the quotations came from peripheral works by unbalanced people. That the author of one of them was a mentor in the major yeshiva in Kfar Chabad was, to put it mildly, highly inconvenient.

From one of the major Lubavitch yeshivas in Israel we move to the major Lubavitch yeshiva in New York. Not long after the appearance of my essay in *Ha'aretz*, Rabbi Keller sent me an article recently forwarded to him, which had appeared in the Fourth Annual Edition of an English-language publication called *Inyaney Moshiach* (Moshiach Matters).[8] Its author, Rabbi Sholom Charitonow, is identified as a *mashpia* in Oholei Torah in Crown Heights, which is, I believe, the largest Chabad yeshiva in the country and probably in the world, claiming a student body of 1,600. It hardly matters that the author himself is not a major authority in the movement. It matters immensely that he is entrusted with providing religious guidance to students at the very hub of the Lubavitch educational system.

All the rebbes, says Rabbi Charitonow, beginning with the Ba'al Shem Tov and his immediate successor and continuing through the Chabad line, reveal the 'pure Essence of God', but they do so 'within and by way of a particular *sefirah*' (one of the ten emanations of the divine in Jewish mysticism). The death of each of these rebbes marked the point where God's revelation through that *sefirah* was completed; nothing more could be revealed by way of this particular form of reality, and it was time for divine Essence to be drawn down by way of the next *sefirah*.

Before proceeding with Charitonow's argument, we might want to ponder the striking similarity between this theology and the Christian assertion that Jesus embodies the particular aspect of God called 'the Son'. At this level, even the argument distinguishing Lubavitch incarnationism from Christianity by pointing to the undifferentiated nature of God in the former loses its persuasiveness as the line between the theologies begins to blur. As in Christianity, the Essence of God *in a specific manifestation* descends to enter a human being, though, unlike dominant Christian doctrine, it may be that this manifestation is not embodied in its entirety. The implications, moreover, go

---

[7] I am grateful to Elie Jacobs for providing me with a copy of this article.

[8] Sholom Charitonow, 'The Rebbeim, the Rebbe, Gimmel Tammuz', *Inyaney Moshiach*, Fourth Annual Edition, pp. 12–26.

beyond the incarnation itself. Sophisticated Jewish polemicists had long argued that the Christian doctrine of the separate incarnation of a particular divine person demonstrates that the alleged unity in the Trinity is illusory; the Jewish insistence that the kabbalistic *sefirot* do not compromise divine unity consequently depends on the assumption that they are never incarnated.[9] For some believers at mainstream Chabad institutions, incarnations perilously close to that of Christian belief have taken place.

Charitonow goes on to maintain that the most recent Rebbe—he would say the current Rebbe—differed from his *sefirah*-bound predecessors by manifesting the unlimited Essence of God in its full purity without even the subtlest concealment. This explains the Rebbe's ability to answer any question the moment it was asked as well as his involvement in every corner of the globe; it explains why there was no difference to him between the physical and the spiritual, heaven and earth, body and soul. It also follows that no interruption is possible in the Rebbe's leadership even in the temporal sense:

Interruptions can only apply where there are borders and limitations (as opposed to Essence), which have been utilized to a maximum, making it necessary to proceed to new borders and limitations. Concerning the Essence, however, in relation to which borders and forms do not conceal at all—on the contrary, they actually become united with the Essence—all causes of interruption do not apply. In other words— not only is the interruption unnecessary, it is in fact impossible. This can apply to something which has a form (whether of a physical or a spiritual nature); it cannot, however, apply to something that is eternal by nature, having no form whatsoever.[10]

What, then, of the Rebbe's body? Even ordinary physical objects have a dual aspect. A table, for example, looks externally like a solid piece of wood, but deeper examination reveals a multitude of revolving atoms. Thus, what happened in June 1994 'affected only the relationship between the body and the world, but with the body itself no change has taken place, even in the physical sense'. During his visible lifetime, we saw with our own eyes that 'the Rebbe's holy body was not restrained by or confined to the limits of nature'. His illness too was not due, God forbid, to any deficiency in his holy body, in which no change ever took place. 'May we merit to see the Rebbe, body and soul in 770 [Eastern Parkway], when he will redeem us, and the entire world will declare in unison, "Long live our Master, Teacher, and Rebbe, King *Moshiach*, for ever"'.

---

[9] See Daniel J. Lasker, *Jewish Philosophical Polemics against Christianity in the Middle Ages* (New York, 1977), 75, 81–2, referring to Profiat Duran (d. *c.*1414) and R. Judah Aryeh da Modena (1571–1648).　　　　　　[10] Charitonow, 'The Rebbeim, the Rebbe, Gimmel Tammuz', 19–20.

The piece speaks for itself: a Messiah manifesting the unconcealed, infinite Essence of God in its full purity, able to respond to any question instantaneously, and surviving in a real, unchanging, but invisible body. What religion, one is tempted to ask, does this sentence best describe?

On the other hand, the *Ha'aretz* article also elicited encouraging reactions from some Chabad quarters. A statement denouncing deification and discouraging messianic activism was issued and widely publicized by fourteen rabbis constituting the Executive Committee of the Central Committee of Chabad-Lubavitch Rabbis in [the] United States and Canada. Though this organization is far less important and influential than its ambitious title would indicate, the statement was meaningful and certainly merits attention:

1. The deification of any human being is contrary to the core and foundation of the Jewish faith.

2. The various talmudic, midrashic and other sources which seem to ascribe superhuman spiritual attributes to certain righteous people were never meant to be deification and great care must be taken when quoting them.

3. Belief in the coming of Moshiach and awaiting his imminent arrival is a basic tenet of the Jewish faith. It is clear, however, that conjecture as to the possible identity of Moshiach is not part of the basic tenet of Judaism.

4. The preoccupation with identifying the Rebbe *zy"a* [may his merit protect us[11]] as Moshiach is clearly contrary to the Rebbe's wishes.

I could not have asked for anything better on the subject of deification. The first paragraph standing alone would not have sufficed, because even Sholom Charitonow and Levi Yitzchak Ginsberg probably have reservations about the flat formulation, 'The Rebbe is God', for reasons that I shall suggest later. What is needed is the affirmation that phrases like 'his entire essence is divinity' are simply not true in their literal sense. This, I hope and believe, is what the second paragraph means, and it tells me that a significant segment of Lubavitch is free of the taint of *avodah zarah*. One Lubavitch hasid, in fact, passed me on the street around this time and said a cryptic 'thank you', which I took as an acknowledgement that the article had helped to generate internal denunciation of theological extremism.

The paragraphs on the Rebbe as Messiah, though welcome, are considerably more ambiguous. The statement discourages the sort of 'preoccupation' that produces public propaganda, but it does not reject the belief itself.

[11] This formula, used of the righteous dead, is avoided by most messianists when referring to the Rebbe. Thus, even so routine an expression can be a marker in the Messiah wars. The widespread notion, however, that the use of this and similar formulas provides a guarantee that the author rejects the belief in the Rebbe's messiahship is emphatically incorrect.

Indeed, a story in the *Forward* quoted one of the signatories to the effect that his personal conviction is that the Rebbe is in fact the Messiah. The most regrettable drawback, however, is not in the statement itself but in the gulf between the name of this group and the quite minimal influence of its geographically diverse signatories on the large majority of Lubavitch hasidim.

Some of the more revealing Lubavitch reactions to the article came in the *Algemeiner Journal*. The paper's main Israeli correspondent, Naftali Krauss, was highly critical of me in his initial report. Within the next few weeks, however, further investigation transformed the tenor of his dispatches entirely, and he began to place primary emphasis on the terrible damage done by the messianists to the Rebbe's memory. A letter writer took particular umbrage at Krauss's call for the appointment of a new leader, asserting that only a dog would seek a replacement for the Lubavitcher Rebbe.[12]

If Krauss was a dog, I was a veritable menagerie. An internet attack directed at me was cleverly entitled 'The Messiah and the Ass', a Lubavitch rabbi in Michigan described me in a sermon as a snake rather than a rabbi, and a pseudonymous article in the *Algemeiner* invoked the animal that Jews revile the most. The author began with a fable of Aesopian proportions. A nightingale and a crow, he wrote, argued as to which of them sings more beautifully. To resolve the dispute, they agreed that they would accept the judgement of the first passer by, and the winner would then peck out one of the loser's eyes. As luck would have it, the first passer by was a pig. Not surprisingly, he ruled in favour of the crow, who proceeded to peck out the nightingale's eye. As tears began to trickle from the remaining eye, the crow asked, 'Why are you crying? Wasn't this our agreement?' The nightingale replied, 'I'm not crying about my eye. I'm crying because the "expert" on music was a pig.'

Similarly, said the author, we now live in a world where a professor can emerge from a college swamp and become an expert on Judaism. Still, he continued, 'May the pig of the parable forgive me', since however little it might know about music, David Berger knows even less about Judaism.[13]

This column provided me with sorely needed comic relief, but for the most part the reactions were no laughing matter. I sadly had to acknowledge the reasonableness of the argument that only renowned rabbis of unquestioned authority may properly level such grave accusations. I had to tell myself that in this narrow area I did have the required expertise and that I could also fall back on the dictum that the deference owed to distinguished rabbis is suspended in an instance where the name of God is being desecrated.

[12] *Algemeiner Journal*, 13 Mar. 1998.

[13] B. Malkovitch, 'Is there a Limit to Presumptuousness?' (Yiddish), *Algemeiner Journal*, 6 Feb. 1998, pp. 4, 6.

Rabbi Butman's lengthy attack in the *Algemeiner* was surely not amusing.[14] My presumed expertise in these matters, he wrote, emerges from the study of Christianity rather than Judaism, and 'from there, from the darkest filth of impurity', I want to understand 'one of the most delicate and profound topics in Hasidism, which deals with the divine Essence itself'. And this is the least of my sins. He explained that he had endured the misfortune of reading my earlier writings, which make it clear that my problem is not that Lubavitch hasidim believe in the messiahship of the Rebbe. My problem, rather, is that I do not believe in the resurrection of the dead at all. Rabbi Butman had already made this assertion in the typescript of his response to my original article in *Jewish Action*, but the editors, who knew what that article actually said, refused to print such a blatant misrepresentation. The editor of the *Algemeiner*, who probably never read the *Jewish Action* piece, did publish it, but, to his credit, also published my brief letter the following week saying, 'This is a simple lie; there is no basis for it whatsoever' (*Dos iz a posheter lign. Lo hoyu dvorim me-'olom*).

Beyond the personal level, Rabbi Butman's piece revealed the deep problems the movement faces in coming to grips with a theology whose language *begins* at the precipice of *avodah zarah*, so that the tiniest step towards literalism hurtles the believer into the abyss. In a single sentence, he asserts that I borrowed a classic antisemitic tactic by utilizing the statements of 'a few atypical people who say wild things' to stigmatize an entire movement. But the remainder of the article is devoted to asking what the fuss is about. There is, after all, firm authority for the proposition that a supremely righteous man has no essence of his own but is rather 'only God Himself, Essence and Being. That is a rebbe.' Nothing in the remainder of the article so much as suggests that this assertion is anything but literal.

In the light of the theology in this and similar Lubavitch works that we have already examined, one wonders about the strong objections to the overt formula calling the Rebbe 'Our Creator'. Why are such expressions 'wild'? Why are those who use them marginalized? With respect to the hasidim who reject the literal understanding of the formulations endorsed by Rabbi Butman, the answer is clear: they object on deep principle to characterizing the Rebbe as God. But it is difficult to escape the conclusion that those who take those formulations literally object to a term like 'Our Creator' only because they think it implies that the Rebbe is a separate, independent deity or

---

[14] 'Once He is So Presumptuous . . .' (Yiddish), *Algemeiner Journal*, 13 Feb. 1998. The ellipsis in the title represents the completion of the talmudic passage from which it is taken. That final phrase reads, 'One can deduce that he is a wicked person.'

that the Essence of God does not extend beyond the dimensions of a particular human being.

In fact, however, the extremists who use the term do not mean it that way. They understand it as an expression—and not an unreasonable one—of the very theology that Avraham Baruch Pevzner, Sholom Charitonow, Levi Yitzchak Ginsberg, and Shmuel Butman appear to endorse. The Rebbe is our Creator because his entire essence has literally been annulled and replaced by the Essence of the one Creator God. Thus, the difference between the promulgators of this theology who use the term and those who do not is essentially semantic, though I am sure the reluctance to use it also stems from a deep-seated Jewish taboo that the majority cannot quite overcome.

All parties imagine that their denial that the Rebbe is an independent deity or that the divine Essence is limited to this human being serves to distinguish their position adequately from that of Christianity. In fact, it distinguishes their belief from a caricature of Christianity, not from genuine Christian doctrine. Classical Judaism, on the other hand, sees even sophisticated Christianity as a form of non-pagan *avodah zarah*, at least when practised by Jews. There are, of course, differences between the specific Christian belief in the incarnation of the second person of the Trinity to form a God–man and the literal belief that the Rebbe is nothing but pure divinity, but I do not believe that those differences are halakhically material.[15]

In fairness, the evidence that Rabbi Butman takes the unalloyed divinity of the Rebbe in completely literal fashion is marginally less decisive than it is in the case of someone like Rabbi Charitonow; nonetheless, his article points in that direction and provides us with yet another indication that the problem of *avodah zarah* in Lubavitch is not confined to the tiny number of hasidim who use a liturgical formula calling the Rebbe God. It reflects a theology that is widespread and deeply rooted in the very heart of the messianist camp, and to some degree even beyond.

As I pondered this material, I came to realize that I had written an uninformed critique of an article that I had been asked to evaluate several years earlier. In 1993 the *Journal of Ecumenical Studies* had requested that I referee an article entitled 'One God: Toward a Rapprochement of Orthodox Judaism and Christianity', by an Orthodox woman who had studied Chabad theology. The article, which was published in the following year, argued that even with respect to incarnation the two religions were not far apart: 'the main difference beween *chasidus* and Christianity is that Christianity restricts this divine interaction with humans to the person of Jesus whereas *chasidus* applies it to

---

[15] For a much fuller discussion, see again App. II.

all humans but, in particular, all Jews'. The author went on to say that this approach is especially characteristic of Chabad, and despite some 'dark mutterings' that Lubavitch constitutes a form of heresy, 'there is no serious movement to excommunicate the Lubavitchers', who 'are generally regarded as within the bounds of Orthodox Judaism'.[16]

My referee's report was marked by a regrettable degree of naivety. I had not read Pevzner's then two-year-old book, and so I wrote to the journal that the author did not directly confront the difference between 'divine interaction with humans' and

the assertion that someone actually *is* God. Does she really mean to say that Lubavitch believes that any person can become God? Let her ask herself (and the reader) a simple question to test the assertion . . . In Judaism, would it be appropriate or permissible to worship a person who had attained this level of 'interaction'? Could one bow down [in worship] or sacrifice to such a person . . .? Without confronting this question the analysis does an end run around the core of the issue.

I hope that the author, as an Orthodox Jew, has not lost her bearings to the point where she thinks that a positive answer to this question is possible. Indeed, her essentially sociological point about the absence of a serious movement to excommunicate Lubavitch is correct only because hardly anyone—with the exception of R. Schach and some of his followers—really thinks that Lubavitch maintains an incarnationist position virtually identical to that of Christianity. I confess that this article has served to heighten my concern about Lubavitch theology and its more extreme exponents.

As I look back at these paragraphs, I tell myself that ignorance really was bliss. Although I wrote that the article heightened my concern, I did not really internalize its full implications. A very bright individual apparently familiarized with Chabad theology by Lubavitch hasidim emerged with the understanding that there is no material difference between that theology and the Christian doctrine of the Incarnation. This is a highly suggestive indication of convictions current in the movement. At the time, however, the notion that such beliefs could really be prevalent seemed so alien and bizarre that I succumbed to what can only be described as denial. I am thus acutely aware of the obstacles that this book must overcome. It must persuade readers to look squarely and unflinchingly at evidence from which I myself averted my eyes not long ago and to recognize the reality of a phenomenon that every Jewish instinct declares impossible. I am now capable of absorbing the information that the late Rabbi Shmuel Yaakov Weinberg told an enquiring student even before the Rebbe's death that he should pray alone rather than in

---

[16] Barbara J. Redman, in *Journal of Ecumenical Studies*, 31 (1994), 307–31.

a Chabad synagogue because 'they pray to a different deity [*eloah*]'.[17] A few years ago, I would have dismissed such a report with puzzled, even annoyed, incomprehension.

In the wake of the *Ha'aretz* article, an Israeli scholar familiar with Pevzner's book who is both an observant Jew and a passionate exponent of interfaith cooperation made a striking remark that he asked me not to quote in his name. This development, he said, is the best thing that has happened to Jewish–Christian dialogue. I suppose it is. Along with belief in the Rebbe's messiahship, it is also the best thing that has happened to the Christian mission to the Jews.

At the same time, Daniel Lasker, the pre-eminent historian of the medieval Jewish philosophical debate against Christianity, made a light remark reflecting a profound truth. Adherents of this theology, he told me, should study Christian theology so that they will not have to reinvent the wheel. I should add that if they do, they will discover an analogous, though not quite identical Christian heresy called Apollinarianism that ascribed a human body and even soul to Jesus but asserted that his spirit, defined as his mind and will, was purely divine. They will see how generations of impressive thinkers struggled to define his relationship with the remainder of the Godhead, an issue that hasidim of this stripe must address with particular urgency with respect to the deceased Rebbe. If, after all, his entire essence is divinity unaffected even by sefirotic limitations, how can he still be invoked separately from the rest of God once his body has ceased to exist? Does he constitute a separable element in God comparable to the second person of the Christian Trinity? Is he no longer pure divinity? Is this, rather, one reason to insist, like Christians, that the body survives in a transcendent state?[18]

These are fascinating questions. Since they are likely to be addressed in ignorance of the works of the Church Fathers and the scholastics, the relationship between the systems will be particularly instructive to historians of

[17] This information comes directly from the student, who lived in my neighbourhood until very recently.

[18] Pevzner (pp. 99–100) wonders why the Rebbe spoke of 'the Essence and Being [of God] *placed in a body*' and responds that because only Torah study and observance of the commandments can produce the requisite conditions for the emplacement of full divinity, the disembodied soul in the upper spheres cannot attain this state. The discussion that follows refers to the soul before its descent to this world, and although the point is not explicit, Pevzner almost certainly means to restrict his observation to that early stage. Once a supremely righteous soul attains its exalted state it does not lose it after the death of the body. This conclusion follows from the very fact that Pevzner's argument takes the form of an interpretation of the Rebbe's words, which refer primarily though not exclusively to the current status of his recently deceased father-in-law. If a rebbe's soul after death is no longer the 'Essence and Being', the passage becomes incoherent.

religion. In my case, however, religious commitment trumps academic interest, so that I hope that the theology will be aborted with some of the questions for ever unanswered. At the same time, much of the wheel has already been reinvented, and there is more than enough material for the study of a neo-Christian theology in the heart of the Orthodox Jewish world.

The *Ha'aretz* article continued to generate considerable discussion through the power of the internet, where it was widely circulated. In addition, the English version was reprinted in the *Australian Jewish News* and the Hebrew version in the New York *Hadoar*. In the wake of the article, a *rosh yeshiva* (professor of Talmud in an advanced yeshiva) sent me an electronic message confiding his distress at the toleration of what he described as heresy. He lay awake at night, he wrote, but believed that he could not speak out because of the silence of the great rabbis of the generation (*gedolim*), who must have reasons that he cannot divine.

Here, in part, is my response:

R. Elya Svei is . . . a rabbi of stature, and he has spoken out. Another member of the *Moetzes*, who asked for anonymity, wrote me to say that I would be remembered as a *loḥem milḥamos Hashem neged kittos hasheker* [fighter of the wars of the Lord against sects of falsehood] and that he has not spoken publicly only out of concern that a non-unanimous statement would invite the implication that other[s] . . . do not disapprove of what is happening. R. Elya [commented favourably] in his yeshiva after the RCA resolution, and [another member of the *Moetzes*] made a congratulatory comment to several people. R. Yaakov Weinberg told [a member of the editorial board] that *Jewish Action*'s decision to print my article was exceedingly important. . . . In short, the absence of the unanimous consent needed for a statement from the *Moetzes* hardly means that a statement by you and other *roshei yeshiva* and *rabbonim* [rabbis] would in any way constitute placing your judgement above that of people you regard as your betters. Many—perhaps most—of them would welcome it.

I should add that I received a second letter on a later occasion from the member of the Council who had written about the need for unanimity in which he urged me to continue writing about this subject and said that he considered me 'a hero fighting a historic battle'.

My e-mail correspondent responded by asserting that he regarded the collective silence as tantamount to a *pesak* (a rabbinic ruling) and emphasized that he did not know the reason for this silence, which presumably reflects wisdom superior to his own.

I replied, perhaps too sharply, as follows:

1. You have no right to remain silent about an issue like this because you deduce the existence of an implicit *pesak*. You worry that there may be a *pesak*? Ask them,

whoever you think the appropriate 'them' may be. You already know from my message that in many cases 'they' will say, 'I can't act, but I urge you to do so'.

2. You don't know why 'they' are silent? Ask them. . . . In the one lengthy conversation I had with a member of the *Moetzes* (someone other than the people I alluded to in my previous [message]) near the very beginning of this whole affair, he said that he is not an expert on the subject of messianic texts and is concerned about *machlokes* [dissension]. Near the end of the conversation, he said, 'Maybe you're right, but it's not going to happen.' I am told that he has since changed his position and been won over by letters that I've sent the *Moetzes*, and when I saw him at a fund-raiser in [my neighbourhood] this September, he greeted me with exceptional warmth, though neither of us raised this issue. 'Gedolim' are not an undifferentiated glob. They are individuals; they can be talked to; they can acknowledge error; they don't believe all the press notices about their infallibility.

One Israeli *rov* [rabbi] who runs a *kollel* [advanced institute for talmudic study] in Jerusalem told me that if things don't improve *gedolim* will eventually act. One of my responses is made even more troubling by your messages. I told him that the next generation will say, 'If *gedolim* x, y, and z in the previous generation were silent, who are we to question their judgement?'

Are you really comfortable telling the *beis din shel ma'lah* [the heavenly court], 'I saw what I believed to be heresy spreading through a major sub-community and affecting the core beliefs and rituals of Judaism; I was a significant rabbinic leader; I spoke out about many issues without asking *shayles* [questions]; I did and said nothing because I saw that others did and said nothing; I didn't approach them to ask why or to inquire what course of action they might recommend for me'?

On 1 February, just two days after sending this message, I found myself at a wedding with a member of the Council whom I had never met. With some trepidation, I approached him, and we had a conversation consisting of two short sentences on each side:

'Rabbi X, I'm David Berger. I've written to the *Moetzes*.'
   'I did my best. It wasn't good enough.'

In fact, however, something positive did occur in Agudath Israel circles. The March 1998 issue of the *Jewish Observer* published an important article by Rabbi Keller entitled 'G-d-Centered or *Rebbe*-Messiah Centered: Which is Normative Judaism?'. A prefatory author's note informed the reader that the article, as well as the relevant section of the summer 1997 piece to which I have already alluded,[19] 'were reviewed, before they were published, by several widely respected *Gedolei Torah*—both Chassidic and non-Chassidic—who

---

[19] Keller, 'The Best of Times, the Worst of Times'.

urged their publication'. It was evident to informed readers that these rabbis must be members of the Council of Torah Sages.

Rabbi Keller cited a number of the messianist writings that refer to the divinity of the Rebbe, accused them of a dangerously literal interpretation of certain respected texts, reinforced his earlier warning about *avodah zarah*, and pointed to the illegitimacy of the belief in the messiahship of the departed Rebbe in and of itself. When I received a copy of the journal from the editor via express mail I was more than pleased, despite the objections of some Modern Orthodox Jews who were upset that the article acknowledged neither my work nor the RCA resolution. On one level, this omission is indeed a tragic and depressing reflection of the dismissal of Modern Orthodoxy in Traditionalist circles, but at this point I considered it a relatively minor irritant. I knew of Rabbi Keller's personal regard from numerous phone conversations that he had initiated, and I had to accept his judgement about the approach that would best serve our common objective within the community represented by the *Observer*. Short of a declaration by the Council itself, this was the most authoritative forum for a statement of policy by the rabbinic leadership of Agudath Israel.

The article unquestionably had a significant impact and helped to mould attitudes towards messianists in segments of what is sometimes called the yeshiva world; at the same time, it could not fully effect the needed transformation. Not long after it appeared, a friend of mine asked a rabbi in Boston why he would not provide guidelines to his congregation regarding this matter, and he responded that notwithstanding Rabbi Keller's article, the *gedolim* as a group had not spoken.

The most important Lubavitch reaction to Rabbi Keller's article came from Jacob Immanuel Schochet, a rabbi and academic who has written widely on theological topics.[20] Rabbi Schochet agreed that 'the grotesque and disgusting publications . . . quoted by Rabbi Keller' contain material that is 'tantamount to *avodah zarah*'. Nonetheless, pointing to what he called 'theomorphic ascriptions' applied to the righteous in accepted works, he went on to berate Rabbi Keller and the unnamed rabbis who urged publication of the article for their ignorance of kabbalistic and hasidic theology, and encouraged interested readers to peruse his own discussion of the matter in a book entitled *Chassidic Dimensions*. In that book he had used the term 'theomorphic metaphors' and explained that 'whatever is attached to something can be referred to by that which it is attached to. A messenger is thus referred to by the name of the one who sent him. This applies to the *tzadikim*. For

[20] 'G-d-Centered or Machloket-Centered'.

their mind is always cleaving unto G-d, and just as they are constantly attached to Him, so He is attached to them and never forsakes them.'[21]

Would that all Lubavitch hasidim understood the formulations under discussion in this fashion. Nothing in Rabbi Keller's article makes me think that he would pose any vigorous objections to this presentation, so that despite the heated tone of Rabbi Schochet's attack, I see no fundamental disagreement on this critically important point. With respect to the messianist position, however, there are deep divisions that I have addressed at length in Chapter 5. Rabbi Schochet, we recall, combines a vigorous rejection of the messianist belief with a vigorous affirmation of its essential legitimacy.

Even before the appearance of Rabbi Keller's article and Rabbi Schochet's response, I became concerned that the emphasis I had placed upon *avodah zarah* in *Ha'aretz* had obscured the danger of Second Coming messianism, and so I decided to follow up with an additional piece in the Israeli press. Intimidated by the criticism that I should not have published the initial article in an irreligious, even anti-religious, paper, I sent the new one to *Hatzofeh*. The English translation that follows in Chapter 11 is an effort to bring this succinct summary of my essential argument to a wider audience.

---

[21] *Chassidic Dimensions* (Brooklyn, NY, 1990), 100–1. The issue of the use and misuse of kabbalistic doctrines and debate about their literal or metaphorical meaning played a role in the Sabbatian controversies as well. See e.g. Elisheva Carlebach, *The Pursuit of Heresy* (New York, 1990), 99–104, 137–43.

ELEVEN

Judaism is Changing Before Our Eyes

O N 13 TEVET (11 January), I published an article in *Ha'aretz* that
aroused a stormy discussion is Israel and the diaspora. I noted a new
rabbinic ruling requiring all of us to believe in the messiahship of the Lubavitcher Rebbe as well as developments that I regard as manifestations of
avodah zarah.

In the wake of the article, we have seen defences of even the most frightening formulations, but we have also been privileged to hear sharp denunciations of the practitioners of *avodah zarah* emanating from various Chabad
circles, including those of committed messianists. It remains to be seen
whether participants in extremist publications who have not repented will be
removed from their posts as educators, spiritual mentors (*mashpi'im*), and
directors of Chabad Houses.

If this does not happen, the aura of danger and suspicion that now
envelops the movement will remain intact, and the argument that we are
dealing with entirely marginal phenomena will be publicly exposed as worth-
less. If it does happen, we will be able to feel reassured at least with respect to
avodah zarah.

On the other hand, the rabbinic ruling itself has not been the object of
vigorous criticism on the part of the movement's leadership. On the contrary,
the latest advertisement indicates that the plague of messianism has spread to
the point where the number of signatories on the ruling has grown from six
to fifty, among them rabbis of cities and heads of rabbinic courts.

Let us imagine that, ten years ago, we would have approached a rabbinic
decisor with the following question:

'Before us is a candidate for a position as head of a rabbinic court, or as a rabbi,
or as a principal or teacher or ritual slaughterer or *kashrut* supervisor. He com-
mands broad knowledge and is endowed with superb talents. Nonetheless,

Originally published in *Hatzofeh*, 22 Feb. 1998. Reprinted by permission. The material included in
the original manuscript but omitted by the editor appears in square brackets.

we feel conflicted as a result of one small drawback that concerns us a bit. This individual is a major spokesman for a movement of false messianism that has attracted thousands of observant Jews.

'He declares that a person who was buried in Queens, New York three years ago is Messiah son of David. With reference to this deceased individual, he fervently declares in his daily prayers, "May our Master, Teacher, and Rabbi, the King Messiah, live for ever", and he encourages others to do the same. He has issued a legal ruling that every Jew is obligated to recognize that this man is the Messiah and to accept the yoke of his kingship. Should this belief serve as an impediment to the appointment of the candidate?'

Is there the slightest doubt that the decisor would have proposed that we seek urgent psychiatric attention?

When a fantasy that is so clearly the stuff of comedy suddenly becomes reality, it is evident that a profound and fateful transformation has taken place.

In the course of generations, Jews explained to representatives of the Christian mission that one of the fundamental reasons for rejecting the messiahship of Jesus, a reason sufficient in itself to excuse us from the need to examine his personality or views, is the principle that Messiah son of David will not die and be buried in the midst of his redemptive mission. Various formulations of this position, some explicit and some in the form of references to prophetic promises that remain unfulfilled, are found in numerous polemical works by ordinary authors as well as in the statements of great figures like Rabbi Sa'adiah Gaon, Maimonides, Nahmanides, and Rabbi Chaim [Soloveitchik] of Brisk.

[By way of illustration, here is a brief, striking example from the end of the eighteenth century:

We are obligated to believe that a Jewish man will come who will begin to save Israel and will complete the salvation of Israel in that generation. One who completes the task is the one, while one who does not complete it in that generation but dies or is broken or is taken captive [Exod. 22:9] is not the one and was not sent by God.[1]]

In the last three years, a critical element of our age-old messianic faith has been lost—and no one is paying attention [Isa. 57: 1]. This catastrophe has occurred not as a result of a convention of rabbis that has decided after serious and lengthy deliberations that the great rabbinic authorities through the

---

[1] R. Phinehas Elijah Hurwitz of Vilna, *Sefer haberit hashalem* (1797; Jerusalem, 1990), 521. I am grateful to Prof. Shnayer Z. Leiman for bringing this passage to my attention.

ages made a fundamental error because they forgot the sources regularly cited by the messianists, but as a result of indifference and considerations that have nothing whatever to do with the messianic faith.

At this moment, a Jew who appeals to the classical Jewish argument against Christian messianism confronts a new, hostile world that has been created *ex nihilo*—and overnight (*yesh me'ayin ukeheref ayin*)—thanks to our silence and indifference. [The missionary will respond to his rival with a contemptuous, crushing reply: 'Do you have the presumptuousness to try to convince me that you are serious about this? Is it not the case that communities of pious Jews appoint judges, rabbis, and kashrut supervisors who proclaim in the loudest tones precisely the belief that you are attempting to place outside the parameters of Judaism?'

There is no answer to this question.]

Anyone who recognizes the authority of messianist rabbis and of rabbinic courts headed by them causes an alien belief to be entwined into the warp and woof of the communal structure of Judaism, ensures the utter smashing of a central, millennium-old argument against the Christian mission, and effects a deformation of the Jewish religion—perhaps without hope of correction—with regard to a matter that cuts to the very core.

We stand witness in our generation to public protests and posters decrying every minor deviation in matters of religious law, custom, and stringency. Yet with respect to this matter, we sit contentedly, without sound or response [2 Kgs. 4: 31], as Judaism changes before our eyes.

*

I sent this article to the American Council of Torah Sages and to a handful of particularly influential Israeli rabbis along with somewhat different covering letters.

To the Council:[2]

In the two months that have passed since my article in *Ha'aretz* on false messianism and *avodah zarah* in the Chabad movement, we have, thank God, seen positive movement both within the movement and outside it. Attacks were also not slow in coming, and there is no doubt that the anti-messianist article that has just appeared in the *Jewish Observer* will intensify the controversy.

On the one hand, we hear assertions that perceptions of the Rebbe as Deity are hardly to be found in Chabad, and on the other hand we read 'proofs' from talmudic passages, the Zohar, and hasidic works that there is not a tinge of impropriety in prostration and prayer to a human being who is considered the Creator of the world

---

[2] Translated from Hebrew.

in the full sense of the term. (According to this last group, all the commentators toiled in vain to interpret Isa. 9: 5 differently from the 'straightforward' Christian interpretation, and if not for that toil, we would have no doubt been offered 'proof' from this verse as well.[3])

I enclose an article that I published in *Hatzofeh* dealing with the danger of Chabad messianism even without the component of *avodah zarah*. It is worth noting that several weeks ago, after he signed the ruling that we are all obligated to believe in the messiahship of the Rebbe, Rabbi Yitzchak Handel of Montreal was elevated to the position of head of the rabbinical court of the entire city.

Only the rabbis of this generation can save Judaism from the religious disaster that confronts us. We now find ourselves in a very short period that will determine the boundaries of our messianic faith over the long term. If the rabbis will rule that one who believes in the messiahship of the Rebbe is disqualified from serving as a rabbi or rabbinic judge, our accepted tradition will survive in its full purity. If not, here is its burial place. . . .

In the letter to the chief rabbis of Israel, I urged—as I had much earlier—that messianist rabbis be removed from their posts, difficult as such a step would be:

Other rabbinic figures will be able to argue before the heavenly court—and before the court of history—that their responsibility for this fateful tragedy is limited to a sin of omission, but the Chief Rabbinate bears direct responsibility for the system of rabbinical courts in Israel. Precisely for this reason, it has the power to rescue our messianic faith from a tragedy that 'the heavens and their outermost reaches cannot contain, how much less this' letter that I have written [cf. 1 Kgs. 8: 27].[4]

After hearing from a third party that a highly distinguished, religiously observant Israeli academic in the field of Jewish Studies had expressed interest in my article in *Ha'aretz*, I sent him the new piece along with some unrelated scholarly material. The reaction was exceptionally gratifying, but it also shook me deeply because it revealed a terrible side effect of this affair: a dramatic decline in respect for rabbinic leadership. There are sharp formulations in the letter he sent me that I would not write, and I have deleted a phrase or two that I am not even comfortable reproducing. To some degree his indictment is

---

[3] The verse in question appears to describe a royal son as 'mighty God' and 'eternal father'. If not for its christological history, it is precisely the sort of verse that would be used by Lubavitch hasidim who 'demonstrate' that a righteous man becomes pure divinity by pointing eagerly and without nuance to the Rebbe's citation of a Zoharic statement (Zohar ii, 38a) that 'the Lord, Lord of Hosts' (Exod. 34: 23) refers to R. Simeon bar Yohai. For a popular presentation of Jewish approaches to Isa. 9: 5, see my discussion in *Jews and Jewish Christianity*, 42–4.

[4] Translated from Hebrew. I also sent the article along with similar letters to two of the most influential authorities in Israel: R. Yosef Shalom Elyashiv and R. Ovadiah Yosef.

unfair; Rabbi Schach, for example, certainly did react, and his followers are now silent because they take his position for granted. The author was also unaware of the article in the *Jewish Observer*, which does not reach non-Agudah circles in Israel. At the same time—setting aside the compliments to me—this letter expresses sentiments that I have formulated to myself all too often in some of my darkest moments.

I would like to express my heartfelt thanks for the offprint of your important article [from *Judaism's Encounter with Other Cultures*] and for the text of your observations in *Hatzofeh*. I read them both avidly. I was unaware of your comments in *Hatzofeh* because I do not read that paper. My regard for it has grown because it served as a vehicle for your wise remarks. I will not hide the fact that I was surprised that the editors agreed to publish the article. . . . If this is a sign of some awakening from the contemptible fear that paralyses the entire religious establishment, this is an additional merit that has been set into motion by a meritorious individual such as yourself.

The situation in our world depresses many good people, but no one, including those with the capacity to protest, has the courage to open his mouth. They all examine the calculus of their own world and do not suffer for the world of Israel that has been destroyed. The processes that are destroying Chabad hasidism are serious, but perhaps even more serious are the silence and indifference and cowardice of those who are (one would think) not involved in this insanity. There is no more frightening sign of the overall degeneration in which we are immersed. It may be that there has never been such a terrible scene in our history—that the name of Heaven should be desecrated in utter degradation on every street, and not one representative of the community of loyal Jews zealously defends the honour of Israel and the honour of their religion with even a still small voice. From their shame there emerges your own great praise.

I believe with complete faith that the day will come—and it is not far off—that historians will scrutinize the sources to find at least a small indication of some tangible awareness on the part of the members of this generation of the seriousness of the developments that occurred in their midst, and they will refuse to believe that no one among the hundreds of Torah scholars and heads of yeshivas . . . raised his voice with respect to this matter. Your words, remarkable in their wisdom and force, will atone in some small measure for the sin of their disgraceful silence, but these words will also condemn them before the heavenly court with an absolute condemnation from which no excuse will save them.

I have already written to [so-and-so] that I envy your portion in the world to come. One can be confident that He who provides reward for those who fear him will not withhold your portion in this world as well.[5]

Regrettably, my correspondent, to whom I was of course deeply grateful,

---

[5] Translated from Hebrew.

is not empowered to allocate portions in this world or the next, and I wish I could feel as confident as he about my ultimate destiny. I suspect that the assessment of most Lubavitch hasidim would be rather different. Still, this powerful letter underscores with eloquent pathos the incredible silence that impelled me to write this book. It may already be too late, but let us turn now to an examination of current realities and what might be done to change them.

TWELVE

From Margin to Mainstream: The Consolidation and Expansion of the Messianist Beachhead

T HE PRIMARY OBJECTIVE of this book is to establish the principle that anyone who proclaims the messiahship of the Rebbe stands outside the parameters of Orthodox Judaism and must be treated accordingly. From this perspective, the question of the size of the Lubavitch movement and the percentage of hasidim who affirm this belief is secondary. Nonetheless, the importance of the Chabad community and the nature of its messianic profile have major implications along a broad front of halakhic, sociological, and public policy issues, and I have no choice but to confront them.

With respect to the movement as a whole, the Lubavitch Youth Organization publishes a directory including an incomplete but very impressive list of emissaries in countries covering the alphabetical spectrum from Armenia to Venezuela. After consultation with official spokesmen in New York, a journalist reported that 'Chabad's facilities have grown by almost a third in [the] six years [since the Rebbe's death]. The movement has established more than 500 Chabad institutions throughout the world, raising the global total to 2,600, with 3,700 couples serving as emissaries.'[1]

Even as we recognize the fluidity of the term 'institutions' and the possibility that these numbers are exaggerated, there is no question that the worldwide Chabad presence is growing at a stunning rate. I have made some random enquiries from what I believe to be reliable local sources to supplement publicly available information, and they reinforce this impression to a degree that will surprise even knowledgeable observers.

I was taken aback to learn that Chabad rabbis constitute 50 per cent of the English rabbinate. Milan has a powerful Chabad presence, Venice boasts a Chabad centre where many Jewish tourists eat and spend the Sabbath, and

[1] Bob Keeler, 'The Lubavitchers of Long Island', *Newsday*, 23 Oct. 2000.

the most important ritual slaughterer in Rome is a Lubavitch hasid. Any Jewish traveller to France, where the Lubavitch directory lists thirty-five major emissaries, will testify to the visibility and significance of Chabad institutions and services there. Half the twenty-six synagogues in Sydney are led by Chabad rabbis, and, in the words of my informant, 'Kashrut, including shechita (ritual slaughter), is governed in Sydney by the Kashrut Authority, which is supervised by one rabbi only—Habad, of course'. Chabad, he went on to say, 'has completely dominated the efforts to bring Russian immigrants into the community'. A Dutch Jewish journalist informs me that more than half the major Orthodox rabbis in Holland are Lubavitch hasidim. We already know that the head of the rabbinical court of Montreal is a Chabad rabbi. The Lubavitch directory lists eighteen major centres in Brazil.

The role of Chabad in the former Soviet Union deserves special attention. The recently formed Federation of Jewish Communities has installed a Chabad emissary named Berel Lazar as the country's chief rabbi. This step is part of a larger power struggle within the community, and the existing chief rabbi has not relinquished his position. Nonetheless, the new group enjoys the sympathy of the government, and the activities of Chabad dwarf those of all other Jewish religious movements. A recent article reports that although

it seems strange to American ears . . . Habad is the mainstream denomination here, with no one having more synagogues or a larger annual budget—a staggering $20 million, 22 times more than what is spent by Reform, the second most active denomination. According to Reform's figures, Progressive Judaism in the entire FSU [Former Soviet Union] operates on a budget of $900,000, much of it raised abroad. A single Ukrainian Chabad shul [synagogue] raised more than that, $1 million, among the Jews of Dnepropetrovsk alone.[2]

In December 2000 a very well informed Russian Jew pursuing a doctorate in Jewish history in New York told my class that, based on his experience, Chabad would come to be seen as synonymous with Judaism, and all other Jewish religious groups would be perceived as sects. The movement bestrides a vast territory with a population of half a million Jews.

Observers who imagine that Chabad is in irrevocable decline in the wake of the Rebbe's death—and readers who believe that they have been perusing a book about an interesting but marginal sect—need to think again. Upon reflection, the success of Lubavitch outreach is not surprising at all. I shall later return to an analogy with Mormonism from a different perspective, but at this point we need only ponder the key ingredient in the worldwide expan-

[2] Jonathan Mark, 'Chabad's Russian Revolution', *Jewish Week*, 1 Dec. 2000.

sion of this recent American religion. Its adherents combine deep commitment with an obligation to devote a few years to missionary work. Lubavitch hasidim display no less commitment, and the best of them become missionaries not for two or three years but for the remainder of their lives. Since their target is not the entire world but the Jewish community alone,[3] their impact is swift and abiding.

What, then, is the messianic profile of this highly significant movement? The factions within provide dramatically contradictory information to outsiders, so that messianists tell us that virtually everyone believes, even if some oppose public affirmations, while the non-messianist leadership would have us conclude that the believers are a very small number of mostly marginal hasidim of relatively recent vintage who know how to make noise and intimidate. Statistical precision is elusive, dependent partly on the reading of minds, and some of what I shall say is necessarily tentative. Nonetheless, the broad outlines are not difficult to discern, and they are far from reassuring.

The central synagogue in 770 Eastern Parkway—the hub of worldwide Lubavitch hasidism—is indisputably the headquarters of a messianic sect, where the *Yehi* messianist slogan is a regular component of the liturgy. A large sign displaying the *Yehi* adorns the front of the Lubavitch Women's Organization Headquarters in Crown Heights. Rabbi Shmuel Butman serves as Director of the Lubavitch Youth Organization. Oholei Torah/Oholei Menachem in Crown Heights, the largest school for boys and young men, employs faculty who play prominent roles in messianist publications; the web page (apparently discontinued) of its student journal proclaimed the messiahship of the Rebbe as of February 2000, and we recall that the recitation of the *Yehi* imperilled its place in AARTS. The head of Tomchei Temimim, another major men's yeshiva in Crown Heights, signed a messianist approbation to a major messianist book published in 1999, and a mentor there participated in its preparation.[4] Machon Chanah, an important seminary for women, also in Crown Heights, teaches messianist doctrine to the point where a recent convert from Christianity left the school after a short while, complaining that this was what she had abandoned when accepting Judaism.[5] A non-Lubavitch Traditionalist Orthodox couple who sent their daughter to a Lubavitch-run elementary school in Boston were startled to hear her recite

---

[3] The Rebbe encouraged efforts to teach non-Jews about the seven Noahide laws incumbent upon all humanity, but such outreach plays a very small role in the activities of Chabad emissaries.

[4] *The Era and the Redemption in the Teachings of the Lubavitcher Rebbe*, letter of approbation and p. 6 (which also lists four staff members of Oholei Torah).

[5] I was informed of this by R. Yosef Blau of Yeshiva University, whom the young woman approached for advice.

the Grace after Meals with an added line calling upon God to bless the Rebbe.

We are already all too familiar with the theology of Rabbi Levi Yitzchak Ginsberg of Yeshiva Tomchei Temimim in Kfar Chabad, the major population centre of the movement in Israel. A religious mentor in the Jerusalem yeshiva Torat Emet told *Siḥat hage'ulah* that 'we know for certain that the Rebbe remains alive in the physical world and no change applies to him, not even that of being hidden away, [though] we do not see him'.[6] A student in that yeshiva confirmed to a friend of mine that the *Yeḥi* is recited,[7] and he gave an evasive answer when asked if the Rebbe is still alive. ('What is "alive"?' he asked.) Recent issues of *Beis Moshiach* carried a multi-part interview with nine messianist *mashpi'im* from eight Lubavitch yeshivas around the world (in Kfar Chabad, Crown Heights, Lod, Montreal, South Africa, Bnei Berak, Safed, and Jerusalem).[8]

In a survey of activities in the large, strongly messianist Chabad community in Safed, *Beis Moshiach* reported on a school system with more than 1,500 students. The elementary school for girls has grown from 100 to 420 students, 'who come not only from the Chabad community, but from all over the city and even neighboring cities, such as Kiryat Shmoneh, Yesod HaMaaleh, Katzrin in the Golan Heights, Teveria, Rosh Pinah, Dishon and other settlements. The school is so popular that this year there will be five first grades, the most they've ever had.' The administrator was asked whether 'a school which had garnered prizes from the Ministry of Education, Aliyat HaNoar [Youth Immigration], and from the education department of the northern district, openly discussed Moshiach or perhaps toned things down a little'. She replied, 'What do you mean? We clearly teach that the Rebbe is *Melech HaMoshiach* and nobody is ashamed of it. Although they don't always agree with our faith, parents of other groups send their daughters here and they see that our faith is sincere. "*Yechi adoneinu*" is printed on every document, including those we send to the government offices.'[9] One is reminded of sixteenth-century Jesuit schools whose excellent quality enticed even Protestant parents to enrol their children despite the strong likelihood that they would emerge as Catholics.

---

[6] *Siḥat hage'ulah* no. 156, 13 Tammuz 5757 (18 July 1997).

[7] When pressed by unsympathetic questioners about the recitation of the *Yeḥi*, spokespersons for Lubavitch institutions have been known to assert that they cannot control unruly participants, as if one could imagine their tolerating a declaration of the messiahship of Rav Schach at the end of the prayer service.

[8] *Beis Moshiach*, 296–8 (Erev Sukkos, Parshas Noach, and Parshas Lech Lecho, 5761; 24 Sept., 15 Oct., 22 Oct. 2000).

[9] *Beis Moshiach*, 291 (Parshas Shoftim, 5760; 1 July 2000). I have left the spelling of place names as they appear in the original.

The impact of such an education is precisely what one would expect. Numerous students have celebrated the birthday of the deceased Rebbe by participating in caravans consisting of dozens of 'mitzvah tanks' with messianist slogans. A student Chabad Club at a university in New York distributed song sheets containing the following text: 'I accept upon myself the positive commandment of declaring, "May the King Messiah live forever. May our Master, Teacher, and Rabbi, the King Messiah, live for ever".' Youngsters who walk from Crown Heights for hours to dance in the synagogues of Queens on the festival of Simhat Torah arrive with skullcaps adorned with the *Yehi*, sometimes partially obscured by hats, sometimes not. A New York rabbi heard a Lubavitch boy identify an abstract picture as that of the Rebbe. When he questioned the identification, the boy replied, 'The Rebbe is everywhere'. Clever techniques draw children to this belief. A recent issue of *Sihat hage'ulah*[10] announced that any child who calls a designated phone number and says the *Yehi* will automatically be entered in a raffle for a new bicycle. I shall return later to the meaningless, anaesthetizing mantra that messianists are crazy, but it should be perfectly evident that this cannot apply to children brought up in this belief. Once they are raised to accept this, it is their religion, and they are not crazy to believe it.

From educational institutions we turn to rabbis. We are already familiar with the 'rabbinic ruling' requiring all Jews to accept the messiahship of the Rebbe as a consequence of the obligation to obey a prophet. As we recall, it was originally issued in late 1997 by six rabbis. Even that number was significant since it included the chief rabbi of Kfar Chabad, the soon to be head of the rabbinical court of the city of Montreal, and the head of the Crown Heights rabbinical court (since deceased), a central institution that not only hears cases but provides kashrut supervision for much of the community. By the end of 1998 the number of names had swelled to approximately seventy, and on 17 January 2000 the ruling was advertised in *Hatzofeh* with a list of 150 signatories from all over the world. Many known messianists do not appear on this 'partial list',[11] and there can be no doubt that more cautious believers did not sign because such a public affirmation can complicate their work as emissaries. Thus, it is perfectly evident that this is very far from an exhaustive enumeration of rabbinic believers. At the same time, the willingness of so many to sign reflects both zealous faith and the judgement that a profession of messianist belief is not so damaging after all. Years of indifference have shown that the risk is eminently manageable.

[10] No. 298, 28 Iyar 5760 (2 May 2000).

[11] I should like to believe that even some convinced messianists could not bring themselves to endorse the reasoning in this ruling, but this is almost certainly wishful thinking.

This list is also a useful tool for assessing the oft-repeated assertion that whatever the situation may be in the main population centres, Lubavitch emissaries doing God's work all over the world are virtually free of the messianist taint. It is certainly the case that the situation among emissaries, some of whom genuinely do God's work, is indeed better than it is in Crown Heights, Kfar Chabad, and Safed. But this is not saying much.

A perusal of these names is the stuff of nightmares. The eighteen signatories from the Former Soviet Union are, I am told, the leading Lubavitch emissaries there.[12] Their posts range from Moscow to Riga to Kazakhstan, from Tashkent to Rostov to Kishinev and beyond. Even knowledgeable observers have been misled into believing that these representatives are not messianists. A rabbi who attended a recent conference of European rabbis told me that he heard no reference to the Rebbe's messiahship from the FSU emissaries, and a very well informed non-messianist Lubavitch hasid of the highest intellect and integrity insisted to me that they are in no way, shape, or form messianist. But they are. The name of the new chief rabbi, Rabbi Berel Lazar, has appeared on the ruling on at least five occasions from 1998 to 2000 in English, Hebrew, and Russian, and an official of the World Jewish Congress who is by no means hostile to Lubavitch told me that he was present at a major Jewish event in Moscow in 1998 where Rabbi Lazar began by reciting the *Yeḥi*. Official Judaism in the FSU threatens to become the Judaism of a deceased Messiah.

And this is by no means the end of it. Messianism abounds in France, where, according to an interview in *Beis Moshiach*, the head of a significant Lubavitch institution called Hadar Torah utilizes both that publication and *Siḥat hage'ulah* in his educational activities, holds mass gatherings on the Messiah and the redemption attracting 'huge numbers of people', and coordinates programmes with the Matteh Moshiach (Moshiach Staff) in Antwerp and Brussels.[13] The messianist head of the rabbinical court of Montreal is not alone in his beliefs. There is a significant messianist presence in Toronto as well, and the emissary in Calgary, who signed the ruling, wears a skullcap inscribed with the *Yeḥi*. A fervent messianist, also a signatory, sits on the non-Lubavitch rabbinical court of Sydney. A friend who led a group of American Jewish tourists to Venice informed me that they were approached with an aggressive messianist message. A Milwaukee rabbi of Russian extraction

[12] R. Pinchas Goldschmidt, the chief rabbi of Moscow engaged in a struggle with Chabad, told me that the ruling was subsequently printed in Russian with all the FSU signatories, that the translation contained an error describing the Rebbe as the Deity, and that only one of the rabbis (from Armenia) disavowed his involvement.

[13] *Beis Moshiach*, 267 (Parshas Ki Sisa, 5760; 25 Feb. 2000).

published a calendar for his synagogue proclaiming the divinity of the Rebbe.[14] In the *Jewish Chronicle* of 1 June 2001 the vice-president of the Chabad Community Centre in Oldfield Street, London N16 wrote that 'every true Lubavitch' hasid is a messianist. Finally, since the school system producing emissaries is suffused with messianism, it is difficult to see why future Lubavitch missionaries should be any less committed to this belief.

We have also reached a point where a theologically respectable, though still not very robust, explanation has been constructed to explain the disaster of 3 Tammuz. Rabbi Gedalyah Axelrod, one of the initial signatories with whom we are already acquainted, has pointed out in an article in *Beis Moshiach* that 2 Chronicles 36: 16–17 attributes the Babylonian exile to the fact that Jews 'mocked the messengers of God and despised His words, and scoffed at His prophets'. To 'correct the original defect that led to the [exile] in the first place, i.e., lack of faith in G-d's prophets', we are now called upon to exercise transcendent faith by accepting the message of the prophet of our generation despite the event of that terrible day.[15] In other words, the Rebbe's passing occurred to create the test of faith needed to undo the effects of an original absence of faith. I do not know whether such an explanation can sustain a movement indefinitely, but it is not at all bad as an initial effort.

The widespread commitment of Lubavitch hasidim to this belief is rooted in more than psychology. I am very hesitant to address the Rebbe's role in creating this movement, a subject I touched on lightly and fleetingly in Chapters 2 and 5. Nevertheless, observers convinced that faith in the Rebbe's messiahship will surely fade away or that its proponents are crazy need to understand the hurdles faced by anti-messianists within Chabad. The messianists' most important ammunition in the inner debates is not the few passages in the standard literature about a resurrected messiah but the Rebbe's own statements over the years.

Before turning to the Rebbe himself, we must look at a theology wide-

[14] The *Wisconsin Jewish Chronicle*, 4 Dec. 1998, published a story about this rabbi, including a reproduction of the picture of the Rebbe with the Russian word for God underneath ('Bog', spelled B-g out of respect for the divine name). The story reports that the main Lubavitch emissary there denounced the rabbi. In late May 2000, a resident of my neighbourhood gave me a picture of the Rebbe with the word G-d underneath that he had just removed from a wall in a Manhattan business district. Needless to say, no large conclusions can be drawn from a poster of unknown provenance. Similarly, an unbalanced hasid from Safed, who took out advertisements proclaiming the divinity of the Rebbe and even scratched such a message on the Western Wall, was arrested after intentionally injuring R. Levi Bistritsky with his car because of the latter's vigorous opposition. On the one hand, such atypical manifestations deflect concern by convincing outsiders that the problem of *avodah zarah* is limited to lunatics; in fact, they are symptoms of a deep problem at the core.

[15] 'So too is He Alive'. Posted on <www.moshiachnow.org/articles> on 5 Jan. 1999. I do not know in which issue of *Beis Moshiach* the article appeared.

spread in Chabad regarding the role of the movement in the divine economy. We recall that not long after the Rebbe's death, an Israeli hasid named Yehezkel Sofer wrote a book arguing that the Rebbe's words need not be construed in a manner supportive of the messianist position.[16] In this work, Rabbi Sofer asserted that when the Messiah comes there will immediately be a limited resurrection of extraordinarily righteous people. At that point we shall ask the resurrected Rebbe whether this apparent Messiah is genuine, and if the Rebbe confirms his status we will recognize him 'even if he is a *Litvak* [a (non-hasidic) Lithuanian Jew]'.

Rabbi Shalom Dov Wolpo responded in a sarcastic sixty-four-page booklet entitled *Sefer sofer vesipur* (A Book, a Writer [*sofer*], and a Tale). Here is his comment on Sofer's assertion:

> In this passage we find not only a denial of our belief that the Rebbe is the Messiah but a decision *that the Messiah has no connection to the teachings of the Baal Shem Tov God forbid* [emphasis in the original]. Not only this, but the author is convinced that the Rebbe will confirm for us that the Messiah, who is divine truth, is a *Litvak* with no association with the teachings of Hasidism! And this is the divine truth for which we have been waiting two thousand years! And for this all the sufferings of exile were worthwhile.[17]

To an outsider, Wolpo's remarks have a more than faintly comic tinge. But, as a fervent messianist explained to me, they reflect a deeply held Chabad belief. The reason for the length of the Jewish exile is to allow for the gradual revelation of the inner meaning of the Torah at a pace deemed appropriate by the divine wisdom. The Zohar became widely known only in the thirteenth century and the kabbalistic system of Rabbi Isaac Luria (1534–72) in the sixteenth. Then, in the eighteenth, the Ba'al Shem Tov emerged armed with reassurance from the Messiah himself that the end would come when hasidic teachings spread. This mission and the leadership role that comes with it were then channelled primarily into the Chabad line of rebbes beginning with Rabbi Shneur Zalman of Lyady. It is worth recalling the stunning sense of self-importance reflected in the assertion with which we are already familiar that with the death of each of the previous Lubavitch rebbes, the revelation of God through the particular divine emanation embodied in that rebbe was completed. For this process to reach its culmination in a non-hasidic Messiah is problematic in the extreme, and, to Wolpo, flatly absurd.

It is evident from all this that Chabad beliefs create a powerful presumption that the Messiah will be the Lubavitcher rebbe of whichever generation

---

[16] See Ch. 4 n. 1.   [17] Page 56.

merits the redemption. With this in mind, we turn to the most recent Rebbe. The messianists point to a substantial number of interlocking assertions that convince them that he expected to be the Messiah. His deceased father-in-law, whose soul he is believed to have shared and who consequently serves as a surrogate or code for Rabbi Menachem Mendel himself, is the prince (*nasi*) of this generation and will redeem us. The prince of the generation is the Messiah of the generation. This is the generation of the redemption. The metaphysical process of separating the sparks of holiness from the domain of evil has been completed. The Messiah has already been revealed; all that is necessary is to greet him. The Messiah is coming right away. 'The time of your redemption has arrived.' The final Temple will descend from heaven to a spot in Crown Heights adjoining 770 Eastern Parkway, and only then will the two buildings be transferred to Jerusalem. The Messiah's name is Menachem.[18] Sympathetic outsiders will be shaken—as I have been over the past several years—to discover that the Rebbe actually said all these things, but they are indisputably on the record.[19]

Non-messianists are put in the position of arguing that the end is indeed imminent but the Messiah is, or may be, someone other than the Rebbe, that these statements were conditioned upon the merit of this generation, or that the Rebbe, like other great Jews, allowed his love for the Jewish people and his burning desire for redemption to generate excessive confidence that the messianic age was at hand. The last formulation is particularly difficult in a movement where most hasidim see the Rebbe as virtually—or literally— infallible. On the substantive question of his claim to messiahship, the non-messianists can point to a report by his long-time aide Rabbi Yehudah Leib Groner that the Rebbe told him on an unspecified occasion, 'The man who is the Messiah has to have this revealed to him from above, and at present this has not been revealed to me.'

The messianists are considerably more vulnerable when the argument shifts to the Rebbe's position on messianic propaganda. Though in his last years he tolerated and even appears to have encouraged the singing of the *Yehi* as well as messianist events sponsored by Chabad women's organizations, he also remarked that he should really walk out when the slogan is sung and

---

[18] Menachem, which means 'consoler', is one of several names proposed for the Messiah in *Sanhedrin* 98*b*.

[19] For a succinct list containing most of these remarks and more (but without sources), see Wolpo's *The Last Trial*, 16–17. A larger sampling with references to the sources appears in Anon., *And He Will Redeem Us*, 17–28. For a fuller discussion, see *The Era and Redemption in the Teachings of the Lubavitcher Rebbe*. The peregrinations of the final Temple are set forth in R. Menachem Mendel Schneerson, *Pamphlet on the Small Temple, the House of our Rabbi in Babylonia* (Heb.) (Brooklyn, NY, 1992).

remains only because leaving would do no good. In the 1980s he expressed strong criticisms of people like Shalom Dov Wolpo for attempting to publish messianist material, and he made some similar remarks as late as 1991. On one occasion, he is reported to have responded to a petition addressed to him in his capacity as the Messiah by saying, 'When he comes I will give it to him.' I certainly do not believe that he would have wanted people to proclaim his messiahship after his death in an unredeemed world.[20]

Control of the overarching, official Chabad institutions in the United States and Israel, including the coordinating body for emissaries, is in the hands of leaders who oppose messianist proclamations and are in some cases genuinely non-messianists. To assess the situation in an informed fashion, we need to survey the spectrum of opinion regarding this question so that we will understand the available options.

On one end, there are a relatively small number of hasidim who recognize that the Rebbe is not and will not be the Messiah. Then there is a considerably larger group of those who say that he may or may not be. Among these, some add that he is the most likely candidate. In the fully messianist camp, there are both tactical and theological divisions. The tactical question is whether to proclaim this belief to the world or to keep it private because of the Rebbe's directive to publicize only those teachings that are likely to find a receptive audience. On the theological front, there are those who believe that the Rebbe died in a sense no different from any other righteous man, but will soon be resurrected to assume his messianic mantle. Others believe that he survives physically in a state that is at least in some sense transformed, while the remainder insist that there has been no change whatever.

Cutting across these lines, there is the question of how to interpret the assertion, proffered by the Rebbe himself, that a rebbe is the Essence and Being of God. While even some non-messianists can and do maintain an understanding of this principle amounting to *avodah zarah*, most of them have habits of mind that militate against a literal reading. Messianists, who begin with the belief that the Messiah-Rebbe is greater than Moses and the ministering angels, are much more likely to adopt the theology that I have discussed at length in an earlier chapter and analyse more fully in Appendix II.

It is my tentative assessment that the non-messianist American establishment consists largely of those who believe that the Rebbe may or may not be the Messiah. They control some educational institutions but are substantially

---

[20] For a balanced discussion of the Rebbe's 'complex' position on this subject, see Binyamin Lipkin, *Reckoning of the World* (Heb.) (Lod, 2000), 142–6. The unpaginated series of documents at the end includes a photocopy of Rabbi Groner's letter reporting his conversation with the Rebbe.

outnumbered by messianists. They generally avoid the movement's main synagogue, and they cannot remove messianist influence even from their own institutions. Efforts by the unequivocally anti-messianist minority to start a truly uncontaminated school in Crown Heights have encountered considerable difficulty, though I am informed that they have very recently achieved some modest success. There are certainly Chabad institutions in a variety of cities led by emissaries who thoroughly reject the messianist position. To the degree that they make their disbelief in the Rebbe's messiahship—not merely their annoyance with the messianists—public in explicit, absolutely unambiguous terms, including assurances that they will not engage in joint projects with believers, they merit enthusiastic support and encouragement. For the most part, however, even genuine non-messianists will not go this far. In human terms, it is impossible not to sympathize with people who resist a complete break with their own flesh and blood, but the future of a religion is at stake.

In Israel, the situation is even worse. Menachem Brod, the most visible spokesman for 'establishment' Chabad, opposes public messianist declarations. I cannot know his inner convictions, but messianists assert that he is a believer and he reacted to a journalist's direct question as to his belief in the messiahship of the Rebbe by saying, 'I am unwilling to comment on this matter.'[21] When another journalist asked Brod's reaction to the messianist belief, his reaction was, 'So what?'[22] After some initial resistance, the 'establishment' group has agreed to sponsor public events with the messianists, and a joint programme dedicated to 'greeting the Messiah' was held on the festival of Shavuot in 2000. There are surely genuine non-messianists in Israel, but they appear to be greatly outnumbered.

When we examine the Israeli signatories of the ruling, our nightmare intensifies. Many are identified as chief rabbis of cities, towns, or settlements, including Kiryat Bialik, Holon, Kiryat Yam, Natzeret Ilit, Kiryat Malachi, and many more. Others are synagogue rabbis, judges in rabbinical courts, members of local offices of the rabbinate, instructors in advanced yeshivas; a few of these even appear to come from outside the Chabad community.[23] A non-messianist Lubavitch hasid who saw a report of the endorsement of this ruling

[21] *Hatzofeh*, 6 Kislev 5760 (12 Nov. 1999), Sabbath supplement, p. 7.

[22] Sari Bashi, 'Hasidic Movement Grapples with Split over Messiah', Associated Press dispatch, 18 June 1999.

[23] I checked issues of *Hatzofeh* for the full month after publication of the ruling. Unless I missed something, only one signatory (R. Amnon Sugarman of Yeshivat Hagolan) wrote to disavow the use of his name. That leaves sixty-six Israeli signatories whose silence gives us every reason to accept the authenticity of their signatures. On the FSU signatories, see above, n. 12.

by non-Chabad rabbis sent me an electronic message asking whether every-one had gone crazy. Most of these rabbis surely preach belief in the messiah-ship of the Rebbe to their constituents, Lubavitch and non-Lubavitch. I am reliably informed that some non-religious Jews persuaded to don tefillin on the streets of Jerusalem and in the mitzvah tanks of New York are instructed to say the *Yeḥi* before 'Hear, O Israel. The Lord is our God the Lord is one.'[24]

Many observers imagine that if they have not recently heard about this subject, it follows that the messianists are being vanquished. Precisely the reverse is true. Little is heard because much of the opposition has been stilled. Jews shrug, go about their private and communal business, and assume that all is well, while their traditional messianic belief collapses around them. The fact that the issue has receded from the public arena is a sign not of the mes-sianists' defeat but of their largely silent march to the threshold of victory. We have seen that Lubavitch hasidim, including a significant number of messian-ists, constitute a majority or near majority of the Orthodox rabbinate in many important centres. Hardly anyone asks them hard questions about their beliefs, and few people care even when their messianist convictions are pub-licly proclaimed. Through the criminal negligence of the Orthodox commu-nity, Lubavitch messianism has positioned itself to proselytize, spread, and ultimately define the contours of Orthodox Judaism in numerous cities and not a few countries all over the world.

The recent publication of the messianist ruling finally inspired a formal, very important reaction from the Chief Rabbinate of Israel:

ANNOUNCEMENT

At the meeting of the Council of the Chief Rabbinate of Israel held on 10 Shevat 5760 [17 January 2000], a discussion was held regarding the newspaper advertisement signed by many rabbis *shlita* [may they live a good, long life, amen] requiring that one obey the words of a prophet including the assertion that he is the King Messiah. By agreement of the Chief Rabbis of Israel and the members of the Council of the Chief Rabbinate of Israel, the following decision was adopted unanimously:

To Remove a Stumbling-block from the Midst of my People

In recent days announcements and declarations are being publicized that can confuse and mislead simple people with messianic propaganda that a certain hasidic rabbi is the King Messiah and one should call to him with various proclamations.

---

[24]   These reports were confirmed by Levi Yitzchak Ginsberg's article, 'Sealed with the Stamp of the Kohen Gadol', *Beis Moshiach*, 305 (Parshas Mikeitz 5761/29 Dec. 2000): 'It is very important that . . . a "Kriyas Shma" sheet with "Yechi Adoneinu" printed on it be used. By this I mean a "Yechi" that isn't just a headline on the page, but part of the text for the person to recite, after "hareini mekabel" ['I accept upon myself' (the commandment of donning tefillin)].'

We have no intention God forbid of diminishing the greatness and the global activities of the Rebbe of blessed memory, but because we are dealing with the foundations of the faith and there is danger in this propaganda, it is necessary to warn against this approach. It is concerning such matters that the Sages said, 'Wise men, be careful with your words.'

Individuals who are undesirable in the eyes of rabbinic scholars are exploiting the signatures of rabbis and turning the simple faith in the coming of the Messiah into propaganda whose end cannot be foreseen. One must be careful and warn people that one must believe in the straightforward faith that the Messiah will come as our Rabbis have taught us, and anyone who adds diminishes.[25]

This is an excellent text, and I do not wish to minimize its importance. For the first time, the Chief Rabbinate has issued a forthright declaration that at least implies that this doctrine undermines one of the fundamental doctrines of Judaism. For reasons of politics and diplomacy, however, it continues to refer respectfully to messianist rabbis whose signatures were somehow 'exploited' by undesirables issuing improper propaganda. What is the signing of that ruling if not the issuing of messianist propaganda? Does the rabbinate imagine that the signatories *shlita* expected the ruling to be kept in an inaccessible vault?

There was an immediate messianist counter-attack, and one member of the Council complained about improper procedures.[26] As recently as June 1999, Chief Rabbi Lau reportedly agreed to attend a 'unity' gathering of Lubavitch as long as the *Yeḥi* sign would be placed on a side wall rather than on stage.[27] Time will tell whether this is a one-time declaration or whether it heralds a significant change leading to a series of courageous actions to delegitimate messianist rabbis. The most important effects thus far appear to be the emboldening of genuine non-messianists in Israeli Chabad to press their arguments and the strengthening of efforts by 'moderate' messianists to persuade their more militant colleagues to refrain from public declarations. The 'moderates' understand all too well that if controversial slogans disappear from the mass media for two or three months, most observers assume that the belief has receded, and messianists can proceed to broaden and strengthen their worldwide activities with little or no opposition.

The legitimation of Second Coming Judaism has not been lost on interested Christians. Two people have told me that Cardinal Lustiger of France,

[25] *Hatzofeh*, 11 Shevat 5760 (18 Jan. 2000), 5. The advertisement containing the ruling covered two full pages of the previous day's *Hatzofeh* (pp. 12–13). The rabbinate's statement took up one-eighth of a page at the bottom of p. 5 and could easily be missed. Many people with a lively interest in this subject have never heard of it. [26] See *Siḥat hage'ulah*, no. 283, 28 Shevat 5760 (4 Feb. 2000).

[27] AP dispatch of 18 June 1999 (above, n. 22).

who was brought up as a Jew, has warned Jewish friends that this is how Christianity began. A stranger approached a rabbi from my neighbourhood on the streets of Manhattan, showed him a picture of the Rebbe, and asked, 'How is he different from the lord Jesus?'

Far more important than these random observations is the growing utilization of this movement by skilled and committed missionaries. A convert to Orthodox Judaism living in Minneapolis informs me that the local head of a missionary organization greets him with the question, 'What about the Lubavitchers?' Three people have told me of a billboard or poster in California with the phone number of a missionary group, a picture of the Rebbe, and the message, 'Right Idea. Wrong Person.' Another spoke of a Jews for Jesus T-shirt with the Rebbe's picture. None of this is the least bit surprising. No missionary with a modicum of intelligence could fail to exploit the gift-wrapped opportunity that Orthodox Jewry has bestowed upon proselytizing Christianity.

A very recent, major missionary tract has made full use of Lubavitch messianism, noting both the doctrine of the Second Coming and the ascription of divinity to the Rebbe. On the first point, the author writes, 'If I did not see and hear and read these things for myself, it would be difficult to believe them, seeing that they form such an exact parallel to the suffering and death of Yeshua [Jesus] . . . along with his resurrection, and his awaited return.' On the second, he observes, 'It is ironic, of course, that these Hasidic Jews, who so vehemently reject Yeshua and find the New Testament teaching on the incarnation offensive, can speak of their deceased leader as "master of the Universe" and point to his alleged divine nature. They implicitly recognize some aspects of the Messiah's divinity, but they have pinned those aspects on the wrong candidate. Jesus alone fits the bill and fulfills the description.'[28] The profound theological differences between Judaism and Christianity have been reduced to a matter of mistaken identity.

An insightful analysis by Professor Martin Lockshin has recently looked at the erosion of the Jewish–Christian divide from a broader perspective in which the Lubavitch issue is but one, critical component. I have focused on the parameters of Orthodoxy. Lockshin asks what it is that keeps Jews for Jesus out of the accepted boundaries of the Jewish community writ large. The Jewish perception of Christians as the quintessential enemy is, he notes, receding to the vanishing point for reasons that must surely be welcomed. Observance of the commandments is no longer a useful dividing line in an age

---

[28]   Michael L. Brown, *Answering Jewish Objections to Jesus*, ii: *Theological Objections* (Grand Rapids, Mich., 2000), 228–9, 220. I am grateful to Gerald Sigal for bringing these passages to my attention.

of Reform Judaism. Disbelief in God does not exclude secular Jews from active communal involvement.

That leaves our issue. 'Jews used to be sure', writes Lockshin, 'that they could agree about one thing: whether they believed in a personal messiah or not, they certainly did not believe in the idea of a dead messiah who was going to come back soon to finish the work that he started before he died. That, one used to "know", was Christianity, not Judaism.' But now, he continues, alluding to my articles in *Jewish Action* and *Ha'aretz*, neither this belief nor even the belief in divine incarnation automatically excludes a Jew from the community. 'It seems inevitable', he concludes, 'that Jews for Jesus will take their place alongside of other Jewish denominations. It is my hope, though, that this will not occur' and that the Jewish community will somehow devise effective criteria to prevent the definition of Jewishness from devolving into a state of anarchy.[29]

Partial confirmation of Lockshin's bleak forecast was forthcoming in a recent issue of *Moment* magazine.[30] Dennis Prager, a popular commentator with strong Jewish commitments, proposed that Jews for Jesus be embraced by the Jewish community as long as they change their name, cease proselytizing, formally declare that they accept the messiahship of Jesus but not his divinity, and break off relations with those who reject these requirements. He builds this proposal upon an analogy to 'some wonderful Chabad Jews who believe the last Lubavitcher rebbe was the messiah'. One reader of the article could not bring himself to believe that it was meant seriously, especially when he reached the section in which Prager proposed that a rabbinical court solicit an oath from these semi-repentant Jews for Jesus to abide by his conditions. But it is serious. While no one will actually pursue this plan, the article itself is a striking symptom of the potential of Lubavitch messianism to erode the boundaries of the Jewish community.

Before examining the explanations accounting for the widespread legitimation of this phenomenon, we must remind ourselves that the current state of Lubavitch messianism in the eyes of the Orthodox community is marked by contradiction, even paradox. In important respects, the belief *has* been delegitimated. The Rabbinical Council of America is on record. We have just seen the recent statement of the Israeli Rabbinate. A number of the most important yeshivas in the world—Ponevezh, Telshe, Chofetz Chaim, Philadelphia, much of Lakewood, some of Ner Israel—have placed Lubavitch

[29] Martin Lockshin, 'Judaism, Christianity, and Jewish-Christianity: What the Future May Hold', in *Cult and Culture: Studies in Cultural Meaning*, Les Cahiers du CICC 8 (July 1999), 137–48.

[30] Dennis Prager, 'A New Approach to Jews for Jesus', *Moment* (June 2000), 28–9.

messianists (and in some cases all Lubavitch hasidim) beyond the pale of Orthodoxy. Followers of Rabbi Schach regard recent developments as confirmation of what they have known all along. There are ad hoc prayer services in Jerusalem where messianists are not counted towards a quorum, and I have been told of a yeshiva in Brooklyn that threatens its students with expulsion if they pray in the messianist institution down the block. I have already alluded to Rabbi Shmuel Yaakov Weinberg's directive that a student pray alone rather than in a Chabad synagogue. Rabbi Yehudah Amital of Yeshivat Har Etzion in Israel told me of his public remark to the students that the failure of more people to join my campaign on this issue is a scandal. Individuals in the Traditionalist Orthodox community have approached me on various occasions with comments like 'Your reward will be very great' (*sekharekha harbeh me'od*). Some members of the Council of Torah Sages have made supportive remarks, and one has sent me two congratulatory letters of encouragement. An influential layman in Agudath Israel recently observed, 'Those close to the *gedolim* know that they have given up on Lubavitch.' The *Jewish Observer* published Rabbi Keller's article. A distinguished rabbi in Brooklyn told a friend of mine in his congregation, 'I hope you don't eat Lubavitch meat.'

And yet none of this comes close to a genuine communal policy. On the contrary, as we have seen throughout this book, messianists are granted full rabbinical status in central posts in the Orthodox world. Oholei Torah is a member in good standing of the Association of Advanced Rabbinical and Talmudical Schools, which represents most of the yeshivas listed in the previous paragraph. Hasidic rebbes send their representatives to speak at events held there. Many RCA rabbis support messianist institutions despite the resolution. That Brooklyn rabbi has never expressed his views publicly even in his own synagogue. We have just surveyed the situation in Israel, in the Former Soviet Union, and around the world. Many if not most observers regard my efforts as symptoms of a personal idiosyncrasy. They may find it admirable or destructive or merely peculiar, but they do not give it much chance of success.

I am occasionally told by representatives of synagogues inviting me to lecture that I should choose a topic less controversial than Lubavitch messianism. While I am perfectly willing to accommodate them and in fact welcome the opportunity to catch my breath by escaping the sometimes suffocating coils of this self-imposed controversy, I cannot help but ponder the irony. If I had proposed a lecture ten years ago on the unacceptability of believing in a Messiah who was buried a short while earlier, the response would have been, 'What will your next lecture argue? That the sun rises in the East?' Now, what was once self-evident is too hot to handle. Ten years ago, an Orthodox Jew who was asked if he would eat in a restaurant festooned with propaganda announcing the messiahship of a dead rabbi would have wondered what drug the questioner was taking; today, it is the refusal to do this that elicits musings about unhealthy obsessions.

Not only has this transformation been effected; public resistance has been so sporadic and ineffectual as to appear quixotic. What, then, can account for such collective indifference and complicity in a community marked by intellect, sensitivity to religious deviation, and deep commitment to faith?

THIRTEEN

Explaining the Inexplicable

I N   M Y   F I R S T   A R T I C L E   in *Jewish Action* (above, Ch. 2), I briefly proposed some tentative explanations for Orthodox Jewry's blithe betrayal of
one of its fundamental beliefs. The question, however, cries out for fuller
treatment. I regret to say that the reasons for this phenomenon now strike me
as broader and deeper than they did in 1995, so that despite their utter lack of
substantive merit, their sociological force will be very difficult to overcome.

The Ideal of Unity and the Avoidance of Communal Strife

The point is self-evident. Every practising Jew has heard countless sermons
about the imperative to love one's neighbour, particularly one's Jewish neighbour. At the barest minimum, the annual Torah reading about Korah's
rebellion against Moses (Num. 16–17) generates discourses about the severe
prohibition against fomenting disputes within the community. (I heard one
of these just two days before writing this sentence.) While rhetoric about this
value cuts across all Orthodox—and Jewish—lines, in our context it is especially compelling for Modern Orthodox Jews who maintain cordial, even formal relations with other denominations and pride themselves on embracing
an ideal of tolerance.

Nonetheless, the refutation of this argument is no less self-evident than its
initial attractiveness. A few weeks after the Torah reading about Korah, very
different sermons are preached about the zeal of Pinchas (Num. 25). I will
not burden the reader with a detailed recapitulation of arguments that have
appeared throughout this volume. No Orthodox Jew believes that everyone
committed to the Jewish community has the right to serve as an Orthodox
rabbi because of the value of unity. The appeal to this principle is relevant
only after one has concluded that Lubavitch messianism is essentially within
the boundaries of Orthodoxy. Since this is precisely what is at issue, the argument begs the question.

Orthopraxy and Appearance

Two distinguished academic observers of contemporary Orthodoxy have chided me for incurable naivety in imagining that matters of faith play any significant role in the community. Anyone who looks and acts the way Lubavitch hasidim do will be treated as an Orthodox Jew. Period. A traditional talmudist in full agreement with my position told me, 'If the messianists looked like you, people would react differently.' Similarly, two other academics argued that issues of faith can be relevant, but only when the deviations come from the left, that is, from a group seen as more modernist than that of the critic.

In several conversations with fully Orthodox Jews, both Traditionalist and Modern, I have heard startling formulations that come close to an unalloyedly orthoprax position, to wit, that any Jew who observes the commandments remains within the fold. During the height of the *avodah zarah* discussion, I responded to this argument by saying that the Second Commandment is also part of Jewish law. It is no accident that enemies of Lubavitch through the years have laid special stress on deviations from the straightforward requirements of halakhah. This argument rests upon Chabad justifications for not sleeping in a sukkah (the hut used during the festival of Sukkot), not eating the third Sabbath meal, waiting till well into the night to recite the afternoon prayer upon the Rebbe's return from his father-in-law's gravesite, and, on one occasion in 1991, delaying the morning prayer on Sukkot till 3.30 p.m.[1] But the weightiest objection to orthopraxy as sole benchmark is that Judaism in fact has a doctrinal element no less important than practice in determining its contours.[2] I am not prepared to reconcile myself to the position that belief does not matter as long as the individual in question fulfils certain criteria of behaviour and appearance. Nonetheless, my critics may well be correct in arguing that precisely such an instinct has played a key role in discouraging a serious, effective reaction to this development.

To the degree that this is the case, I am compelled to reformulate my earlier definition of *avodah zarah*. *Avodah zarah*, it would appear, is the formal recognition or worship as God of an entity that is in fact not God provided that the believer is someone other than a Sabbath-observing Jew wearing a wig or a black hat. Beliefs and actions that any knowledgeable Jew would

---

[1] With respect to the first two issues, the problem was less with the practice itself than with the seemingly principled rejection of the requirement. On that Sukkot day in 1991, see Lipkin, *Reckoning of the World*, 112–13.

[2] Cf. my review of Menachem Kellner, *Must a Jew Believe Anything?*, in *Tradition* 33/4 (Summer 1999), 81–9.

unhesitatingly describe as *avodah zarah* if presented in the abstract cease to be *avodah zarah* the moment the perpetrators are identified as Lubavitch hasidim. Judaism, which was once a great faith, is now an agglomeration of dress, deportment, and rituals.

Prior Delegitimation

We recall that this very point about external appearance and ritual observance was made in *Yated ne'eman*, a newspaper published by followers of Rabbi Schach, in the wake of my article in *Ha'aretz*. The challenge, said the author, is to transcend externals and recognize the illegitimacy of these superficially Orthodox Jews. This sector of Israeli Orthodoxy and its counterparts in some American yeshivas do not act because they think they have already acted.

The Balkanization of Orthodoxy, or the Orthodoxy of Enclaves

How can such Jews fail to see that whatever they have done on this front remains inadequate and incomplete? While part of the explanation lies in despair born of frustration and another, conflicting part in a rose-coloured belief that by now everyone sees that Rabbi Schach was correct, there is a deeper issue that plays a very important role in other sectors of the Orthodox community as well. The challenge of modernity and the growth of religious deviationism have impelled much of Orthodoxy to turn inwards. One consequence of this orientation has been the attenuation of the instinctive sense of a Jewish religious collective extending beyond one's own group. Moreover, and very much to the point, 'group' does not even refer to Orthodoxy as a whole but to a much smaller entity.

I was once scheduled to give a talk entitled 'Varieties of Orthodoxy'. Before I began, someone approached me and asked, 'So how many varieties are there?' I replied, 'I don't know. All I know is that it's not a rational number.' Quips aside, the main focus of many Orthodox Jews is on their own subgroup, *anshei shlomeinu* in the terminology of hasidic communities, *yeshiva layt* in non-hasidic groups, and so on. Consequently, the key argument of this book, namely, that something called Judaism, even Orthodox Judaism, has changed because of the legitimation of Lubavitch messianists, invokes categories that have lost much of their force. I do not mean to suggest that Orthodox Jews—even in Traditionalist circles—have entirely rejected their responsibilities to the larger community, but instincts have undoubtedly changed. The question posed—even in Modern circles—is, 'Does anyone in my immediate environment believe that the Rebbe is the Messiah?' If the answer is no, then the rise of this movement becomes a curiosity or at most a mildly disturbing development. A blinkered, myopic question produces a blinkered, myopic response.

Orthodox Interdependence, or the Interlocking of the Enclaves

Paradoxically, another critically important explanation stands in stark contrast to the psychology of balkanization, namely, the reality of interdependence. The cancer of messianism is contiguous to, even entwined with, healthy tissue. This, of course, makes it all the more dangerous, but it also makes excision all the more difficult.

I have had more than one conversation in which an Orthodox Jew would tell me that I am overreacting because Lubavitch is after all a relatively small, ultimately peripheral movement, and then agree under questioning that he or she would have considerable practical difficulty living without it. Messianist rabbinical courts interact regularly with other courts. How should they be regarded? What is one to do with non-Chabad courts on which messianists serve? How easy is it to depose rabbis of Israeli towns who have signed the messianist ruling? We have already seen that Lubavitch rabbis, many of them messianists, play a disproportionately large role in a significant number of countries throughout the world. How realistic is it to propose that they be marginalized? A respected, Lubavitch-run kashrut organization is the supervisor of choice for restaurants full of messianist propaganda. How does one deal with it? Rejecting Lubavitch ritual slaughter or refusing to attend a messianist synagogue would cause no little inconvenience to Orthodox travellers and require significant modification of vacation plans. How realistic is the expectation that concern with a matter of abstract theology will change established behaviours? Jews have made great sacrifices for their faith, but sacrificing a vacation—or a favourite food—may well be too much to expect. A friend formulated this point even more sharply and cynically than I. 'People who act religious', he said, 'would actually have to be religious.' To place the challenge in perspective, I am inclined to say that masses of Orthodox Jews would have to muster one-tenth of one per cent of the religious devotion exhibited by Lubavitch emissaries.

While I believe that with respect to most Jews in Israel and North America the sharp tone of the preceding sentences is entirely justified, there is a significant group facing far more serious problems. Many Jews throughout the world live in cities and countries that residents of the largest Jewish centres merely visit on business or vacation. When the food, school, and synagogue on which you depend are suddenly rendered unacceptable, you face a religious challenge not one whit less daunting than that of the most devoted Lubavitch emissary.

Compounding these difficulties is the fact that not all Lubavitch hasidim are messianists and not all messianists endorse a theology of *avodah zarah*. It is much easier to accept false assurances that a majority maintain Orthodox beliefs than it is to take the very difficult steps implied in the previous paragraphs and outlined explicitly in the following chapter. Rather than face these consequences, Jews force themselves to conclude that Second Coming messianism promoted by people whose services we need is not really Second Coming messianism, that legitimation is not legitimation, that *avodah zarah* is not *avodah zarah*. Many Orthodox Jews react negatively to assertions that Jewish law has changed in response to social or economic pressures. Such Jews will have to look intently into the mirror and into their hearts and ask whether they are not redefining the most central laws and beliefs in the Jewish religion for precisely such reasons. Of all the causes of inaction, this is the most intractable, and it may well result in a permanent and profound betrayal of Judaism.

'Good Things'

'But they do so many good things.' I cannot count the number of times I have heard this sentence or its equivalent. Some of these 'things' are acts of kindness that are not specific to Judaism; others involve the teaching of Torah and the successful dissemination of Jewish rituals to the proverbial four corners of the earth. Much of the loyalty to Lubavitch on the local level flows from personal relationships established with Jews of all stripes—Orthodox, Conservative, Reform, even secular—in need of an understanding heart, a sympathetic ear, a favour large (sometimes very large) or small. In an increasingly impersonal society, Lubavitch emissaries exult in the joy of others and empathize with their sadness, forging bonds that cannot be broken by mere theology. On the ritual level, they not only encourage the wearing of tefillin and the lighting of Sabbath candles; they provide travellers with kosher food, a Passover seder, a prayer service, and more. The beneficiaries of this largesse cannot help but feel deep gratitude. Chosen by the Rebbe as a global elite assured special standing in the messianic age,[3] the emissaries live lives of remarkable devotion at which ordinary mortals can only marvel.

[3] Note the little vignette in *Kfar Chabad*, 731 (Eve of Sukkot 5757; 27 Sept. 1996), where the Rebbe tells the discouraged wife of an emissary, 'We are on the verge of being privileged to experience the coming of the Messiah. You must decide where you want to be at that time—pushed far back among the masses or together with the emissaries who see the face of the king and sit first in the kingdom.'

And yet—if the emissary is a messianist, all this good turns to ashes. This is not to say that acts of kindness are not admirable in and of themselves. One who performs such acts is deserving of appreciation. But once they are part of a messianist mission, they become instruments of a campaign to deform Judaism. A rabbi with blunter inclinations than mine reacted to another rabbi's reference to the kindness shown by Lubavitch emissaries by saying, 'Jews for Jesus do the same thing.' Even I found this jarring, but, like it or not, the point is precisely on target. Fundamental beliefs cannot be compromised because of kindness, nor can we trade such beliefs for a myriad of additional Sabbath candles—or even a myriad of additional observant Jews.

News of Lubavitch successes that would have once lifted my spirits now hurl me into depression. Not long ago, I received a brochure from the Lubavitch Development Fund announcing a dramatic $30 million project to build ten new Jewish community centres in the Former Soviet Union with significant funding from a wonderful Modern Orthodox philanthropist whom I know very slightly. Instead of rejoicing, I reminded myself of the multitude of FSU signatures on the messianist ruling. Immense energies and resources are being invested by the most well-meaning people to help undermine the Jewish religion.

Transient Insanity

I have heard the assertion that the messianists are crazy no less frequently than the argument that 'they do good things'. Sometimes this appears to mean that because the belief is insane it will surely not last and should therefore be treated with benign—or malign—neglect. Wrong-headed as I think this is, it is at least a coherent contention. In most cases, however, such terms as *meshugoyim* (crazy people) or *meshuga'as* (craziness) seem to be regarded as a self-defining argument, minimizing the gravity of the messianists' belief. Because they are crazy, they cannot be taken seriously and should be ignored —or even supported for their 'good things'.

This strikes me as so incoherent that I have difficulty spelling out what it means. Most people who proffer this argument appear to agree that the belief stands in fundamental contradiction to the classical Jewish messianic faith. But if it is in fact antithetical to that faith, how does the fact that it is also a form of craziness qualify the believer to be a rabbi, judge, principal, or teacher? Does the very fact that it is crazy somehow make it compatible with Judaism?[4] Imagine a colloquy in which someone objects to hiring a

---

[4] For those concerned with the posthumous destiny of people who might be heretics, the assertion that they are crazy can serve as mitigation. This, however, is not my concern here, nor is it the primary context in which the argument is used.

messianist rabbi. A supporter of the appointment responds, 'It is true that he maintains a profoundly un-Jewish belief, but this drawback is neutralized by a countervailing consideration that works in his favour. He is crazy.'

Moreover, the large majority of messianists are not crazy in any clinical sense; to suggest that they are is crazy. I have already explained the difficulties that Chabad non-messianists face in interpreting teachings of the Rebbe that appear to point to his messiahship. Against this background, for a hasid to defend the messianist position through the strategies detailed throughout this volume is decidedly not a violation of the canons of reason. An outside observer is, of course, free to argue that belief in the resurrection of the dead, or in a personal Messiah, or, for that matter, in God, is itself irrational. By that criterion, however, all serious Orthodox Jews, myself included, are crazy.

I should, I suppose, be gratified if readers of this book have been so persuaded by its argument that they consider a contrary position insane. Probably the percentage of unbalanced individuals is higher in the messianist population than in the Jewish population as a whole. But in general terms I had no intention of arguing that believers are crazy in any serious sense of the term, and this is simply not the case. Would that it were. The messianist position needs to be rejected because it fundamentally distorts Judaism, not because its adherents require medical attention or even because the belief itself violates reason any more than many other doctrines of supernaturalistic religions.

This point, of course, also bears on the confident predictions of the inevitable, imminent disappearance of belief in the messiahship of the Rebbe. In *Jewish Action*, I already noted that a religion called Christianity, which also believes in a redeemer who dies and is resurrected, has not yet disappeared. Let me reinforce this by pointing to a much more recent example to which I have already alluded.

Mormonism was born in modern times as a dramatically deviant form of Christianity. It makes highly problematic historical assertions about relatively recent events. Its theology makes that of Lubavitch messianists appear like the very soul of rationality. It has a sophisticated, well-educated constituency. It sends emissaries to the ends of the earth to make converts and is, I believe, the fastest-growing religion in the world. Whatever one thinks of the rationality of the first generation of believers, I have already noted that children brought up in such a faith can surely accept it without damage to their rational faculties. If Mormonism flourishes, why is Chabad messianism necessarily condemned to extinction?

I will not hazard a prediction as to the medium- or long-term survival of this belief. Menachem Friedman, the most distinguished sociologist of Orthodoxy in Israel, believes that in a leaderless movement, the group with the most fervent message is likely to prevail. If so, then all the worldwide institutions of Chabad will eventually be mobilized to spread this version of Judaism. However that may be, I certainly do not see what will destroy this faith as long as the rest of Orthodoxy legitimates messianist rabbis and the bulk of the Chabad educational system remains in messianist hands. Confident prognostications of imminent demise fly in the face of reason.[5]

*

In addition to these major causes of communal inaction, there are four miscellaneous factors that deserve brief consideration. First, some observers have no doubt been persuaded by messianist arguments that this belief is not so terrible. The most egregious examples are the few non-Chabad signatories of the rabbinic ruling. With the decline of a pervasive Christian threat, familiarity with messianic texts and sensitivity to messianic deviationism has waned to the vanishing point even among learned Jews.

Second, a distinguished head of a well-known yeshiva recently remarked that at least one of the hasidic representatives in AARTS opposed the expulsion of Oholei Torah on the grounds that hasidism itself would be threatened if hasidim were told to reject what they believe their rebbe taught them. This argument appears to maintain that hasidim have carte blanche to do whatever they wish to Judaism; it is hard to think of a stance that would threaten the standing of hasidism more than this.

Third, this is not an easy battle to fight. To begin with, it takes time and effort. The talmudic scholar who initially argued that he does not act because of the silence of great rabbis ultimately wrote that he does not have the time needed for what would inevitably become an all-consuming struggle. Though I have managed to do other things in the last six or seven years, I can testify to the fact that he is not entirely mistaken. The difficulty is greatly magnified by the fact that Lubavitch messianists are part of an influential movement with impressive human and financial resources that defends its interests vigorously. Few people have the stomach to pursue a campaign that will cause them to be publicly labelled haters, dividers, liars, heretics, egotistical seekers of fame and fortune, ignoramuses, snakes, asses, and pigs. The

---

[5] The failure to take this development seriously has led more than one person to suggest that I stop wasting my time on it. A very distinguished scholar who is an observant Jew urged me to remain focused on the area where I do important work, the Middle Ages. In other words, I should spend all my time studying what is really significant, namely, Jewish arguments against Christianity in the Middle Ages, rather than diverting my attention to the trivial issue of whether Jews still believe those arguments. I wonder what this scholar tells his students about the uses of history.

reluctance to 'start a fight with Lubavitch' is palpable, particularly on the part of those whose institutions might lose support from Lubavitch sympathizers or whose positions might even be jeopardized. The unfathomable enormity of what has occurred to Judaism in less than a decade finds striking expression in the fact that excluding believers in the messiahship of a recently buried rabbi from Orthodox Judaism is widely seen as a courageous act. However absurd and incredible this perception ought to be, it reflects a grim reality. I anticipate the reaction to this book with no small measure of apprehension.

Finally, several people have chided me for attributing so much significance to this development. After all, they say, I am a historian, and a historian of ideas no less. I should know better than most that beliefs change, that religions evolve. Hasidism itself was an innovation. Religious Zionism was an innovation. Why must I remain in a state of arrested development, embalmed in the world of the Barcelona disputation?

It should not be necessary to say that historians are permitted to have commitments to abiding principles. The decision to study history is not a decision to embrace change as one's supreme value. The challenge is always to determine the legitimacy of a given innovation, and in this case I believe that a core element of Judaism is at stake. Here is my response to one of my critics:

I consider this issue [especially] serious for roughly the following reasons: (1) It involves a key element in the fundamental understanding of one of the *ikarei ha'emunah* (fundamentals of the faith). (2) Comparable movements throughout Jewish history have been thoroughly, vehemently, angrily delegitimated by *kelal yisra'el* [the Jewish collective]. I refer both to the movements that persisted after the candidate's death and the movements that died with his death precisely because their posthumous survival was unthinkable. (3) Denial of such a belief has been a part of the very definition of Judaism in innumerable confrontations with the Christian mission. Accepting it as a harmless enthusiasm awards victory to Christianity on a fundamental matter of principle. (4) It has led to *avodah zarah* in both past instances and shows signs of doing so again.

Explaining a catastrophe does not diminish it or neutralize the obligation to confront it. Jews have remained loyal to their deepest commitments in the face of greater obstacles than these. Medieval believers in astrology insisted that the decree of the stars was not immutable, that concerted, sometimes heroic human effort could overcome it. The same must be true of the decree of the sociologists.

FOURTEEN

What Must Be Done?

JUDAISM stands on the threshold—perhaps beyond the threshold—of a fundamental transformation. If we are to return to the *status quo ante* of 1993, we must first take steps that would have seemed self-evident in that so recent but so distant past. For purposes of clarity and impact, I will present my position in language appropriate for definitive rulings. No one realizes more clearly than I that I do not have the standing to issue such rulings.

The most important principle is that no messianist should be treated as an Orthodox rabbi or functionary in good standing. No such person should be permitted to head or even serve on a rabbinical court. Every Jew must categorically refuse to appear before a court headed by a messianist even if legitimate rabbis only are hearing this particular case. If there is no other rabbinical court in that city, one must insist on an ad hoc tribunal of three rabbis or on a trip to the nearest city with an acceptable court. This means that no one may appear before the court of Crown Heights or of the city of Montreal or the one presided over by Rabbi Gedalyah Axelrod in Haifa. Other rabbinical courts should interact with these courts or recognize their decisions only in cases of extreme emergency such as jeopardy to someone's eligibility to marry. If a messianist does not head the court but merely serves on it, I might agree under sufficient duress to appear before a kosher panel of that court, though I would make every effort to avoid this.

No messianist should serve as a communal or synagogue rabbi. Anyone with the authority to remove such a rabbi is obligated to do so. A resident of that community should not recognize its rabbi as his or her religious authority in any respect. An organization like the National Council of Young Israel must immediately expel a synagogue that refuses to dismiss a messianist rabbi. One must pray in private rather than attend a synagogue in which the standard messianist formula is recited.

No messianist should be appointed as Jewish Studies principal or teacher in an Orthodox yeshiva. A communal rabbi told me that a rabbinic authority had permitted him to hire a principal who gave an evasive answer about his messianist beliefs and who would almost certainly be attending a synagogue with an overtly messianist rabbi. The reason was the familiar one that this is merely a *meshuga'as*. Thus, students have a rabbinic role model who believes in a deceased Messiah.

Messianist institutions, no matter how many 'good things' they do, must be excluded from the Orthodox community. Any school where the *Yeḥi* is recited or where messianist educators teach should be removed from AARTS. Orthodox Jews should not attend the functions of such institutions or raise money for them. When a rabbi asked me about criteria for evaluating Lubavitch institutions, I replied that I would contribute (or allow its leader to give a class in my synagogue) only if I received a written statement that read, 'I recognize that the Lubavitcher Rebbe *zatzal* is not and will not be the Moshiach, and I would not permit anyone who believes that he is to teach Torah in my institution.' No one should even dream of sending a child to a Lubavitch-run school or summer camp without receiving such a letter from the director, and an equivalent statement must be elicited from every Lubavitch candidate for a position as rabbi or teacher. I know a rabbi who imposes a comparable requirement and says that no one has ever agreed to sign. This may be because even non-messianists regard such a loyalty oath as an insult, but there is simply no alternative. A presumption of acceptability (*ḥezkat kashrut*) on this matter no longer exists.

If the messianic faith of Judaism is to survive intact, these guidelines must be followed even in difficult cases. One of the contexts in which even my resolve weakens is that of the Former Soviet Union, where messianist rabbis provide many communities with the only access they have to Jewish rituals and education. But support of those rabbis by Orthodox Jewry means that a massive sector of world Jewry will be led by a messianist rabbinate recognized as an integral part of Orthodoxy, precisely the outcome that must be avoided at all costs. Fortunately, there are alternatives. To my knowledge, the most wide-ranging of these is the Traditionalist Orthodox Va'ad L'Hatzolas Nidchei Yisroel, which runs programmes in thirty-five locations. Its director assures me that, with a major infusion of funds, it could provide permanent religious services and institutions in these and many more venues. Though my own identification is with Modern Orthodoxy—and I strongly urge support of the FSU programmes of the Orthodox Union, the Yeshiva and University Students for the Spiritual Revival of Soviet Jewry (YUSSR), and other such organizations—the Va'ad probably provides the best hope of serving the religious needs of this Jewry without undermining Judaism itself. Anyone tempted to support Chabad in the FSU should triple his or her intended contribution and direct it to the Va'ad and its Modern Orthodox counterparts. This is a genuine emergency.

We now move from legitimation and support for messianist Judaism to more detailed issues of Jewish ritual law. The messianist belief in itself, with its abolition of Judaism's criteria for identifying the Messiah, is seen by some as heresy. I have studiously avoided that term, though I do not quarrel with those who use it. Since consuming meat slaughtered by a heretic is at least problematic, some people who avoid Lubavitch shechitah probably do so on these grounds alone.

We confront, however, an even greater problem than 'mere' messianist heresy. One who habitually engages in *avodah zarah* is disqualified as a ritual slaughterer, and any animal that he does slaughter is not kosher.[1] I will not recapitulate here the theological and halakhic discussions to which I have devoted several chapters and a lengthy appendix. Nonetheless, we must remind ourselves that mainstream Lubavitch has produced literature justifying prostration to a righteous man because he is pure divinity, mainstream figures quote this literature with admiring approval, and religious mentors in the major yeshivas in the movement from New York to Kfar Chabad to Jerusalem advocate a theology of *avodah zarah*. Highly educated lay people are comfortable with the term 'man-God', asserting that when you speak to the Rebbe you speak to God, and a sophisticated author emerges from exposure to Chabad principles with the conviction that there is no material difference between Lubavitch beliefs about the righteous and the Christian affirmation of the divinity of Jesus. To dismiss adherents of this theology as so marginal that they can be ignored in making halakhic assessments is to close one's eyes to reality. At the very least, we are dealing with a level of heresy more egregious and unambiguous than that of messianism alone. It is with very good reason indeed that significant segments of Traditionalist Orthodoxy avoid Lubavitch shechitah.

Mainstream Orthodoxy, both Modern and Traditionalist, has made it quite difficult to implement this policy. I recently attended a board meeting of an important Modern Orthodox organization of impeccable religiosity where we were served meat sandwiches from a Manhattan restaurant that has distributed brochures to its customers calling upon them to accept the messianic

---

[1] Babylonian Talmud, *Ḥulin* 5a. A worshipper of *avodah zarah* who believes in the authority of the Torah and its commandments is hardly typical, but I do not believe that this point undermines the prohibition against meat slaughtered by such a person. Many of the ramifications of this issue are analysed in R. Ovadiah Yosef, *Yabia omer*, vol. 1, responsum 11. The responsum deals primarily with wine rather than shechitah and with Sabbath violators rather than worshippers of *avodah zarah*, but it surveys a voluminous literature touching on all the relevant issues.

kingship of the Rebbe. I do not eat any meat supervised by the organization that certifies the kashrut of this and other messianist establishments, but most Orthodox Jews certainly do. The Orthodox Union has a somewhat better record on this issue than most supervisory organizations. It usually avoids joint supervision with overt messianists and makes at least perfunctory efforts to enquire about the theology of its Lubavitch ritual slaughterers. I still rely on the OU supervision of a largely Lubavitch shechitah, in part because a caterer who claims to feel even more strongly than I about this matter guaranteed to me that the ritual slaughterers there are not 'believers'. Nonetheless, I wonder whether I am deceiving myself.

The issue of shechitah is a particularly good illustration of the extent to which the usual rules of Orthodox behaviour are suspended when dealing with Lubavitch. Two distinguished rabbis with direct access to a member of the Council of Torah Sages informed me on separate occasions that Rabbi Yosef Shalom Elyashiv, the most respected Ashkenazi rabbinic decisor today, told the Council member that he considers the shechitah of messianists forbidden. Additional evidence of this stance was forthcoming in June 1999, when I received the following e-mail message from a friend in Israel:

My son is now in the *Kollel Zioni* [Zionist-oriented institute for advanced talmudic studies] in Moscow. He called me last week with the following *she'elah* [question of religious law]. The only shochet in Moscow is a Chabadnik who each morning says the *Yeḥi adonenu verabbenu* . . . [may our Master and Rabbi (the King Messiah) live, etc.] out loud after the davening [prayer service].

The question came up about eating meat in Russia. One of the kollelniks called Rav Simcha Kook in Rechovot [Israel]. He didn't answer directly but said that he indeed did verify that Rav Elyashiv said the meat is *treif* [non-kosher] even *bedi'eved* [after the fact; that is, one must not only make an effort to find a different shochet if available; one may not eat the meat at all].

I later checked with Rabbi Pinchas Goldschmidt of Moscow, who said that chickens from a non-problematic shochet are available, but there is sometimes a problem with meat. Since I do not have access to Rabbi Elyashiv, I cannot be certain of his position. What I do know is that many Orthodox rabbis who would normally treat a report of Rabbi Elyashiv's views with the utmost seriousness generally ignore this one with little or no investigation.

Unless one is to disqualify all Lubavitch ritual slaughterers, the task of a supervisory organization is to ask whether the candidate for a post believes that the Rebbe is the Messiah. If the answer is *unequivocally* negative, my own tentative inclination would be to stop there since such a person is unlikely to endorse a theology of *avodah zarah*. If the answer is not unequivocally negative, I would not hire him. However, I can understand the view that this is not enough to disqualify someone. In that case, one absolutely must ask the following questions: 'Do you believe that the Rebbe is the Essence and Being of God placed in a body? Do you take this to mean that the Rebbe's entire being is divinity? If so, let us see how literally you understand this. Do you believe that the Rebbe knows everything? That he can effectuate anything he wants? That he was (and is, if you believe that he remains literally alive) incapable of sin?' I would not quarrel with someone who insisted that these questions must be asked even of non-messianists. Failure to follow this admittedly unpleasant procedure is an abdication of responsibility and generates a grave risk of providing the unsuspecting public with non-kosher food.

Serious problems also arise with respect to the writing of Torah scrolls, tefillin, and mezuzas. Scribes are required to write the divine names in these documents with special concentration and intent. Even a learned rabbi who is unwilling (on what I consider idiosyncratic grounds) to forbid the shechitah of a Lubavitch adherent of *avodah zarah* told me that the need for intent persuades him that a scribe is probably different. This means that one should not purchase any of these items from a Lubavitch scribe whose theology has not been determined. In the light of the extraordinary efforts made by the Rebbe to encourage every Jewish man to don tefillin, it is excruciatingly ironic that the tefillin provided by Lubavitch hasidim cannot be presumed kosher. If they were written by an adherent of the literal belief that the Rebbe is pure divinity, whoever puts them on not only fails to fulfil the commandment but is guilty of reciting improper blessings and taking the name of the Lord in vain. I stopped attending a convenient morning prayer service on days when the Torah is read because a new Lubavitch Torah scroll was donated to the synagogue and the donor, who is himself a non-messianist hasid with impeccable views, did not respond to a request for assurances regarding the theology of the scribe.[2] For analogous reasons, a congregation retaining the services of a Lubavitch cantor must determine his stand on these questions, and here false messianism alone is more than sufficient reason to seek a different candidate.

[2] See R. Eliezer Fleckeles, *Teshuvah me'ahavah*, nos. 110, 112, for an exchange between the author and R. Yechezkel Landau about a Sabbatian scribe in the waning days of the movement. R. Fleckeles notes that Sabbatians oscillate between calling Shabetai Tzevi the Messiah and calling him God, and points to a single instance in which tefillin were found containing a picture of a turban along with a verse about God applied to Shabetai. Although there was a wide spectrum of beliefs in late Sabbatianism, this was enough to persuade him that the Torah in question may not be used. The evidence for *avodah zarah* in contemporary Chabad seems eminently sufficient to meet this standard.

Finally, Lubavitch witnesses at weddings and especially divorce proceedings require special scrutiny. While every effort must be made to seek grounds for leniency in cases where the validity of a divorce is challenged, the potential consequences of using an unacceptable witness are so grave that there is little room for error and none for inertia and complacency.

While I consider all of these very difficult changes in the current behaviour of most Orthodox Jews to be absolutely mandated by Jewish law, I do not expect most lay or even rabbinical readers to implement them without consultation with their own rabbinical authorities. Very few rabbis, however, no matter how learned they are, are fully aware of the material presented here, and they do not usually take seriously even what they have heard. Anyone who wants a meaningful ruling should lend the book to his or her rabbinical authority and request an answer only after the rabbi has read it with care.

This discussion of practical issues has wrenched me away from the prime focus of the book, which has nothing to do with meat, tefillin, and divorce. A reader can disagree with every word that I have written about these matters while still recognizing the crucial need to delegitimate Second Coming Judaism. The tortuous personal trajectory detailed in this account began with messianism, not *avodah zarah*, and that is where it will end.

Epitaph

THE CLASSICAL MESSIANIC FAITH of Judaism is dying. Most Orthodox Jews may still adhere to it, but their willingness to grant full rabbinical, institutional, educational, and ritual recognition to people who proclaim the messiahship of a dead rabbi conveys the inescapable message that such a proclamation does not contradict an essential Jewish belief. Mainstream Orthodoxy now appoints heads of rabbinical courts, teachers, and principals who conclude their prayers on the Day of Atonement with the passionate, twin affirmations, 'The Lord is God! May our Master, Teacher, and Rabbi, the King Messiah, live for ever!' By extending this recognition, Orthodox Jewry has repealed a defining element not only of the messianic faith but of the Jewish religion itself.

As we observe the death throes of a fundamental Jewish belief, let us not deceive ourselves as to the identity of its executioners. They are not the messianists. Sectarians can establish sects; only the mainstream can transform a religion. It is not the former who are the perpetrators and the latter the facilitators. Quite the contrary. The messianists may have launched the assault, but Orthodox Jewry writ large has administered the fatal blow.

In spite of everything, I continue to cling to a slender thread of hope that it is not too late, that the patient can be revived, that Judaism's criteria for identifying the Messiah can still be rescued from the brink of extinction. This hope may well prove illusory. If so, then let this book serve as a eulogy, an obituary, and an epitaph.

תהא נשמת האמונה המשיחית הצרופה של עם ישראל צרורה בצרור החיים
עם נשמות קדושי עליון שמסרו את נפשם עליה.

*May the soul of the authentic messianic faith of the Jewish people
be bound up in the bond of life along with the souls of the exalted martyrs
who sacrificed their lives to preserve it.*

On a Messiah who Dies
with his Mission Unfulfilled:
Selected Quotations

JEWISH LITERATURE, especially polemical literature, is replete with arguments that the Messiah could not have come—or that Jesus could not have been the Messiah—because the prophecies of the end of days remain unfulfilled. In most cases, these two formulations appear interchangeable. Since the very definition of the concept 'Messiah' is rooted in biblical descriptions of visible, global redemption, Judaism properly recoiled from scenarios without a shred of biblical justification in which the Messiah's mission is interrupted by death in an unredeemed world. The God of the Hebrew Bible sends the messianic king to accomplish his end, not to follow a two-part script in which the hero tragically dies and the words 'to be continued' suddenly appear on the screen.

The Jewish denial of this possibility has been expressed in various forms through the ages. This appendix presents a small but, I hope, representative sampling of relevant texts. Three of these, from Maimonides, Nahmanides, and *Sefer haberit*, have appeared in whole or in part earlier in the book.

1. *Midrash Bereshit Rabba* 98:

Our father Jacob saw Samson [in a prophetic vision] and thought that he was the King Messiah. Once he saw that he died, he said, 'This one too has died. For your salvation I wait, O Lord.'

2. Jacob ben Reuben, *Milḥamot hashem* (c.1170), ed. Judah Rosenthal (Jerusalem, 1963), 78:

'And this is the name by which he shall be called: the Lord our Righteousness' (Jer. 23: 6). You [the Christian] said that the Messiah is called 'the Lord our Righteousness'. Now according to your words, how can you say that this messiah of yours 'reigned as king and prospered'? How were 'Judah and Israel delivered in his days', and how did they 'dwell securely' (Jer. 23: 5–6)? . . . [This figure] is the [true] messianic king, as it is written afterwards, 'Assuredly, a time is coming—declares the Lord—when it shall no more be said, "As the Lord lives, who brought the Israelites out of the land of Egypt", but rather, "As the Lord lives, who brought out and led the offspring of the House of Israel from the northland and from all the lands to which I have banished them." And they shall dwell upon their own soil' (Jer. 23: 7–8). And all of this has not yet come to pass.

3. Maimonides (1138–1204), *Mishneh torah*, Laws of Kings 11: 4, in the uncensored version.

If a king arises from the House of David who studies the Torah and pursues the commandments like his ancestor David in accordance with the Written and Oral Law, and he compels all Israel to follow and strengthen it and fights the wars of the Lord—this man enjoys the presumption of being the Messiah. If he proceeds successfully, defeats all the nations surrounding him, builds the Temple in its place, and gathers the dispersed of Israel, then he is surely the Messiah. But if he does not succeed to this extent, or is killed, it is evident that he is not the one whom the Torah promised; he is, rather, like all the complete and righteous kings of Israel who have died. . . .

Jesus of Nazareth, who imagined that he would be the Messiah, [caused Israel to stumble]. But no human being can grasp the thoughts of God, for our ways are not his ways, and our thoughts are not his thoughts. In fact, all the events surrounding Jesus of Nazareth and the Ishmaelite [Muhammad] who came after him were for the purpose of straightening the way for the King Messiah and preparing the entire world so that all will serve the Lord together, as it is written, 'For then I will make the peoples pure of speech, so that they all invoke the Lord by name and serve Him with one accord' (Zeph. 3: 8). How is this so? [Because of Christianity and Islam,] the entire world has been filled with discussion of the Messiah, the Torah, and the commandments. These matters have spread to the distant isles and to many benighted nations, who debate these issues and the commandments of the Torah. Some say that they were true but have been annulled in our time since they were not intended for all generations. Others say that there are hidden meanings in them so that they are not to be understood according to their plain sense; rather, the Messiah has already come and revealed their secrets. But when the King Messiah will truly arise, succeed and be exceedingly exalted, they will all repent and realize that their forefathers inherited falsehood and their prophets and ancestors misled them.[1]

---

[1] In pondering the fate of Jewish belief during the past seven years, I have allowed myself to speculate half-seriously about a narrower providential explanation for the rise of Christianity. I wondered whether God might have allowed a form of non-pagan *avodah zarah* centred on a deceased messiah to grow to maturity outside the Jewish community so that Jews could formulate a response that they would be able to draw upon in resisting such a development when it unfolds within. The extraordinary hurdles that I face in this campaign would be insuperable if not for the long history of Jewish rejection of Christian belief. Nonetheless, I hesitate to ascribe such a motive to God when it appears that the preparation that He has provided us to meet this challenge is proving insufficient when put to the test.

4. **Nahmanides, The Barcelona Disputation (1263), in *Kitvei ramban*, ed. Chavel, 311.**

I cannot believe in [Jesus'] Messiahship, for . . . the prophet said that in the time of the Messiah, 'No longer will they need to teach one another and say to one another, "Know the Lord", for all of them shall know me etc.' (Jer. 31: 34). And it says, 'For the earth shall be filled with knowledge of the Lord, as waters cover the sea' (Isa. 11: 9). And it says, 'They shall beat their swords into plowshares. . . . Nation shall not take up sword against nation; they shall never again know war' (Isa. 2: 4). And from the days of Jesus till today the entire world is full of pillaging and robbery . . . indeed, how difficult it would be for you, my lord the king, and for your knights, if they would never again know war. Furthermore, the prophet says concerning the Messiah, 'He shall strike down a land with the rod of his mouth' (Isa. 11: 4). The aggadah explains . . ., 'If the messianic king is told, "This nation has rebelled against you", he will say, "Let the locust come and destroy it"' . . ., and this was not true of Jesus.

5. **R. Meir ben Simeon Hame'ili (13th century), *Milḥemet mitzvah*, in *Shitat hakadmonim al masikhtot nazir, zevaḥim, arakhin, utemurah vesefer milḥemet mitzvah*, ed. Moshe Yehudah Hakohen Blau (New York, 1973).**

[Jesus] called himself king and maintained that the verse 'Behold, your king is coming to you etc.' (Zech. 9: 9) was said of him. Yet he granted kingship to Caesar and commanded that tax be paid to the publicans, which is not the behaviour of a king. Thus he gave the lie both to himself and to the prophecy of the prophets that the King Messiah will be exalted above all the kings of the earth, and that all of them will serve him, not that he and his fellowship will have to pay them tax. Rather, they will all be subordinate to him and subservient to him, as it is written in a psalm that they interpret to refer to him, 'Let all kings bow to him and all nations serve him' (Ps. 72: 11). This man, on the contrary, was subservient to kings and fearful of them. (p. 318)

It is written about the Messiah who is to come in the future, 'The righteous will flourish in his time, and well-being will abound till the moon is no more' (Ps. 72: 6), and it is written, '[And he will judge] among many nations' (cf. Isa. 2: 4), 'and he shall strike down a land with the rod of his mouth' (Isa. 11: 4). It is also written, 'He shall proclaim peace to the nations' (Zech. 9: 10). Here is proof that this prophecy will be fulfilled in the future and has not yet been realized, since none of this was to be found in your messiah. It is clear, then, that it will be fulfilled in the days of our Messiah, who will come speedily in our days. (p. 351)

6. **Moses Hakohen of Tordesillas, *Ezer ha'emunah* (14th century), in *Rabbi Moses ha-Kohen of Tordesillas and his Book Ezer ha-Emunah— A Chapter in the History of the Judaeo-Christian Controversy*, ed. Yehuda Shamir, Part II (Coconut Grove, Fla., 1972), 64.**

There will be great peace in the world when our Messiah comes . . . as Isaiah said, 'In the days to come, the Mount of the Lord's House etc. and the many peoples shall go etc.', and it is written, 'He will judge among the nations' (Isa. 2: 2–4). And Micah too prophesied similarly. Consequently, Isaiah says here, 'They will do nothing evil nor vile etc.' (Isa. 11: 9). And if you say that Jesus was the Messiah, how was this prophecy fulfilled in his time?

7. R. Yom Tov Lipmann Muelhausen, *Sefer nitzaḥon* (1390), ed. T. Hackspan (Altdorf, 1644), sect. 227, p. 126.

'A shoot shall grow out of the stump of Jesse, a twig will sprout from his stock. The spirit of the Lord shall alight upon him: a spirit of wisdom and insight, a spirit of counsel and valour, a spirit of devotion and reverence for the Lord.' Here too the Christians stumbled and referred this to the Nazarene. . . . [But] it is explicit in the passage that this king will come regarding the redemption of Judah and Israel, as it is written, 'In that day . . . as there was for Israel on the day when it left the land of Egypt' [Isa. 11: 11–15], and these matters have not yet come to pass.

8. R. Shimon ben Tzemah Duran (1361–1444), '*Keshet u-Magen*: A Critical Edition', ed. Prosper Murciano (Ph.D. diss., New York University, 1975), 45.

[Jesus'] mistake was that he thought he would be the Messiah, but when he was hanged his thought was annulled.[2]

9. Solomon ibn Verga, *Shevet yehudah* (early 16th century), ed. Azriel Schohet (Jerusalem, 1947), in an account of the Tortosa disputation (1413–14) referring to the rabbinic assertion that the Messiah was born on the day of the destruction of the Temple (p. 105).

Our belief and the belief of every Jew is that if a man comes, gathers the dispersed of Israel, builds the Temple, and all the nations gather to him and call out unanimously in the name of God, then we will say that he is the Messiah. Any statement that [appears to] contradict this has an interpretation.

10. Isaac ben Abraham Troki (*c.*1533–94), *Ḥizuk emunah* (New York, 1932), I: I, p. 23. Troki was a Karaite, but his work was immensely popular among mainstream Jews, who amended it, translated it, and disseminated it widely.

We have many valid proofs contradicting the Christian position by demonstrating that Jesus was not the Messiah at all. . . . The fourth is that the promises designated for the time of the awaited Messiah were not fulfilled in his time, and these matters are required conditions for believing in the true Messiah.

11. R. Judah Aryeh da Modena (1571–1648), *Magen vaḥerev*, ed. S. Simonsohn (Jerusalem, 1960), 73.

Once we are speaking about the Messiah and whether he was Jesus, we cannot refrain from investigating the terms 'Messiah' and 'king', which are so inappropriate to the

---

[2] In the edition reprinted by Makor (Jerusalem, 1970), p. 11a, an erroneous reading (*keshenitgalah* instead of *keshenitlah*) renders the sentence incoherent.

life he lived and the deeds he did. . . . Let us begin with the universal practice of calling the future redeemer Messiah; they too call him *Christo* in Greek, which in the ver-
nacular is 'anointed', and in Hebrew *mashiah*. Let us see how it is possible to say that
this was the Nazarene. When and where was he anointed, and who anointed him?
Everyone knows that those actually anointed were the king and the priest. [Though
the term *mashiah* can sometimes be used metaphorically, in this case it surely refers to
a real king with genuine authority like that of David] who will rule over Israel and the
nations and whose kingship will be powerfully established. But where and over
whom did Jesus rule, and where were the judgement and justice that he did in the
earth? [Christians cite Zech. 9: 9 to show that the Messiah will be poor], and from
this they 'prove' a second fantasy—that the Messiah will come twice. . . .

12. R. Phinehas Elijah Hurwitz of Vilna (1765–1821), *Sefer haberit hashalem* (Jerusalem, 1990), 521.

We are obligated to believe that a Jewish man will come who will begin to save Israel
and will complete the salvation of Israel in that generation. One who completes the
task is the one, while one who does not complete it in that generation but dies or is
broken or is taken captive (Exod. 22: 9) is not the one and was not sent by God.

13. David Berger and Michael Wyschogrod, *Jews and 'Jewish Christianity'* (New York, 1978), ch. 2, 'Jesus and the Messiah' (reprinted by permission).

Both of us share responsibility for the full content of the book, but this chapter was assigned to me. Needless to say, I do not include this selection because
it carries any authoritative weight but because it reflects my best effort to present the standard Jewish position in a polemical context. It also illustrates the
ongoing importance of this argument to the Jewish defence against the
Christian mission, a point that was brought home to me just two days before
I wrote this appendix, when a sophisticated activist in an anti-missionary
organization approached me to enquire about the means of responding to the
Lubavitch belief in a Second Coming. *Jews and 'Jewish Christianity'* was aimed
at a popular audience, including people of high-school age, and so its arguments are formulated in colloquial language.

Let us begin with the fundamental belief that Jesus was—and is—the Messiah. Since
the very word *Christ* means Messiah, this belief lies at the heart of the Christian faith.
But how do we go about testing the claim that Jesus was the Messiah? The first thing
to remember is that the term *Messiah* gets its basic meaning from biblical prophecy; it
is only because of such prophecy that people expected the Messiah in the first place.
Any person claiming to be the Messiah must, therefore, be able to pass a very exact-
ing test: has he done what the Bible expects of the Messiah?

We must begin, then, by taking a look at the Bible as a whole. How would the
Messiah of the Hebrew Bible be described by someone who had just read the text for

the first time without any knowledge of either Judaism or Christianity? If our hypo-thetical friend were a perceptive reader, his first observation would be that the word *messiah* simply refers to any king or high priest who was anointed with oil in accor-dance with the custom of ancient Israel. There is, however, a rather special king from the House of David who is described in several biblical passages as the man who will preside over a redeemed and perfected world. Eventually, Jews came to use the word *Messiah* (this time the capital *M* is justifiable) to refer to that king, and it is in this con-text that any man claiming to be the Messiah must be judged.

In other words, the only way to define 'the Messiah' is as the king who will rule during what we call the messianic age. The central criterion for evaluating a Messiah must therefore be a single question: Has the messianic age come? It is only in terms of this question that 'the Messiah' means anything. What, then, does the Bible say about the messianic age? Here is a brief description by a famous Christian scholar: 'The recovery of independence and power, an era of peace and prosperity, of fidelity to God and his law, of justice and fair-dealing and brotherly love among men, and of personal rectitude and piety' (G. F. Moore, *Judaism* (Cambridge, Mass., 1927–30), ii. 324). If we think about this sentence just for a moment in the light of the history of the last two thousand years, we will begin to see what enormous obstacles must be overcome if we are to believe in the messianic mission of Jesus. If Jesus was the Messiah, why have suffering and evil continued and even increased in the many cen-turies since his death?

We don't know much about messianic figures between the period of the Hebrew Bible and the lifetime of Jesus. The first Christian century, however, was a time when tensions between Jews and Romans were reaching the boiling point, and we know of at least three or four 'Messiahs' during that century. In that sense, Jesus' career was not unique; it reflected a fairly common tendency in Jewish society at that time. In fact, at least one of the other Messiahs was also killed by the Romans. Unlike the other move-ments, the one started by Jesus survived its founder. The direction that Christianity took differed from what Jesus had in mind (as we shall see, he would have protested his designation as God with every fibre of his being), and it is very important to under-stand how the belief that Jesus was the Messiah survived his death.

In the light of what was universally understood to be the function of the Messiah, the crucifixion was a terrible logical and psychological blow to Jesus' followers. The Messiah was supposed to redeem Israel, bring peace and justice to the world, make the wolf live peacefully with the lamb, and see to it that 'they learn war no more' (Isa. 2: 1–4, 11: 1–10). Something, it seemed, had gone terribly wrong. How could the paradox of a crucified Messiah be explained? . . .

There can be little doubt that many of the first-century Jews who had been attract-ed by Jesus' preaching sadly submitted to the conclusion forced upon them by his death. They had been mistaken. God had not yet chosen to redeem his people. They would have to wait once more, however long it might take, however much their hearts might be aching for redemption.

But for others this was impossible. The belief was too strong, the hurt too great, to face the terrible truth. There simply had to be an explanation, and such an explanation was found.

First of all, Jesus was said to have been resurrected. Secondly, the Bible was examined with the purpose of finding what no one had ever seen there before—evidence that the Messiah would be killed without bringing peace to the world or redemption to Israel. . . . Thirdly, there was the expectation of a second coming, at which time Jesus would carry out the task expected of the Messiah. And finally, there had to be an explanation for the first coming and its catastrophic end. The basic structure of this explanation was to shift the function of the Messiah from a visible level, where it could be tested, to an invisible one, where it could not. The Messiah's goal, at least the first time around, was not the redemption of Israel (which had clearly not taken place) but the atonement for original sin, which was seen as a sort of inner redemption. Whether or not such an atonement was necessary is something we'll discuss later, but at least no one could *see* that it hadn't happened.

Please don't misinterpret this as an argument which describes Jesus' disciples as cynical manipulators of religious beliefs. These are beliefs which resulted from powerful psychological and historical pressures and were surely sincere. But an understanding of the process that formed these beliefs should arouse some scepticism, not about the sincerity with which they were held, but about their truth.

At this point, a little digression of about sixteen hundred years might be helpful in giving us another glimpse of this process. You may have heard about Shabetai Tzevi. He was the most successful Jewish Messiah since the time of Jesus, and in 1666 there were very many Jews throughout the world who believed in him. In September of that year, however, he was forced to become a Muslim, and ten years later he died.

The conversion was as great a shock to Shabetai Tzevi's followers as Jesus' crucifixion was to his. Again, most Jews overcame the need to continue believing and bitterly resigned themselves to yet another disappointment. But others could not, and the similarities between their explanations and those of the early Christian are really striking. (Historians, by the way, generally agree that the basic similarities result mainly from the similarity in the problems faced and not from Christian influence on these seventeenth-century Jews, many of whom lived in Muslim countries.) Shabetai Tzevi was said to have predicted his conversion. He too was expected to return again—first from his converted state and later from beyond the grave. The reality of his death was denied, and here too we find a story about an empty grave. Once again people examined the Bible to find what no one had ever found before—this time, evidence that the Messiah could *convert* without bringing peace to the world or redemption to Israel. And once again they were 'successful'; where Christians, for example, found that Isaiah 53 prophesied that the Messiah would be 'pierced', Shabetai's followers found that he would be 'profaned'. (The word *meholal* in verse 5 can be translated either way.) And finally, there had to be an explanation for the first coming and its catastrophic end. Once more the solution was a shift of the Messiah's function, at least the first time around, from a visible to an invisible level. Here the Messiah had to enter the world of evil to liberate invisible 'sparks of holiness', and while we can't go into details here, the explanation is quite as brilliant as its Christian counterpart, if not more so. Eventually, the ultimate step was taken, and Shabetai Tzevi too came to be considered God.

These are both fascinating episodes in the history of religion. In both cases, a Messiah ended his career in a way that made continued belief in him impossible; in both cases, the impossible was made possible by *redefining the role of the Messiah so that it would fit this man's career*.

The Jewish people have refused to take the easy way out. If the Bible's description of the Messiah has not been fulfilled, there is only one conclusion to be reached: he has not yet come. To Jews, who were often subjected to mockery and contempt when asked where their Messiah was, this conclusion was painful, sometimes excruciatingly painful. But an honest facing of the facts made it—and still makes it—inescapable. In adversity and joy, through holocaust and statehood, Jews faithful to the Torah and the prophets can only repeat the words of their forefathers: 'I believe with complete faith in the coming of the Messiah, and though he may tarry I shall wait for him every day, hoping that he will come.'

The Parameters of Avodah Zarah

Avodah zarah, which I have defined as the formal recognition or worship as God of an entity that is in fact not God, has played an important role in this book. I have argued that Chabad theology utilizes language capable of leading to *avodah zarah*, which is possible even in the context of an essentially monotheistic theology, and that this step has in fact been taken by people who function in the central institutions of the movement. While I hope that the fundamental points were established in the body of the work, they demand a more careful treatment that will do at least some justice to their delicacy and complexity.

I noted in Chapter 1 that very early in the Rebbe's tenure, he asserted on a single occasion that a rebbe is 'the Essence and Being [of God] placed into [*areingeshtelt in*] a body' and that once the expression came to public attention at a much later date, it led Rabbi Schach and others to level the accusation of *avodah zarah*. It was in response to these attacks that Avraham Baruch Pevzner published *Al hatzadikim* (On the Righteous) in 1991, where he compiled and analysed an imposing list of mainly hasidic sources to defend this formula. As far as I can determine, the work, published by the House of the Union of Chabad Hasidim (Beit Agudat Ḥasidei Ḥabad) in Kfar Chabad, emerged out of circles at the heart of the Lubavitch community, where it is widely respected as a standard explication of the Rebbe's remarks. In addressing its theology, then, I will be engaging a mainstream work of considerable influence. This excursus is by no means a diversion into the exotic byways of Chabad.

Since any discussion of 'the Essence and Being of God placed in a body' and what this might mean must take place against the background of the Jewish rejection of the Christian doctrine of the Incarnation, we must first look at the standing of that belief in Jewish law and theology. Classical Christianity affirms that the second person of a triune God took on flesh in Jesus of Nazareth. In our context it is essential to stress that whatever the special characteristics attributed to the 'son', he is understood to be an integral part of the one God, and some Christians even proposed that the persons of the Trinity refer to divine attributes such as power, wisdom, and will.

Jews argued that the Trinity cannot be explained so innocuously in the light of the belief that one and only one of the persons took on flesh. But in the course of their arguments they made it perfectly clear that their objections to Christian theology would not be diminished if Jesus were seen as the incarnation of all or part of an undifferentiated God. Jewish polemicists and theologians regarded the belief that a human being could be God as philosophically untenable, and rabbinic authorities condemned it as heresy and, when translated into practice, as *avodah zarah*.[1]

For Christians, the fact that Jesus was seen not as a separate deity but as the embodiment of the one Creator God made all the difference in the world. Many Jews agreed, some of them with emphatic enthusiasm, that this point distinguished Christianity from paganism; nonetheless, even the belief that the true, unitary God was incarnated in a man was enough to cross the critical line, at least if the believer was a Jew. While numerous Jewish texts assert that Christianity is *avodah zarah*, Rabbi Meir ben Simeon Hame'ili, a thirteenth-century talmudist and polemicist from Narbonne, formulated the most explicit response I know to the argument that the monotheistic character of the Christian belief in the Incarnation should render it acceptable:

[Even non-Jews, said the Jewish protagonist, must believe] that the world has a Creator who is one true [God], primeval with no beginning or end, who exercises providence over created beings, treating each man in accordance with his deeds. The [Christian] responded, 'We too believe this'. The [Jew] replied, 'Take someone who believes this and ask him if he knows who this Being is. If he answers that he is a man born of a woman affected by all physical experiences including death—and he is the Creator God—then [the person questioned] has denied the Creator of the world if he is mistaken.[2]

---

[1] The most recent discussion of the legal sources in a rabbinic mode is a series of responsa by R. Yehuda Herzl Henkin, *She'elot uteshuvot Benei Banim*, vol. iii (Jerusalem, 1997), nos. 34–6. Jacob Katz's *Exclusiveness and Tolerance* (New York, 1961), best read in the Hebrew *Bein yehudim legoyim* (Jerusalem, 1960), addresses much of the relevant material from an academic perspective. Cf. my forthcoming article on Katz's contribution to the understanding of medieval Jewish–Christian relations in the proceedings of a May 2000 Harvard University conference on the legacy of Jacob Katz. See too Rabbi J. David Bleich, 'Divine Unity in Maimonides, the Tosafists and Meiri', in Lenn Evan Goodman (ed.), *Neoplatonism and Jewish Thought* (Albany, NY, 1992), 237–53. For a thorough analysis of the philosophical arguments against the Trinity and Incarnation, see Lasker, *Jewish Philosophical Polemics against Christianity*, 45–134. See too my *The Jewish–Christian Debate in the High Middle Ages*, app. 5 ('Who Was Incarnated?'), pp. 366–9.

[2] *Milḥemet mitzvah*, Parma MS, fo. 43ᵛ. Hebrew text also in William Herskowitz, 'Jewish–Christian Dialogue in Provence as Reflected in Milḥemet Mizvah of R. Meir ha-Meili' (DHL diss., Yeshiva University, 1974), 111.

A 16th-c. Italian Jew under detention during a period of persecution asserted that because

Rabbi Meir was a sophisticated polemicist well aware that Christians see Jesus as a manifestation of one aspect of the triune God, not as the totality of the Deity. Nonetheless, he asserts that a conception of the Creator that includes His embodiment in an individual who can be described as fully God effectively denies the true Deity. The passage leaves no doubt that in R. Meir's view, worship of such a Creator constitutes *avodah zarah*.

The most influential medieval Jewish text that addresses the special character of Christianity is not in a polemical work but in the classical compilation of northern European talmudic commentaries known as Tosafot.[3] The Tosafists address the character of an oath in which a Christian swears in the name of God without any explicit reference to Jesus. According to the dominant Jewish interpretation of this passage of Tosafot, it describes such an oath as an act of 'association' (*shituf*) because a Christian taking it is thinking of Jesus of Nazareth along with the Creator of heaven and earth. Tosafot concludes that such an oath is not forbidden to non-Jews. It is clear from their discussion, however, that it is forbidden to Jews as a form of *avodah zarah*. If this were not an oath but an analogous act of worship, i.e. if someone prostrated himself to God while including Jesus in his mind, this might be prohibited even to non-Jews and would surely be full-fledged *avodah zarah* for a Jew. In sum, Christians are different from pagans because they worship the Creator of heaven and earth; nonetheless, Jewish worship of Jesus as a manifestation of God, and even the worship of God understood to include Jesus, is *avodah zarah*.[4]

Christians regard the Trinity and Incarnation as a manifestation of 'the First Cause', they do not commit *avodah zarah*. Ironically, it was his Christian interrogator, a Jewish convert to Christianity, who reacted incredulously and asked whether 'a person who believes that a particular man is God and accepts him as such is a worshipper of *avodah zarah* or not'. The unfortunate Jew replied that if the believer thinks that this man is 'a god separate unto himself' with no relationship to 'the God who created heaven and earth in whom we the Children of Israel believe', then he is a worshipper of *avodah zarah*. If, however, he believes in the incarnation of the true God, then he is not, even though the belief is forbidden and renders him a sinner. (See Ishmael Hanina ben Mordecai Harofe, *Sheva ḥakirot* (Husiatyn, 1903), 2 ff. = *Hashaḥar* 2, pp. 17–19.) The sincerity of these remarks is of course highly suspect, though compare the argument of Solomon Modena, another 16th-c. Italian Jew, published and discussed in David Ruderman, 'A Jewish Apologetic Treatise from Sixteenth-Century Bologna', *Hebrew Union College Annual*, 50 (1979), 253–76.

In the light of the Lubavitch arguments we shall encounter below, it is interesting that one of Modena's grounds for absolving Christianity of the charge of *avodah zarah* is his (highly dubious) contention that Christians do not maintain that the *essence* of God was incarnated. He also makes a misleading analogy to the position held by R. Abraham ben David of Posquières (Rabad) that although anthropomorphism, or a corporeal conception of God, is an erroneous belief, it is not heretical. Anthropomorphism is a mistaken understanding of God; Christian incarnationism identifies an existing (or once existing) human being with God. There is no question that Rabad, no less than Maimonides, considered worship of that human being *avodah zarah*.

[3] Tosafot on *Sanhedrin* 63*b* s.v. *asur*; cf. Tosafot on *Bekhorot* 2b, s.v. *shema*. See also R. Yeruham ben Meshulam, *Toledot adam veḥavah* (1516), 17: 5.   [4] For a fuller analysis of this Tosafot, see App. III.

The most positive assessment of Christian theology by a significant medieval authority was that of the late thirteenth- and early fourteenth-century Provençal talmudist Rabbi Menahem Hameiri. Hameiri insisted that Christians do not worship idols and drew some very important and reasonably influential conclusions regarding the proper treatment of what he deemed to be civilized people ('nations bound by the ways of religions').[5] Nonetheless, though Hameiri may well have believed that even a Jew who engages in Christian worship does not commit *avodah zarah*,[6] no significant authority after him seriously entertained such a view. When Jews in the early years of the Reformation confronted new forms of Christianity that avoided the use of icons, they did not hesitate to say that Christian prayer even in the absence of an image runs afoul of this most serious of prohibitions.[7]

With all this in mind, let us turn now to the Rebbe's statement and to its explication in Pevzner's book. In one early address the Rebbe remarked that 'the righteous have no essence in themselves; their essence is divinity'. In the discourse that aroused major controversy, he spoke about his deceased father-in-law's continuing presence and raised the question of the permissibility of approaching God through an intermediary. Since a rebbe is a 'connecting intermediary' [who does not interrupt the divine flow], a unity is established between the hasid who is one with the rebbe and the rebbe himself, who is 'the Essence and Being itself placed into a body'. All are one.[8]

As Pevzner demonstrates, rhetoric of this sort regarding the supremely righteous is not unknown in earlier Jewish texts. The tension between divine

[5] The most recent scholarly treatment of Hameiri's view is in Moshe Halbertal, *Between Torah and Wisdom: Rabbi Menahem Hameiri and the Maimonist Masters of Halakhah in Provence* (Heb.) (Jerusalem, 2000), 80–108.

[6] R. Henkin, *She'elot uteshuvot benei banim*, iii. 121, is certain that Hameiri would have considered this *avodah zarah*, but I have difficulty reconciling some of Hameiri's rulings with this understanding. See my discussion in 'Jews, Gentiles, and the Contemporary Egalitarian Ethos: Some Tentative Thoughts', in the forthcoming proceedings of the Orthodox Forum of 2001.

[7] Rabbi Saul Levi Mortera, one of the major rabbinic authorities in 17th-c. Amsterdam, wrote a substantial treatise devoted in significant part to this point. See his *Tratado da verdade da lei de Moises*, ed. H. P. Salomon (Coimbra, 1988), and the discussion in Miriam Bodian, *Hebrews of the Portuguese Nation* (Bloomington and Indianapolis, Ind., 1997), 72–3. Bodian's subsequent point that popular attitudes towards Dutch Calvinism among the former Marranos were more positive than their feelings towards the Catholicism of the Iberian peninsula is of considerable historical interest but has no relevance to the halakhic issue. See also *Ḥazon Ish*, 'Yoreh de'ah' 62: 21–2, where it is asserted that one must worship an existing rather than an imaginary entity to commit *avodah zarah* (rather than to be guilty of *minut* (heresy) alone), but an individual whose soul still exists for the purpose of judgement qualifies. The passage goes on to discuss the status of an image dedicated to such an entity, but the original point of the discussion appears to be precisely that the image is not necessary to generate the act of *avodah zarah*.

[8] Photocopies of the relevant passages from the Yiddish *Likutay sikhes*, ii. 444, 510–11, were provided by Pevzner at the beginning of his book.

immanence and transcendence is central to Judaism, and the relatively mild assertion that a righteous person can be the dwelling place for the divine presence can be found in Nahmanides' commentary on the Torah and in other medieval and modern works. By early modern times, such language becomes stronger in a handful of pre-hasidic authors, and many forms of hasidism speak of the presence of God in all of creation obscured to a greater or lesser degree by real or apparent impediments.[9] The divine presence is particularly strong in the righteous, who can annul their own essence in the service of God. Several of these texts draw an analogy between the righteous and the Temple. Just as the Essence of God rested in the Temple, so it is manifest in these human temples.

Maimonides would certainly have reacted with considerable unease—to put the matter mildly—had he been confronted with such language, and the assertion that I cited earlier by unnamed rabbis in the Association of Advanced Rabbinical and Talmudical Schools (AARTS) that hasidism itself is *avodah zarah* may well have flowed from deep disquiet over this theology. Nonetheless, there is a gulf between a rhetorical or metaphorical use of these formulations in an effort to capture the meaning of God's presence in the world and the belief that a human being is fully and literally divine. Here Pevzner's learned book is dangerously undiscriminating.

What does it mean to say that one's entire essence is divinity? The author's initial explanation is moderate and, given the expressions in some earlier texts, unexceptionable:

When one annuls his essence completely and does not feel himself to be an essence at all but rather feels that his entire essence consists in the fact that God created him and sustains him every hour and moment, so that his entire nature consists solely in doing the will of God through the study of Torah and the observance of the commandments, that righteous man becomes a chariot for God, who dwells within him eternally.[10]

However, the analysis that follows, cited approvingly from another Chabad rabbi, proposes a more radical understanding. It appears to read with absolute literalism a classic Chabad teaching that during Torah study at the highest level of religious devotion, the nullification of essence in the subordinated entity is so complete that such a man does not even possess an essence that is nullified before God and fulfils his command; rather, that man's essence has disappeared to the point where his speech is literally the voice of

---

[9] The strongest version of this position is sometimes described as acosmism. For some relevant texts along with an accessible analysis, see Norman Lamm, *The Religious Thought of Hasidism* (New York, 1999), ch. 1. See too several of the works cited above, Ch. 1 n. 1.   [10] *On the Righteous*, 3.

God. As the discussion proceeds throughout the book, it is clear that this status is understood to persist uninterruptedly during every moment of the
supremely righteous man's life.

To illustrate the fundamental point, the rabbi quotes a parable allegedly
widespread in Chabad circles that unintentionally illustrates the dangers of
avodah zarah inherent in this theology. A king, says the parable, may appro-
priately place his crown on a hook or a piece of furniture but not on the head
of a soldier. The reason for this is that the soldier, despite his subordination
to the king, 'is a self-conscious being; consequently, if the king's crown is
placed upon his head this means that the crown rests on the head of another
person, and this is essentially rebellion against the king'. If, then, it would be
possible for the soldier to annul himself to the point where he becomes like
the hook on the wall, then the crown could be placed upon him. Precisely
this level of self-annulment is achieved by the supremely righteous.[11]

It follows, however, from this very parable that one who does not believe
that the soldier can achieve (or has achieved) this level of self-annulment—or
that he achieves it only sporadically—must maintain that placing the crown
on his head or treating him as the king is indeed an act of rebellion. If the
crown is that of God, such rebellion is the essence of *avodah zarah*. A literal
reading of this parable would require us to believe that the supremely righteous never possess any self-consciousness at all, that when they ask God for
help they are addressing themselves or an aspect of themselves, that when
they repent and ask for forgiveness on the Day of Atonement, their prayers
are incoherent. The moment we reject these absurdities and recognize the
existence of some level of separate self-consciousness in the righteous, we are
impelled to classify the assertion that they are literally nothing but divinity as
an affirmation of *avodah zarah*.

The parable is also helpful in examining the proper limits of the analogy
between the righteous and the Temple. One who prostrates himself before
God while facing the Temple sanctuary may or may not believe that the divine
presence is more fully manifest in that location. But however he understands
the sanctity of the Temple, he is not confusing the stones, which are not sen-
tient beings, with God. Moreover, even in the absence of such confusion,
Judaism places restrictions on bowing to unauthorized inanimate objects
believed to contain the spirit of the true God.[12] When the object of adoration

---

[11] *On the Righteous*, 3–4.

[12] For academic discussions of this and related issues, see Kalman P. Bland, *The Artless Jew:
Medieval and Modern Affirmations and Denials of the Visual* (Princeton, 2000); Lionel Kochan, *Beyond
the Graven Image: A Jewish View* (New York, 1997); Moshe Halbertal and Avishai Margalit, *Idolatry*
(Cambridge, Mass., 1992).

is not an inanimate object but a human being, who thinks and speaks and exercises volition, the assertion that all these thoughts, statements, and volitions are literally those of God confuses this human being with the Deity. One who believes this and proceeds to prostrate himself before that individual commits unambiguous *avodah zarah*.

Pevzner himself goes on to provide some halakhic analogies in a discussion that may betray his own uneasiness with the implication that righteous people have literally no identity of their own at all. Thus, he says, certain foods become legally annulled to other foods when both varieties are eaten together. 'The object that is annulled takes on the definitions and laws of the object to which it is annulled.'[13] While this perception of annulment may avoid the absurdities implicit in the earlier discussion, it still asserts that a supremely righteous individual has the full legal status of God. We would do well to remember that standard Christianity asserts that Jesus is fully God and fully man. Once a human being is identified as fully God, Jewish law regards him as an object of *avodah zarah* whether or not he is also seen as man.

Both Pevzner and A. Avraham, the probably pseudonymous author of the article in *Beis Moshiach* responding to my piece in *Ha'aretz*, cite with apparent approval a passage in *Nishmat adam*, an early seventeenth-century work by Aaron Samuel of Kremenetz (d. *c.*1620), asserting that because certain rabbinic scholars have souls that are a spark of the divine, 'one who serves them [*oved otam*] and bows towards them is actually serving (or worshipping) God'. Such scholars are 'actually God as it were'.[14] Even this author uses the phrase 'as it were', speaks of 'a spark' of the divine inevitably connected to the indivisible Deity, and says that the scholar is 'compared' (*nimshal*) to God; his justification for serving (or worshipping) such God-like scholars is unique, to my knowledge, in all of Jewish literature. Pevzner and my pseudonymous critic not only give every impression of endorsing this unparalleled comment; they speak of the transformation of this object of worship into nothing but divinity.

The difference between the theology of *Nishmat adam* and that of these Lubavitch authors is evident from the earlier work's ensuing discussion, which is not cited by either Pevzner or Avraham. *Nishmat adam* proceeds to speak of the danger that even a small sin can damage the exalted soul of the righteous far more than the ordinary soul of the average Jew. The author warns the righteous to be especially vigilant to avoid even minor sin, and

[13] *On the Righteous*, 4–5.
[14] Ibid. 46–7; cf. A. Avraham, 'And They Believed in God and in Moses His Servant', 39.

surely, he adds, they must avoid major ones.[15] The passage takes for granted that such sin is a real possibility; it knows nothing of the notion that the righteous individual has so annulled himself to the divine that he is nothing but God, a notion that would render the passage incoherent. For Pevzner, on the other hand, it is utterly impossible for such a righteous individual to so much as experience self-satisfaction at his exalted status, an experience that would contradict his very essence.[16]

In the same vein, both Pevzner and Avraham egregiously misuse a passage in a classical hasidic work, *Kedushat levi* of Rabbi Levi Yitzhak of Berdichev (*c*.1740–1810), to justify bowing to a righteous man as the essence of God. As Pevzner presents it, there is a contradiction in Rabbi Levi Yitzhak's book. In one passage, *Kedushat levi* comments on Genesis 33: 20, whose plain meaning is that Jacob named an altar that he set up, 'God, the God of Israel'. The Sages understood the verse differently, taking it not as 'He [Jacob] called it God, the God of Israel', but reading instead, 'The God of Israel called him [Jacob] God'. Rabbi Levi Yitzhak cites the rabbinic statement and remarks, 'The matter is to be interpreted in a manner that will prevent you from asserting God forbid [*ḥas veshalom*] that Jacob was called God so that one should worship him [*la'avod lo*]; Heaven forbid that one should say this.' Pevzner ends the quotation at this point followed by an 'etc.', and for the time being I shall follow his lead.

The allegedly contradictory passage comments on Deuteronomy 17: 3. It asserts, in Pevzner's abbreviated quotation, that 'we find in the Torah that people bowed to the righteous. . . . And we find that the Holy One Blessed Be He called our father Jacob "God", that is, because he observed the entire Torah he had the aspect of "God". Similarly all the righteous have this aspect because of the command of the Torah, and it is permissible to bow to them.'

To Pevzner, this is an outright contradiction. The four classic acts of *avodah zarah* in talmudic law are sacrificing an animal, burning incense, pouring a libation, and prostration. Since prostration is one of these four, how could Rabbi Levi Yitzhak assert that worshipping a righteous man is forbidden despite the ascription of the term God to Jacob and then proceed to permit bowing to him for the very same reason? The answer, says Pevzner, is in the intent of the worshipper. One who bows to a righteous man in the belief that this man possesses sanctity on his own engages in forbidden worship, but one who does so with the understanding that he is bowing to someone who has annulled himself entirely to God acts in a fully permissible manner.[17]

[15] Aaron Samuel of Kremenetz, *Nishmat adam* (Jerusalem, 1989), 100–1.
[16] *On the Righteous*, 7.   [17] Ibid. See too pp. 25–6.

Before we proceed, it is worth pondering the full enormity of this assertion. Since Pevzner stresses that there is no difference between bowing and
the other forms of worship, it follows that it is permissible in principle to
pour a libation to a righteous man, to burn incense to him, and to sacrifice an
animal to him as long as this is done with the realization that the man's own
essence has been completely effaced and replaced by that of God. Though
Pevzner does not say this, I presume that the only reason such acts are not
appropriate is the peripheral consideration that they may be performed only
in the Temple. I do not believe that there is a modicum of exaggeration in
saying that Pevzner would have to conclude that when the Temple is rebuilt,
libations may well be poured to the resurrected Rebbe, whose entire essence
is divinity.

Rabbi Levi Yitzhak of Berdichev had no intention of saying anything of
this sort. The passage in *Kedushat levi* addresses a verse in which the Torah
speaks of a man or woman who turns to the worship of other gods and bows
down to them, 'to the sun or moon or any of the heavenly host which I did
not command'. The final phrase appears awkward, and Rabbi Levi Yitzhak
notes Rashi's comment that it means 'which I did not command you to worship'. He then proposes his own reading of the phrase that explains why one
can bow to a righteous man but not to the heavenly host.

Before examining his interpretation, we must remind ourselves of a fundamental point: Jewish law permits bowing to a human being as long as the
intention is honour rather than worship; in this respect bowing is very different from the other three modes of worship. The author of an important
medieval commentary on the talmudic tractate *Sanhedrin* attributed to Rabbi
Nissim Gerondi (Ran; 1310–?1375) argued that even bowing to someone
whom you do not consider divine can occasionally cross the line from 'prostration of honour' (*hishtahava'ah shel hidur*) to 'prostration of divinity' (*hishtahava'ah shel elohut*). Thus, because he considers 'prostration of honour'
inapplicable after death, he concludes that bowing to any deceased individual
such as Muhammad or a Christian saint is *ipso facto* 'prostration of divinity'
and hence *avodah zarah*.[18] In any event, it is unequivocally permissible to bow
to a living person as a form of honour; consequently, biblical evidence that
people bowed to the righteous presents no fundamental difficulty.

Since Rabbi Levi Yitzhak surely knew this, it is highly improbable that he
raised the problem in a rigorously legal context. *Kedushat levi* is a homiletical
work, and its objectives are pietistic and inspirational. Nonetheless, Rabbi

[18] *Ḥidushei haran, Sanhedrin* 61b. The real author of this work is probably a somewhat earlier
Spanish talmudist.

Levi Yitzhak was apparently uneasy about bowing to someone other than God without a compelling reason. If the person is a king or prince, the reason is obvious and unproblematic. With respect to the righteous, he may have been concerned about Maimonides' ruling that even one who does not attribute divinity to the heavenly spheres commits *avodah zarah* by bowing to them out of a desire to honour God through the servants He Himself has honoured.[19] Since the righteous can be described as precisely such servants of God, Rabbi Levi Yitzhak proposes his distinction.

Here then is a fuller text of *Kedushat levi* on Deuteronomy 17: 3:

'To the sun or the moon which I did not command': See Rashi: 'which I did not command you to worship'. . . . It appears [to me that the likely meaning of the verse is the following]: We find in the Torah that people bowed to the righteous as in the case of Obadiah's bowing to Elijah, for the righteous have God's Torah. And we find that the Holy One Blessed Be He called our father Jacob 'God'; i.e. because he observed the entire Torah he had the aspect of 'God'. Similarly all the righteous have this aspect because of the command of the Torah, and it is permissible to bow to them. But it is forbidden to bow to the sun and the moon, which do not have the command of His holy Torah. This then is the meaning of 'to the sun and the moon which I have not commanded'; i.e. they do not have my command, namely, the Torah that was given to Israel.

It is, then, appropriate to honour the righteous because they possess God's Torah, not because their essence has become full divinity. By honouring them one honours the Torah of God.[20] On the evidence of this passage alone, no one would so much as imagine that Rabbi Levi Yitzhak means to say that bowing to the righteous is permissible precisely and only because they have annulled themselves to the point where one is literally bowing to God Himself. To Pevzner, the evidence pointing towards this understanding lies precisely in the earlier passage's outraged denial that it is permissible to worship the righteous!

Kedushat levi on Genesis had indeed provided an alternative interpretation of the rabbinic statement about Jacob—hardly surprising in a homiletical work. That interpretation was meant to prevent anyone from entertaining the idea that Jacob may be worshipped, and it is no accident that Pevzner does not quote it. The irony is that he and his followers take the earlier passage's

---

[19] *Mishneh torah*, 'The Laws of *Avodah Zarah*' 1: 1. See above, Ch. 10 n. 1.

[20] This formulation is a subtle but, I think, intentional deflection of the passage in *Nishmat adam*, which ends with a reference to this very verse and explains that one can serve the righteous because they are the Temple of God. In that passage the reference is to the divine character of their souls; to R. Levi Yitzhak the point is that they possess the divine command in the form of the Torah.

vigorous protest against the notion that the righteous may be worshipped (or 'served') as God—a protest that may well be aimed against the anomalous passage in *Nishmat adam*—and use it as a foil to transform the passage on Deuteronomy into advocacy of precisely such worship.

Pevzner, we recall, constructed the following distinction: Rabbi Levi Yitzhak in Genesis meant to prohibit worshipping a righteous man only when he is understood to be divine in his own right. The passage in Deuteronomy, which permits prostration, must refer to a worshipper who bows with the correct understanding that the object of his adoration has been completely taken over by pure divinity. The Talmud often argues against a proposed distinction by asserting that the text in question should have made it explicit *(liflog velitnei bedideh, bameh devarim amurim . . .)*. In the Genesis passage, Rabbi Levi Yitzhak explains why the rabbinic text saying that Jacob is God does not mean—Heaven forbid—that it is permissible to bow to him. If Pevzner were correct, this is where the relevant distinction should have been specified. 'God called Jacob God', Rabbi Levi Yitzchak should have said, means that the patriarch is nothing but the Creator, but not that he is a separate deity. Hence, it is forbidden to worship him with the latter understanding, but it permissible to do so with the former. Instead, the passage in *Kedushat levi* on Genesis 33: 20 reads as follows:

'And the God of Israel called him [Jacob] *el*': the matter is to be interpreted in a manner that will prevent you from asserting—Heaven forbid [*ḥas veshalom*]—that Jacob was called God so that one should worship him [*la'avod lo*]; Heaven forbid that one should say this. We will explain why the specific name 'the God of Israel' is used here. The reason is that *el* [referring to Jacob] means powerful and able. Now . . . it is known that a righteous man rules, as it were, over the decrees of God by annulling an evil decree against Israel and turning it into good. It is truly the supernal will, resulting from [God's] love of Israel, that a righteous man annul the evil decree for good. This is the meaning of [the rabbinic dictum], 'Who called Jacob *el*', i.e. the one with the ability to annul what is decreed above and turn it to the benefit of Israel? 'It was the God of Israel', who wants what is good for Israel, not what is bad for them, and wishes only to shower them with all that is good.

In this passage, Rabbi Levi Yitzhak understands *el*, which I have carefully transliterated with a lower case 'e', to mean nothing more than 'endowed with great power'. It is unmistakably clear that he describes God as separate from Jacob; because of His beneficence, God endows the righteous patriarch with the authority to annul divine decrees. The utilization of this passage as a key building block in an argument turning Rabbi Levi Yitzhak of Berdichev into an advocate of *avodah zarah* is both an intellectual and religious offence of unspeakable proportions.[21]

There is also no compelling reason to understand the Rebbe's own statements in the extreme, literal sense suggested in Pevzner's stronger interpretation. A person's essence can be divinity in the sense that he completely subordinates himself to God, and the assertion that a rebbe is the Essence and Being of God and hence not an intermediary must be seen in the light of the simultaneous affirmation that the hasid is one with the rebbe. Even one who believes, as Pevzner does, that a hasid is somehow a part of his rebbe's soul surely does not believe that he loses all identity and in effect becomes the rebbe. I find myself making a deeply ironic argument since from the perspective of Judaism, the interpretation I am trying to rule out, to wit, that the entire essence of a rebbe is literally God, is more absurd than the full identification of hasid with rebbe. Thus, I am proposing a reduction of the already absurd—that a rebbe is fully God—to the slightly less absurd: that a hasid is fully his rebbe. Still, I hope that the approach is illuminating. Just as the Rebbe did not mean that he and his hasidim were literally one to the point where they were suffused with his own knowledge and did not exercise will on their own, so he did not mean that he himself was literally God.

We shall recall that the theology asserting that the Rebbe is literally nothing but divinity, that he is indistinguishable from God, that nothing can occur without his agreement, that no one can tell him what to do, that he could answer any question instantaneously, that he is entirely without limits, can be documented in mainstream figures and institutions in the Lubavitch movement. While this is more than enough to generate the most serious consequences in Jewish law, we must nonethelesss examine an additional, technical question of considerable moment. An idolatrous theology without an

---

[21] It is worth noting that one explanation proposed by the Tosafists for a talmudic regulation prohibiting a person from standing behind his teacher during prayer is concern about the appearance of bowing worshipfully in the teacher's direction. See Babylonian Talmud, *Berakhot* 27*b*, Tosafot s.v. *velo aḥorei rabo*.

Language similar to that of Pevzner's book is sometimes used by hasidim of the long-deceased R. Nahman of Bratslav. See, for example, Gedalyahu Aharon Kenig, *The Book of the Life of the Soul* [*Sefer ḥayei nefesh*] (Jerusalem, 1968), where we read that a very small number of extraordinarily righteous men from Adam to Moses to R. Nahman to the Messiah have been granted knowledge of every detail of the lives and souls of all people in history (pp. 30–4). This status is associated with the quality of extreme self-effacement that enables a figure like Moses to be included in the supernal Nothing that transcends the limits of location (p. 76). Nonetheless, even this theology, deeply troubling as I find it, stops short of the full identification of such figures with God. R. Nahman, for example, 'grasped everything that *one born of a woman is capable of grasping in this world* [my emphasis] with utter completeness' and continues to be elevated further and further after his death (p. 49). (I am grateful to Rabbi Elchanan Adler for bringing this book to my attention.)

idolatrous act is *minut*, or heresy, in Jewish law; only the act makes the believer a *practitioner* of *avodah zarah*. Any hasid who faces the Rebbe's picture while praying because he wants to worship in the direction of a manifestation of pure divinity is certainly practising *avodah zarah*.[22] But even if we set this aside, there are, I believe, several actions performed by believers in this theology that cross the behavioural line.

One of the classic forms of worship in the laws of *avodah zarah* is, as we have already seen, prostration. Orthodox Jews generally prostrate themselves once during the prayer service on Rosh Hashanah and several times on Yom Kippur. Let us say that the God you believe in contains components that embodied themselves separately and in all their purity in successive Lubavitch rebbes, a belief we have encountered earlier that is dangerously close to that of trinitarian Christianity. Depending on the precise contours of this belief, a case could be made that worship of such a deity is *avodah zarah* in and of itself.

Setting this doctrine aside, let us say further that you believe in a God whose infinite Essence is manifested in all its force in the most recent Rebbe, who continues to exist in body or soul as pure divinity. When you prostrate yourself before that God—with or without an image—it is difficult to avoid the conclusion that you are practising *avodah zarah*. This is the case, I think, even if you do not bow to the Rebbe as a separate entity or explicitly address him as God.

A look back at the passage from Tosafot about 'association' strongly supports this conclusion. Tosafot affirms that to worship a Creator who manifests himself in full force in a human being (a perfectly fair formulation of the doctrine of Jesus' divinity) is effectively to worship God along with the human being even if no reference to that 'something else' is articulated in this particular act. One might argue that because Christians habitually worship Jesus, they are almost certain to be thinking of him when they bow to God, while advocates of the theology we have been scrutinizing are considerably less likely to have such intent. This is probably true, but it is a slender reed on which to rest a conclusion that they are guilty 'only' of *minut*. We recall that believers of this sort maintain that bowing to the Rebbe is permitted in principle precisely because he is literally nothing but divinity. Their thoughts of him are obsessive. He is their saviour and their consolation. At a recent Lubavitch affair that evinced no sign of messianism, a rabbinic speaker

---

[22] See above, Ch. 7, p. 79. A friend reported to me that a religious Jewish woman very friendly to Lubavitch provided him with eyewitness confirmation of a published report that when the Rebbe was ill, a significant number of the worshippers in 770 Eastern Parkway prayed towards him rather than towards Jerusalem. See Y. Yanover and N. Ish-Shalom, *Dancing and Weeping* (Heb.) (New York, 1994), 130. I cannot, however, be sure of the theological underpinnings of this practice.

declared that 'the Rebbe runs the world' (*Der Rebbe firt di velt*).[23] Why should we believe that such hasidim never think of him when they prostrate themselves before God?

And so we come to the next point. Lubavitch hasidim regularly direct petitions to the Rebbe. Whatever formulations they use, those who believe that he is all-powerful because of his status as pure divinity are by the very nature of their faith not asking him to intercede with God but praying to him *as* God. The author of the *Beis Moshiach* article calling the Rebbe 'our God' recently wrote a book affirming the Rebbe's messiahship that was carefully reviewed by Professor Herman Branover, a respected scientist and communal leader, who is listed on the title-page as editor and described in the introduction as a virtual co-author. Obviously chastened by the criticism of his earlier formulation, the author vigorously denies that God can be a human being. He has not, however, been sufficiently chastened to prevent him from telling the reader matter-of-factly that Scripture calls Moses 'man-G-d' (Deut. 33: 1) without so much as a hint that the straightforward meaning of the Hebrew is 'man *of* God'. Working now within the parameters of what he and his editor clearly perceive as mainstream Chabad theology, he proceeds to explain how righteous men can be completely transparent vehicles for God, and asserts that 'asking their help is asking God's help'.[24] Prayer directed towards a human being, living or dead, whose thoughts and speech are seen as literally those of

[23] This was related to me incredulously by a rabbi in my neighbourhood who attended the event.

[24] Arnie Gotfryd, *Living in the Age of Moshiach*, ed. Herman Branover (New York, 2000), 40–1. The description of Moses in this passage takes only the tiniest step—if that—beyond the theology presented in the 'moderate' *parashah* booklet *Siḥat hashavua* of 16 Mar. 2001 published by the mainstream Tze'irei Agudat Chabad of Israel. In an analysis of the sin of the golden calf, we are informed that the Jews did not seek a substitute for God; rather, as many Jewish commentators have argued, they sought a substitute for Moses, who served as their link with God. This idea, says the booklet,

> had a basis. The children of Israel saw that God had taken them out of Egypt specifically by means of Moses. . . . They became aware that God enclothed Himself in Moses, to the point where [the latter's] entire essence was united with the divine holiness, so that he had no personal essence of his own. This is why the Torah calls Moses 'man of God', for the divine Presence spoke from his throat.
>
> This unification of the divine holiness with the essence of a man, soul in body, makes possible a deeper, more inward connection between man and God. Without this enclothing [*hitlabeshut*], it is possible only to believe in God and nothing more, but when the divine Presence speaks from Moses' throat, it is also absorbed into the intellect, the emotions, and the overall personality of a human being [who comes into contact with Moses]. So that the overall essence of a human being should be connected with God, the Creator reveals Himself through a human being, whom all can see and hear. Thus is created an inner and all-encompassing closeness between man and the Creator. This was the task of Moses.

As Pevzner has shown, elements of this description can be found in earlier Jewish texts, but the portrait as a whole, with its literal presentation of what Immanuel Schochet properly calls 'theomorphic metaphors', is specifically characteristic of Chabad. Even if we make the charitable and probably

God, is at the very least an appurtenance (*abizrayhu*) of *avodah zarah*, which itself generates the obligation of martyrdom, and it is probably more than that.

Finally, Lubavitch messianists sign and circulate forms accepting the kingship of the Rebbe the King Messiah (*kabalat malkhut*). For those who do not take the assertion that the Rebbe is the Essence of God in the full, literal sense, signing this statement, objectionable as it is, does not entail *avodah zarah*. But accepting a non-divine entity as your deity is a classic form of *avodah zarah*. Those who understand the formula literally, who believe that the Rebbe is omniscient and omnipotent, 'indistinguishable' from God, that when he speaks God is speaking and when you address him you address God, and proceed to 'accept his sovereignty' in this formal document, step over a frightening line.

To shine a harsh and revealing light on this question, we might want to ask if a Jew who embraces classical Christian theology regarding the Incarnation would commit an act of *avodah zarah* if he or she signed a document that did not refer to Jesus' divinity but addressed him with the formula, 'I accept your sovereignty (or kingship)'. It is more than likely that if the religious mentors at Lubavitch yeshivas whose views we have been examining signed the messianist form they committed an act of *avodah zarah* and if they urged those whom they have taught this theology to sign it they engaged in incitement to *avodah zarah*.[25]

The most fundamental theological boundary in Judaism is being breached in both faith and action while Orthodox Jews remain almost entirely oblivious. On the rare occasions when the matter is brought to their attention, they react with transient amazement consisting of disapproval and disbelief in equal measure and then move to a posture of utter indifference and equanimity. One learned Jew insisted to me that only a few lunatics could maintain this belief, but when I reacted by telling him that people with significant positions in the movement have made such affirmations, he responded, 'Well, they do cite sources, don't they?' The sociology of this response is fascinating,

unwarranted assumption that the author of these paragraphs did not quite mean that Moses actually became God, it goes without saying that readers of a publication placed in every accessible Israeli synagogue will take this material literally. The impact on Lubavitch hasidim, who not only read *Siḥat hashavua* but regularly hear such presentations from their teachers and mentors, is evident from Gotfryd's remarks.

[25] It seems probable that fervent messianists such as Levi Yitzchak Ginsberg and Sholom Charitonow have signed the form and urged others to do so. Since I cannot recall seeing Avraham Baruch Pevzner's name on any messianist declaration, I do not know whether or not he believes that the Rebbe is the Messiah.

and I have attempted to analyse it in an earlier discussion. From a religious perspective, however, it is so remarkable that no explanation can suffice to remove it from the realm of mystery.

Tosafot on 'Association' (Shituf)

IN THE PREVIOUS APPENDIX, I made reference to the Tosafists' discussion of what they call 'association'.[1] Because of the importance of this text to a key contention of this book, I present here a more detailed and technical analysis.

A talmudic regulation urged Jews to avoid business partnerships with pagans lest a dispute arise in which the non-Jewish partner would take an oath in the name of his god. The Jew would thus violate a biblical injunction that the Talmud understands to forbid causing someone to invoke the name of 'another god'. What is the standing of this regulation in Christian Europe?

The Tosafists maintain that accepting an oath from Christians is permissible because they swear in the name of the saints, to whom they do not attribute divinity. It is true, Tosafot continues, that they mention 'the name of Heaven' (presumably God) along with the saints 'and their intention is to something else [a better text reads 'Jesus of Nazareth'], but this [i.e. 'the name of Heaven' without explicit mention of Jesus] is still not an idolatrous name. Also, their intention is to the Creator of heaven [and earth].'[2] This last sentence may mean either that in addition to Jesus they have in mind the Creator or, in a formulation more accurately reflecting Christian doctrine, that while they think of Jesus their ultimate intention is the true Creator. In either case, Tosafot maintains that Christians intend to worship the true God but cross a crucial line by incorporating a human being into their conception of the divine. The Tosafists even considered the possibility that one actually pronounces the name of a foreign deity by simply saying the word 'God' with Jesus in mind, and they take for granted that the explicit invocation of his name would run afoul of this prohibition.[3]

---

[1] Tosafot on *Sanhedrin* 63*b* s.v. *asur*; cf. Tosafot on *Bekhorot* 2*b*, s.v. *shema*. See also R. Yeruham ben Meshulam, *Toledot adam veḥavah* 17: 5.

[2] Tosafot appears to be thinking of an oath attested in Christian sources which said, 'I swear in the name of the omnipotent God and these four sacred Gospels [*evangelia*].' See J. Katz, 'The History of Three Apologetic Statements' (Heb.), in id., *Halakhah vekabalah* (Jerusalem, 1986), 279 n. 60.

[3] While some Jews avoid pronouncing the name of Jesus even in a neutral context, there are

This, however, is not quite the end of the text. The enigmatic continuation, which has produced a literature unto itself, says, 'And even though they associate the name of Heaven with something else, we do not find that it is forbidden to cause someone else to associate, and the commandment not to cause a blind man to stumble [i.e. not to cause someone to sin] does not apply because Noahides [i.e. non-Jews] were not commanded regarding this [i.e. association, as an alternative version of the text says explicitly].'

The assertion that there is no prohibition against causing someone to associate is a narrow, technical point. It means that although there is a specific prohibition against causing someone to invoke the name of another god, there is no comparable, focused prohibition against causing 'association' (*shituf*). There is, however, a general prohibition against causing sin, which at first glance should forbid a Jew to create a situation in which his Christian partner will 'associate' in an oath. Tosafot concludes, however, that non-Jews, unlike Jews, are permitted to 'associate', and hence a Jew who causes them to do so has not caused sin.

Rabbinic commentators and decisors have provided two distinct interpretations of 'associate' as it is used in this text. Since the first of these interpretations can yield two quite different explanations of what Tosafot actually meant by the assertion that non-Jews are not commanded to avoid association, I shall refer to the two versions of that interpretation as 1A and 1B. According to both 1A and 1B, 'association' here refers to the unarticulated thought of Jesus included in the Christian's mind when he uses the word 'God' in his oath. One who thinks of Jesus when saying 'God', even if he sees the former as connected with the Creator of heaven and earth, is in effect acknowledging the Creator along with something else. Such an oath is prima facie an act of *avodah zarah*, and a Jew may not cause it.

Interpretation 1A assumes that the Tosafists' final response accepts the premiss that this oath is an expression of *shituf* and hence, in principle, an act of *avodah zarah*. However, it understands that response to introduce the striking principle that Jewish law has a dual standard for *avodah zarah*. For a Jew, an act of 'association' indeed constitutes *avodah zarah*, but for a non-Jew, not merely an oath but even prayer and prostration to God along with 'something else' is flatly permissible. Thus, the Jew is not causing any sin at all. This interpretation was proffered in early modern times and has been embraced in our own day by ecumenically oriented Jews because of its assertion that non-Jews who engage in Christian worship do not commit *avodah zarah*.

substantial grounds to permit this. See, for example, R. Yair Hayim Bacharach, *Ḥavot ya'ir* (Frankfurt, 1699) 1, *hasagot* 11–12, and R. Elijah ben Solomon Zalman of Vilna, *Be'ur hagra*, 'Yoreh de'ah' 157: 3.

Interpretation 1B, while agreeing that 'association' refers to the unarticulated thought of Jesus included in the oath, insists that actual Christian worship violates the prohibition of *avodah zarah* for anyone, Jew or non-Jew. Consequently, if a Jew caused a non-Jew to bow or sacrifice to the God of Christianity, who includes Jesus of Nazareth, that Jew would have caused the blind to stumble. An oath, however, is different. It is not an act of worship and hence does not rise—or sink—to the level of a prohibited form of *avodah zarah* for a non-Jew. Association *in an oath* is permitted to non-Jews; association in worship is forbidden. One proponent of 1B notes the general principle that any act of *avodah zarah* that would not be a capital offence for a Jew is permitted to non-Jews.[4] In this instance, a Jew thinking of Jesus along with the true Creator while taking an oath in the name of God would violate the general prohibition against *avodah zarah* but would not be subject to execution; hence, such an oath is not forbidden to non-Jews at all.

Explanation 2 understands 'association' differently. The problem of causing the name of another god to be mentioned has already been disposed of by Tosafot's earlier comments. The issue now is a lesser prohibition that would rule out taking an oath in the name of both God and a religiously significant entity like a saint even though that entity is not understood to be divine. It is this prohibition, not that of *avodah zarah*, which applies to Jews but not to Noahides.[5]

In sum, both 1A and 1B clearly maintain that if a Jew took an oath in the name of God understood as the Creator of heaven and earth but including Jesus of Nazareth, he would be committing an act subsumed under the prohibition of *avodah zarah*. If he prostrated himself to God so understood, he would be committing classic, full-fledged *avodah zarah*. Even proponents of explanation 2 could agree with this position, and they probably do.

[4] *Ḥazon Ish*, 'Yoreh de'ah' 62: 19.

[5] For a fairly clear exposition of this understanding of Tosafot, see Samuel ben Nathan Halevi Kolin, *Maḥatzit hashekel* on *Shulḥan arukh*, 'Oraḥ ḥayim' 146: 2, s.v. *yitḥayev*. (In one edition, the relevant paragraph was omitted, probably because of its argument that *shituf* is forbidden to non-Jews.)

Glossary

THIS glossary contains only those Hebrew or Yiddish terms that appear at some point in the book without an adjoining translation.

avodah zarah the formal recognition or worship as God of an entity that is in fact not God—literally, foreign worship (see also Ch. 10 n. 1)

daven pray

gedolim great rabbis

gemara Talmud or talmudic passage

halakhah Jewish law

halakhic pertaining to Jewish law

Ḥazal the talmudic Sages

kashrut kosher status

kosher fit for consumption according to Jewish law

lehavdil to distinguish between two phenomena that are morally, religiously, or existentially incommensurate

mashpia (pl. **mashpi'im**) religious guide or mentor, an instructor of hasidic teachings in a Lubavitch yeshiva

meshuga'as craziness

mitzvah (pl. **mitzvot**) commandment or good deed

Moetzes Gedolei Hatorah Council of Torah Sages

mohel performer of a ritual circumcision

moshiach (or **mashiaḥ**) Messiah

parashah weekly Torah reading

pesak din rabbinic ruling

rosh yeshiva (pl. **rashei yeshiva**) head of a yeshiva or instructor in Talmud in an advanced yeshiva

sefirah (pl. **sefirot**) emanation, manifestation, or quality of God in Jewish mysticism

shechitah (**sheḥitah**) ritual slaughter

shlita may he (or they) live a long, good life, amen

shochet (**shoḥet**) ritual slaughterer

3 Tammuz the date in the Jewish calendar when the Rebbe passed away

tefillin phylacteries

tzaddik righteous man, sometimes synonymous with hasidic rebbe

Yeḥi The messianist slogan 'May our Master, Teacher, and Rabbi, the King Messiah, live for ever' (*yeḥi adonenu morenu verabenu melekh hamashiaḥ le'olam va'ed*)

zt"l, zatzal = *zekher tzadik liverakhah*, 'the memory of the righteous is a blessing', an abbreviation placed after the name of a deceased individual

Bibliography

AARON SAMUEL OF KREMENETZ, *Nishmat adam* [*treatise on the soul*] (1611; repr. Jerusalem, 1989).

ABARBANEL, ISAAC, *Perush al nevi'im aharonim* [*Commentary on the Later Prophets*] (Jerusalem, 5716).

—— *Yeshuot meshiho* [treatise on the Messiah] (1828; Jerusalem, 1993).

ANON., *And He Will Redeem Us* [*Vehu yigalenu*] (Brooklyn, NY, 1994).

ANON., *The Era and Redemption in the Teachings of the Lubavitcher Rebbe* [*Hatekufah vehage'ulah bemishnato shel harebe milubavitch*] (Kfar Chabad, 1999).

ANON., *Questions and Answers about the Messiah and Redemption* [*She'elot uteshuvot be'inyenei mashiah uge'ulah*], 2nd edn. (Safed, 1996).

AVRAHAM, A., 'And They Believed in God and in Moses His Servant' ['Vaya'aminu bashem uvemosheh avdo'], *Beis Moshiach*, 170 (17 Shevat 5758), 36–40.

AXELROD, GEDALYAH, 'Do Not Touch My Anointed Ones' ['Al tige'u bimeshihai'], *Ha'aretz* (15 Jan. 1998) (English version published as 'The Prophet of God').

BACHARACH, YAIR HAYIM, *Havot ya'ir* [responsa] (Frankfurt, 1699).

BASHI, SARI, 'Hasidic Movement Grapples with Split over Messiah', Associated Press dispatch, 18 June 1999.

BERGER, DAVID, *The Jewish–Christian Debate in the High Middle Ages: A Critical Edition of the* Nizzahon Vetus *with an Introduction, Translation, and Commentary* (Philadelphia, Pa., 1979; repr. Jason Aronson, Northvale, NJ and London, 1996).

—— 'Jews, Gentiles, and the Contemporary Egalitarian Ethos: Some Tentative Thoughts', forthcoming in proceedings of the Orthodox Forum of 2001.

—— 'Judaism is Changing Before Our Eyes', *Hatzofeh*, 22 Feb. 1998 [repr. in Ch. 11].

—— 'The New Messianism: Passing Phenomenon or Turning Point in the History of Judaism?', *Jewish Action* (Fall 1995), 35–44, 88 [repr. in Ch. 2].

—— 'On False Messianism, Idolatry, and Lubavitch', *Ha'aretz*, 11 Jan. 1998 (reprinted in Ch. 9).

—— Rejoinder on the Second Coming, *Jewish Action* (Winter 5756/1995), 65–8 [repr. in Ch. 4].

—— 'Religion, Nationalism, and Historiography: Yehezkel Kaufmann's Account of Jesus and Early Christianity', in Leo Landman (ed.), *Scholars and Scholarship in Jewish History* (New York, 1990), 149–68.

—— Review of Howard M. Sachar, *Farewell España: The World of the Sephardim Remembered*, in *The New York Times Book Review*, 27 Nov. 1994, p. 18.

—— Review of Menachem Kellner, *Must a Jew Believe Anything?*, in *Tradition*, 33/4 (Summer 1999), 81–9.

BERGER, DAVID, 'The Sea Change in American Orthodox Judaism', *Tradition*, 32/4 (Summer, 1998), 27–31.

—— 'Some Ironic Consequences of Maimonides' Rationalistic Messianism' ['Al totze'oteha ha'ironiyot shel gishato haratzionalistit shel harambam latekufah hameshihit'], *Maimonidean Studies*, 2 (1991), 1–8 (Hebrew section).

—— and Michael Wyschogrod, *Jews and 'Jewish Christianity'* (New York, 1978).

BLAND, KALMAN P., *The Artless Jew: Medieval and Modern Affirmations and Denials of the Visual* (Princeton, 2000).

BLEICH, J. DAVID, 'Divine Unity in Maimonides, the Tosafists and Meiri', in Lenn Evan Goodman (ed.), *Neoplatonism and Jewish Thought* (Albany, NY, 1992), 237–53.

BLIDSTEIN, GERALD, DAVID BERGER, SHNAYER Z. LEIMAN, and AHARON LICHTENSTEIN, *Judaism's Encounter with Other Cultures: Rejection or Integration?*, ed. Jacob J. Schacter (Northvale, NJ and Jerusalem, 1997).

BODIAN, MIRIAM, *Hebrews of the Portuguese Nation* (Bloomington and Indianapolis, Ind., 1997).

BROWN, MICHAEL L., *Answering Jewish Objections to Jesus*, ii: *Theological Objections* (Grand Rapids, Mich., 2000)

BUTMAN, SHMUEL, 'Once He is So Presumptuous . . .' (Yiddish), *Algemeiner Journal*, 13 Feb. 1998.

CARLEBACH, ELISHEVA, *The Pursuit of Heresy* (New York, 1990).

CHARITONOW, SHOLOM, 'The Rebbeim, the Rebbe, Gimmel Tammuz', *Inyaney Moshiach*, Fourth Annual Edition, pp. 12–26.

COHEN, DEBRA NUSSBAUM, 'One Year after Rebbe's Death, Lubavitcher Soul Burns Bright', *JTA Daily News Bulletin*, 73: 121 (27 July 1995).

DAN, JOSEPH, *Modern Jewish Messianism* [*Hameshihiyut hayehudit hamodernit*] (Tel Aviv, 1999).

DEUTSCH, SHAUL SHIMON, *Larger than Life*, 2 vols. (New York, 1995, 1997).

DURAN, SIMEON BEN TZEMAH, '*Keshet u-Magen*: A Critical Edition', ed. Prosper Murciano (Ph.D. diss., New York University, 1975).

EHRLICH, AVRUM M., *Leadership in the Habad Movement* (Northvale, NJ, 2000).

ELIJAH BEN SOLOMON ZALMAN (the Vilna Gaon), *Be'ur hagra* [commentary on the *Shulhan arukh*], in the standard editions of the *Shulhan arukh*.

ELIOR, RACHEL, 'The Lubavitch Messianic Resurgence: The Historical and Mystical Background 1939–1996', in Peter Schaefer and Mark Cohen (eds.), *Toward the Millennium: Messianic Expectations from the Bible to Waco* (Leiden, Boston, and Cologne, 1998), 383–408.

—— *The Paradoxical Ascent to God: The Kabbalistic Theosophy of Habad Hasidism* (Albany, NY, 1993).

—— *The Theory of the Divine in the Second Generation of Chabad Hasidism* [*Torat ha'elohut bador hasheni shel hasidut habad*] (Jerusalem, 1982).

ETKES, IMMANUEL, 'Rabbi Shneur Zalman of Lyady's Career as a Hasidic Leader' ['Darko shel r. shene'ur zalman miliadi kemanhig shel ḥasidim'], *Tziyon*, 50 (1985), 321–54.

FEINSTEIN, MOSHE, *Igerot mosheh*, 'Even ha'ezer' [collection of responsa], 4 (New York, 1985).

FESTINGER, LEON, HENRY W. RIECKEN, and STANLEY SCHACHTER, *When Prophecy Fails: A Social and Psychological Study of a Modern Group that Predicted the Destruction of the World* (New York, 1956).

FLECKELES, ELIEZER, *Teshuvah me'ahavah* [responsa] (1809–21; repr. New York, 1966).

FOXBRUNNER, ROMAN A., *The Hasidism of R. Shneur Zalman of Lyady* (Tuscaloosa, Ala. and London, 1992).

FRIEDMAN, MENACHEM, 'Habad as Messianic Fundamentalism: From Local Particularism to Universal Jewish Mission', in Martin E. Marty and R. Scott Appleby (eds.), *Accounting for Fundamentalisms: The Dynamic Character of Movements* (Chicago, 1994), 328–57.

FRIEDMAN, MOSHE, *A Good Resolution about Moshiach: Many Lubavitchers Thank the RCA* (Brooklyn, NY, 1996).

GINSBERG, LEVI YITZCHAK, 'I Don't Regard the Rebbe as a Basar V'Dam', *Beis Moshiach* (19 Dec. 1997).

—— *Messiah Now* [*Mashiaḥ akhshav*] (Kfar Chabad, 1993).

—— 'Sealed with the Stamp of the Kohen Gadol', *Beis Moshiach*, 305 (Parshas Mikeitz 5761 / 29 Dec. 2000).

—— 'Thoughts before the Yartzeit of our King Messiah—The Holy Day 3 Tammuz' ['Hirhurim likrat yom malkenu meshiḥenu—yom hasegulah gimel tamuz'], *Beis Moshiach*, 41 (9 June 1995).

GORDON, LARRY, 'Has Moshiach Lost the OU?', *Algemeiner Journal*, 3 Nov. 1995, English section, p. B3.

GOTFRYD, ARNIE (ARYEH), *Living in the Age of Moshiach*, ed. Herman Branover (New York, 2000).

—— 'The Rebbe's Answer: A Dream Come True', *Beis Moshiach* (1 Elul 5756 / 16 Aug. 1996), 66–63 [pages numbered in reverse order].

GREEN, ARTHUR, *Tormented Master: A Life of Rabbi Nahman of Bratslav* (Tuscaloosa, Ala., 1979).

GREENBERG, GERSHON, 'Machane Israel-Lubavitch, 1940–1945: Actively Responding to Khurban', in Alan A. Berger (ed.), *Bearing Witness to the Holocaust, 1939–1989* (Lewiston, NY, 1991), 141–63.

—— 'Redemption after the Holocaust according to Machane Israel-Lubavitch, 1940–1945', *Modern Judaism*, 12 (1992), 61–84.

GREENBERG, IRVING, 'The Relationship of Judaism and Christianity: Toward a New Organic Model', in Eugene Fisher, A. James Rudin, and Marc H.

Tanenbaum (eds.), *Twenty Years of Jewish–Catholic Relations* (New York and Mahwah, NJ, 1986), 191–211.

GROSSMAN, AVRAHAM, *The Early Sages of France* [*Ḥakhmei tzarfat harishonim*] (Jerusalem, 1995).

HALBERTAL, MOSHE, *Between Torah and Wisdom: Rabbi Menahem Hame'iri and the Maimonist Masters of Halakhah in Provence* [*Bein torah leḥokhmah: rabi menaḥem hame'iri uba'alei hahalakhah hamaimunim biprovence*] (Jerusalem, 2000).

—— and AVISHAI MARGALIT, *Idolatry* (Cambridge, Mass., 1992).

HALKIN, ABRAHAM, and DAVID HARTMAN, *Epistles of Maimonides* (Philadelphia, Pa., 1985).

HENKIN, YEHUDAH HERZL, *She'elot uteshuvot benei banim* [responsa], vol. iii (Jerusalem, 1997).

HURWITZ, PHINEHAS ELIJAH, of Vilna, *Sefer haberit hashalem* [on science, philosophy, ethics and kabbalah] (1797; Jerusalem, 1990).

IBN ABI ZIMRA, DAVID (RADBAZ), *Teshuvot* [responsa] (1882).

IBN VERGA, SOLOMON, *Shevet yehudah* [historical work], ed. Azriel Schohet (Jerusalem, 1947).

ISHMAEL HANINA BEN MORDECAI HAROFE, *Sheva ḥakirot* [exchanges between a Christian interrogator and a Jew] (Husiatyn, 1903).

JACOB BEN REUBEN, *Milḥamot hashem* [anti-Christian polemic], ed. Judah Rosenthal (Jerusalem, 1963).

JACOBSON, AVROHOM, 'The Service of Refining the World has been Completed —That's a Fact', *Beis Moshiach*, 267 (25 Feb. 2000).

JUDAH ARYEH (LEON) DA MODENA, *Magen vaḥerev* [anti-Christian polemic], ed. S. Simonsohn (Jerusalem, 1960).

KARELITZ, ABRAHAM ISAIAH, *Ḥazon ish*, 'Yoreh de'ah' [commentary on the Shulḥan arukh] (Benei Berak, 1962).

KASHER, MENAHEM, *The Great Era: The Voice of the Turtledove* [*Hatekufah hagedolah: kol hator*] (Jerusalem, 1969).

KATZ, JACOB, *Bein yehudim legoyim* (Jerusalem, 1960) = *Exclusiveness and Tolerance* (New York, 1961).

—— 'The History of Three Apologetic Statements' [Sheloshah ma'amarim apologetiyim begilguleihem'], in id., *Halakhah vekabalah* (Jerusalem, 1986).

KEELER, BOB, 'The Lubavitchers of Long Island', *Newsday*, 23 Oct. 2000.

KELLER, CHAIM DOV, 'The Best of Times, the Worst of Times', *The Jewish Observer* (Summer 1997), 36–9.

—— 'G-d-Centered or *Rebbe*-Messiah Centered: Which is Normative Judaism?', *Jewish Observer* (Mar. 1998), 11–19.

KENIG, GEDALYAHU AHARON, *The Book of the Life of the Soul* [*Sefer ḥayei nefesh*] (Jerusalem, 1968)

KOCHAN, LIONEL, *Beyond the Graven Image: A Jewish View* (New York, 1997).

KOLIN, SAMUEL BEN NATHAN HALEVI, *Maḥatzit hashekel* [supercommentary on the *Magen avraham*, a commentary on the *Shulḥan arukh*], in the standard editions of the *Shulḥan arukh*.

LAMM, NORMAN, *The Religious Thought of Hasidism* (New York, 1999).

LASKER, DANIEL J., *Jewish Philosophical Polemics against Christianity in the Middle Ages* (New York, 1977).

LEVI YITZHAK OF BERDICHEV, *Kedushat levi* [hasidic comments and homilies on the Torah] (Warsaw, 1876).

LEVIN, SHALOM DOV BAER, *The History of Chabad in Soviet Russia, 1917–1956* [*Toledot ḥabad berusiyah hasovi'etit, 1917–1956*] (Brooklyn, 1989).

—— *The History of Chabad in the United States, 1900–1950* [*Toledot ḥabad be'artzot haberit, 1900–1950*] (Brooklyn, 1988).

LIPKIN, BINYAMIN, *Reckoning of the World* [*Ḥeshbono shel olam*] (Lod, 2000).

LOCKSHIN, MARTIN, 'Judaism, Christianity, and Jewish-Christianity: What the Future May Hold', in *Cult and Culture: Studies in Cultural Meaning*, Les Cahiers du CICC 8 (July 1999), 137–48.

LOEWENTHAL, NAFTALI, *Communicating the Infinite: The Emergence of the Habad School* (Chicago, 1990).

—— 'The Neutralization of Messianism and the Apocalypse', in Rachel Elior and Joseph Dan (eds.), *Kolot Rabim: Memorial Volume to Rivkah Shatz-Uffenheimer*, Jerusalem Studies in Jewish Thought 13 (Jerusalem, 1996), 2*–14* (English section).

MAIMONIDES, MOSES, *Ma'amar teḥiyat hametim* [treatise on resurrection], trans. into English as 'The Essay on Resurrection', in Abraham Halkin and David Hartman, *Epistles of Maimonides* (Philadelphia, Pa., 1985), 209–33.

—— *Mishneh torah* [halakhic code], ed. Shabse Frankel (New York, 1975–).

MALKOVITCH, B., 'Is there a Limit to Presumptuousness?' (Yiddish), *Algemeiner Journal*, 6 Feb. 1998, pp. 4, 6.

MARGALIOT, REUBEN, *Margaliot hayam* [interpretations of the talmudic tractate *Sanhedrin*] (Jerusalem, 1958).

MARK, JONATHAN, 'Chabad's Russian Revolution', *Jewish Week*, 1 Dec. 2000.

MEDINI, HAYIM HEZEKIAH, *Sedei ḥemed* [halakhic encyclopedia], 18 vols. (Warsaw, 1891–1912).

MEIR BEN SIMEON HAME'ILI, *Milḥemet mitzvah* [account of disputation with a Christian], partly edited in *Shitat hakadmonim al masikhtot nazir, zevaḥim, arakhin, utemurah vesefer milḥemet mitzvah*, ed. Moshe Yehudah Hakohen Blau (New York, 1973), and in William Herskowitz, 'Jewish–Christian Dialogue in Provence as Reflected in Milḥemet Mitzvah of R. Meir ha-Meili' (DHL diss., Yeshiva University, 1974).

MINDEL, NISSAN, *R. Schneur Zalman of Liadi* (New York, 1971, 1973).

MORTERA, SAUL LEVI, *Tratado da verdade da lei de Moises*, ed. H. P. Salomon (Coimbra, 1988).

MOSES HAKOHEN OF TORDESILLAS, *Ezer ha'emunah* [anti-Christian polemic], in *Rabbi Moses ha-Kohen of Tordesillas and his Book Ezer ha-Emunah: A Chapter in the History of the Judaeo-Christian Controversy*, Part II, ed. Yehuda Shamir (Coconut Grove, Fla., 1972).

MUELHAUSEN, YOM TOV LIPMANN, *Sefer nitzaḥon* [anti-Christian polemic], ed. T. Hackspan (Altdorf, 1644).

NAHMANIDES, MOSES, *Works* [*Kitvei ramban*], ed. Chaim Dov Chavel (Jerusalem, 1963).

PEVZNER, AVRAHAM BARUCH, *On the Righteous* [*Al hatzadikim*] (Kfar Chabad, 1991).

PRAGER, DENNIS, 'A New Approach to Jews for Jesus', *Moment* (June 2000), 28–9.

RAMBAM, *see* Maimonides

RAVITZKY, AVIEZER, 'The Contemporary Lubavitch Hasidic Movement: Between Conservatism and Messianism', in Martin E. Marty and R. Scott Appleby (eds.), *Accounting for Fundamentalisms: The Dynamic Character of Movements* (Chicago, 1994), 303–27.

—— *Messianism, Zionism, and Jewish Religious Radicalism* (Chicago, 1996).

REDMAN, BARBARA J., 'One God: Toward a Rapprochement of Orthodox Judaism and Christianity', *Journal of Ecumenical Studies*, 31 (1994), 307–31.

RUDERMAN, DAVID, 'A Jewish Apologetic Treatise from Sixteenth-Century Bologna', *Hebrew Union College Annual*, 50 (1979), 253–76.

SACHAR, HOWARD M., *Farewell España: The World of the Sephardim Remembered* (New York, 1994).

SASSON, HAYIM, *I Know that my Redeemer Lives: Chapters of Analysis on the Third of Tammuz from the Book* Now I Know [*Va'ani yada'ti go'ali Ḥai: pirkei hitbobenut beyom gimel tamuz mitokh hasefer attah yada'ti*] (Jerusalem, 1999).

SCHNEERSON, MENACHEM MENDEL, *Likutei siḥot* [anthology of sermons] (Brooklyn, NY, *c*.1962–*c*.1993).

—— *Pamphlet on the Small Temple, the House of our Rabbi in Babylonia* [*Kuntres be'inyan mikdash me'at zeh beit rabenu shebebavel*] (Brooklyn, NY, 1992).

SCHOCHET, JACOB IMMANUEL, *Chassidic Dimensions* (Brooklyn, NY, 1990).

—— 'G-d-Centered or Machloket-Centered: Which is Normative Judaism? A Response to Rabbi Chaim Dov Keller of Chicago', *Algemeiner Journal*, 27 Mar. 1998, English section, pp. B3–B4.

SHAPIRA, AMNON, '"Our Master, Teacher and Creator"—The Fundamental Problem' (Heb.), *Hatzofeh*, 16 Jan. 1998, p. 4.

SHAPIRO, MARC B., 'The Last Word in Jewish Theology? Maimonides' Thirteen

Principles', *Torah U-Madda Journal*, 4 (1993), 187–242.

SOFER, YEHEZKEL, *Matters Will Be Purified and Clarified* [*Yitbareru veyitlabenu*] (Beer Sheva, 1995).

STERNHARTZ, NATHAN, *Biography of Rabbi Nahman of Bratslav* [*Ḥayei moharan*] (Bratslav, 1875).

TROKI, ISAAC BEN ABRAHAM, *Ḥizuk emunah* [apologetics] (late 16th cent.; repr. New York, 1932).

TZIKERNIK, YESHAYA WOLF, *Precious Stories and Discourses* [*Ma'asiyot uma'amarim yekarim*] (Zhitomir, 1903); repr. in *Sefer sipurim uma'amarim yekarim* (Shikun Skvere, 1994).

WOLPO, SHALOM DOV, *A Book, a Writer, and a Tale* [*Sefer sofer vesipur*] (Brooklyn, NY, 1996).

—— 'Comfort Ye, Comfort Ye, My People—Double Comfort' ['Naḥamu naḥamu ami—neḥamah bekiflayim'], *Kefar ḥabad*, 106 (5743), 6–7.

—— *The Last Trial* [*Hanisayon ha'aḥaron*] (Kiryat Gat, 1994).

YANOVER, Y., and N. ISH-SHALOM, *Dancing and Weeping* [*Rokedim ubokhim*] (New York, 1994).

YERUHAM BEN MESHULAM, *Toledot adam veḥavah* [halakhic compendium] (Constantinople, 1516).

YOSEF, OVADIAH, *She'elot uteshuvot yabia omer* [responsa], vol. i (Jerusalem, 1986).

ZELIGZON, M. (ed.), *A Voice Announcing and Saying: Anthology of New Torah Interpretations. The King Messiah and the Final Redemption* [*Kol mevaser mevaser ve'omer: kovetz ḥidushei torah. Hamelekh hamashiaḥ vehage'ulah hashelemah*] (1983).

Index

Breningstall, Jena Morris 35, 50
Brod, Menachem 127
Brussels, messianism in 122
Butman, Rabbi Shmuel:
  attack on Berger in *Algemeiner Journal*
    103
  on death of Rebbe 25
  letter to Jewish Action 36, 39–40, 41,
    49–50, 52
  messianic views 39–40, 47, 52, 103, 104
  role 36, 119
  sources cited by 39–40, 43, 44, 45

C

Calgary, messianism in 122
Central Committee of Chabad-Lubavitch
    Rabbis in United States and Canada
    101
Chabad, *see* Lubavitch
Charitonow, Rabbi Sholom 99–101, 104,
    173 n.
Chofetz Chaim yeshiva 131
Christianity:
  Apollinarian heresy 106
  belief in Messiah 30, 155–7
  beliefs shared with Jews 38, 49
  compared with hasidism 104–5
  compared with Lubavitch messianism
    53–5, 131
  death of Jesus 21, 28, 140, 156–7
  divinity of Jesus 51, 159–62
  history of Jewish–Christian debate 74,
    91, 106
  Incarnation, doctrine of the 99–100,
    105, 159–61
  Jewish defence against 27, 31, 33–4, 39,
    91, 155–7
  Maimonides on 72–3
  Second Coming, belief in 53, 129–30
  Trinity, doctrine of the 39, 46, 100, 106,
    159–61
Commentary 17
Conservative Judaism 26, 68, 89–90, 138

Council of Torah Sages:
  attitude to Lubavitch messianism 75, 81,
    107, 108, 132, 146
  Berger letters to 33–4, 76, 77–8, 79–80,
    84–5, 113–14
  membership 80
  role 76
Crown Heights, Brooklyn:
  anti-messianists 79
  messianism in 11, 26, 88, 119, 120
  rabbinical court 56, 92, 121, 143

D

Daniel 25 n., 37, 41, 43, 44, 59
David, House of 18, 21, 30, 40, 60
David, King:
  ancestor of Messiah 1, 36, 40
  as Messiah 11, 25 n., 37, 41, 43, 59
Deutsch, Shaul Shimon, Rabbi 73–4
divorce, improper witnesses invalidate 93,
    148
Dov Baer of Mezhirech, Rabbi 59
Duran, Rabbi Shimon ben Tzemah 154
Dworken, Rabbi Steven 65, 66

E

Eden, Garden of 39, 46
education, Lubavitch involvement in 2,
    93, 120–1, 127, 140–1, 143–4
Elijah ben Solomon Zalman, *see* Vilna
    Gaon
Elyashiv, Rabbi Yosef Shalom 114 n., 146
England, Lubavitch presence 117
Essence and Being of God:
  Christian beliefs 104
  descriptions of Rebbe as 51, 83, 87,
    100–1, 104, 173
  Rebbe's assertion that a rebbe is 7–8,
    106 n., 159, 162, 170
  status of a rebbe in relation to 7–8, 97,
    103, 106 n., 159, 162–3, 170

F

Feinstein, Rabbi Moshe 88
Fleckeles, Rabbi Eliezer 147 n.